Australasian Encounters

UFOs
DOWN UNDER

THE FILES REVISITED

*

Barry Watts

Testimony from Experiencers:

"I didn't panic like I did the first time."

"We signaled the beings by torchlight."

"The thing is just orbiting on top of me."

"A triangle underneath my belly button."

© Barry John Watts 2017

All rights reserved

Without limiting the rights under copyright above, no part of this publication may be reproduced, stored in a retrieval system, or transmitted in any form or by any means (electronic, mechanical, photocopying, recording or otherwise) without the prior written permission of both the copyright owner and the publisher.

Published by Pegasus Education Group,
P.O. Box 223, McCrae, Victoria 3938,
Australia

ISBN: 978-0-9945355-6-6

First printing: July 2017

Author contact:
barrywatts@bookfellows.com.au

CONTENTS

INTRODUCTION

1. FLYING EGGS THE SIZE OF LOCOMOTIVES 1

2. GROUP SEE GIANT FLYING FOOTBALL 6

3. LT. O'FARRELL'S NIGHT-TIME ENCOUNTER 14

4. MERGER IN SKIES OVER ZANTHUS 23

5. VALENTICH VANISHES OVER BASS STRAIT 30

6. CRESSY MINISTER CHANGES HIS TUNE 42

7. MORELAND STORY HIDDEN FROM PUBLIC 50

8. NEW ZEALAND'S 'KIAKOURA LIGHTS' 57

9. HEADACHE BREWING AT 'WILLOW GROVE' 72

10. A RUDE AWAKENING AT CHILDERS 78

11. TULLY FARMER FINDS UFO 'NEST' 81

12. INTRUDER AT A ROSEDALE WATER-TANK 92

13. COUNTRY PUB UNDER SURVEILLANCE 99

14. TEENAGERS SCARED BY GRAVEL-PIT LIGHTS 105

15. RON SULLIVAN'S BENDING HEADLIGHTS 111

16. HUME HIGHWAY MOTORCYCLIST CAUGHT 118

17. ST HELENS FAMILY BUZZED BY UFO 123

18. THE KNOWLES FAMILY AT MUNDRABILLA 126

19. TOM DRURY'S UFO CAUGHT ON FILM? 137

20. REV. GILL'S 'REMARKABLE TESTIMONY' 143

21. SECRECY SHROUDS WESTALL UFOS 154

22. NEW ZEALAND TEACHERS SEE STRANGE OBJECT 173

23. THE MELTON POLICE — UFO FIASCO 178

24. SPOOKS: "YOU SAW NOTHING! GOT IT?" 184

25. MAUREEN PUDDY AT THE 'MEETING PLACE' 189

26. KEMPSEY MAN SUCKED THROUGH GLASS 197

27. KELLY CAHILL'S ABDUCTION 202

INTRODUCTION

Unexplained lights in the sky …reports of strange saucer-shaped craft…mysterious landing marks on the ground…small gray humanoids with enormous eyes…alien messages received by thought transference…unaccountable images on radar…witnesses experiencing lost time…perceived threats to national security.

These are the hallmarks of earth's UFO visitors.

During the last sixty years Australia, New Zealand and Papua-New Guinea — Australasia — have had many reports of such encounters.

Some events were mentioned in long out-of-print books; others are buried away in government archives protected by statute, while still more are kept under wraps by experiencers too frightened of ridicule to talk about them.

What kind of people encounter these unusual phenomena? Everyday people: farmers, pilots, office workers, school children, housewives, pub owners, holiday makers, banana growers, policemen, teachers, teenagers, and ministers of religion. Perhaps, even members of your own family.

Where do they happen? Well…anywhere really…although mostly, it seems, in sparsely populated areas, or near water or power lines or, in several instances, near school-grounds. Perhaps they occur in and around cities, but we are mostly too busy or pre-occupied to look up and see them!

Are these flying saucers/UFOs/spacecraft manned? Do they wish to harm us? Where do they come from? How do these craft travel such enormous distances? Are there different types of aliens? Is it true that they abduct humans?

Questions, and doubts – each answer leading to even more questions and even more doubts!

In this book I have re-examined over thirty UFO encounters in Australia, New Zealand and Papua-New Guinea in detail.

Some of these are well known and I have included extracts from witness statements, newspaper reports, on-line podcasts and expert assessment by informed investigators, including a few scientists! Others are old or obscure, but are nevertheless provocative mysteries.

Look Up,

Barry Watts

Acknowledgements

The material presented here draws on many sources relating to individual UFO sightings — including witnesses — and the research, observations, reactions, judgments, and bias of several individuals and groups who have expressed themselves on the topic – either online, in UFO publications, newspapers and journals, in television programs, on DVD, or at meetings and public lectures, or in official documents, over the past sixty years.

Utilized sources are identified in the text of this work either immediately before or after their inclusion.

The author sincerely acknowledges the expertise, efforts and contributions of each named person or organization in furthering the wider understanding of the 'UFO phenomena' and its implications.

A list of 'References Consulted' appears at the back of this book.

1. Flying Eggs the Size of Locomotives

"They seemed to be floating in the air"

In 1947 Kenneth Arnold's observation of 'nine peculiar-looking, saucer-like disks' flying over the Cascade Mountains near Mt. Rainier, Washington, gave rise to the expression 'flying saucers' and marked the start of the modern era of unidentified flying objects.

But was he really the first?

Over four months earlier, on February 5, 1947, on the opposite side of the globe — that is, Down Under — Australia may have had the world's first modern-era UFO sighting.

The *Adelaide Advertiser* newspaper, in an article by-lined 'Port Augusta, February 6', reported:

STRANGE OBJECTS REPORTED IN SKY

While working in the yard at the Commonwealth Railways workshop yesterday morning Mr. Ron Ellis and two workmates claim to have seen five strange objects in formation pass across the sky from north to south.

The objects were white or light pink and shaped like an egg, Mr. Ellis said he could not give an accurate estimate of the size of the objects, but they were casting shadows and judging by his experience with aircraft in the RAAF during the war he considered they were about the size of a locomotive.

Although the objects kept on a direct course at a height of about 6,000ft., they appeared to be quivering he said. Owing to their great speed they were out of sight within a few seconds.

Any question of the phenomenon being an optical illusion was dispelled by the fact that a few minutes later both Mr. Ellis and his companions gave an identical description of what they had seen. Their description was verified by another member of the workshop who said he had also seen the objects. [*Adelaide Advertiser,* Friday February 7, 1947, p.1]

On the day following the announcement of the Ellis sighting in Port Augusta, this front-page news item appeared:

OBJECTS IN SKY NOT METEORITES

Commenting yesterday on a report from Port Augusta that several men working in the yard at the Commonwealth Railways workshop at about 9am on Wednesday had seen five strange egg shaped objects in formation pass across the sky at a height of about 6,000ft, the Government astronomer (Mr. G F Dodwell) said that the phenomenon did not fit in with anything astronomical and was a complete mystery to him.

Mr. Dodwell discounted the probability of the objects being meteorites. He said that meteorites being so small and traveling at such high speeds did not cast shadows whereas the report stated that the objects had cast shadows about the size of a locomotive. The presence of falling meteorites would have been accompanied by a deafening roar. [*Adelaide Advertiser*, February 8, 1947, p.1]

These newspaper items were read with interest by a 68-year-old machinery agent, Walter Flavel from a small farming community at Lock, on South Australia's Eyre Peninsula. Lock is 300 road miles (483kms) from Port Augusta.

Flavel sat down immediately and wrote to the *Adelaide Advertiser* telling of a sighting made by him and his wife on the same day [5 February], but earlier in the morning.

His letter was published in the Letters to the Editor column on February 17, 1947:

STRANGE OBJECTS IN THE SKY

I saw objects in the sky between 7 and 8 o'clock [a.m.] the same day as you record a report from Port Augusta. I was walking in a north-westerly direction to the house after feeding the pigs. There were five of the strange objects and they seemed to be coming up out of the sea like a shadow with smoky-grayish color around them. They were oblong with narrow points. I saw them quite plainly. They seemed to be floating in the air from north-west to south-east and caused a shadow.

I called the wife to have a look at them, and the Port Augusta men did so an hour later. I have never seen anything like this before, and after reading what others saw, I thought I would let you know that my wife and I saw these objects.

Mr. F W Flavel, Lock, Eyre Peninsula

Veteran South Australian UFO investigator Keith Basterfield began looking again at these early sightings in January 2015. He spent considerable time at the State Library of South Australia, Adelaide, and checked both metropolitan and regional newspapers covering the first few weeks of February 1947. He identified all the items quoted above, plus duplicates of both sightings in the *Quorn Mercury*. Quorn is just over 20kms (12 miles) north-east of Port Augusta.

He subsequently established that an Adelaide-based researcher, Jeff Fausch, conducted his own cold case investigation into the Flying Eggs – Port Augusta case ten years previously. The main witness, Ronald Ernest Ellis, had been found and interviewed by Mishelle [no surname provided]. Ellis lived only a couple of streets away from Mishelle. He died on July 15, 2008, aged 87 years.

Jeff Fausch emailed Keith Basterfield:

Mishelle interviewed Ron Ellis in June 2006 sending me [Fausch] a couple of updates, but in September 2006 told me that her husband was being transferred to Kalgoorlie, Western Australia. When she moved to Kalgoorlie I lost contact with her and have not heard from her since.

In an email sent to me [Fausch] on June 29th 2006 Mishelle said that she had interviewed Ron Ellis who was at the time, 86 years old. His report of the incident conflicts with that of the media article in terms of what he witnessed, who was spoken to, etc.

Mr. Ellis first told Mishelle he saw nothing at first, then changed his story, and was adamant what he witnessed was a weather/observation balloon. This was told to him by unknown benefactors after the article was published [in the newspaper]

During a phone call, Mishelle told me Ellis was approached by two men who told him that it was a weather balloon and to leave it at that. Mishelle felt that there was much more to this sighting than met the eye.

I believe when Michelle approached him, he had been taken by surprise as no one had brought this up for nearly sixty years. [*Magonia-Down Under* blog, Keith Basterfield, January 8, 2016]

Jeff Fausch also mentioned a comment from Mishelle's final email to him:

[Mishelle] had contacted the department of Meteorology, specifically the climate services section, and was informed that the closest area to Port Augusta in which weather balloons were launched was Woomera, but interestingly, upper air observations did not begin at Woomera until March 1, 1949, two years after the Port Augusta incident. [*Magonia-Down Under* blog, Keith Basterfield, January 8, 2016]

In their book *Return to Magonia: Investigating UFOs in History*, writers Chris Aubeck and Martin Shough applied their critical judgment (and considerable knowledge of UFOs) to some of the oldest recorded sightings of strange aerial phenomenon between 1991BC and 1947AD.

They have included a thorough investigation of both the South Australian sightings of 5 February 1947.

In their lengthy assessment they progressively ruled out aircraft, airships, rockets, balloons, and birds as well as clouds and other weather phenomena as likely explanations. In part, their summary states:

Both reports resemble the seminal Kenneth Arnold sighting on June 24 the same year, yet Arnold would not have been exposed to either...

We can find no simple explanation. The relationship, if any, between the two reports from Lock and Port Augusta is not clear...

Nevertheless this is a striking case, and is certainly of great historical and cultural interest. Simply put, this is a modern UFO. [Chris Aubeck & Martin Shough, in 'Giant Flying Eggs', *Return to Magonia: Investigating UFOs in History*, p.350]

**

A decade later (1957), America had its own Blue Egg UFO sighting.

Appropriately, it was recorded in the American Air Force's Blue Book – the name given to their project that received and analyzed the couple of thousand UFO reports between 1952 and 1970.

The project engaged astronomer Dr J. Allen Hynek as a

technical consultant. His job was to see how many reports could be rationally explained as 'meteors, twinkling stars, and bright planets.'

The American Blue Egg sighting happened at 7.30pm on November 4, 1957, three miles (4.8kms) southeast of El Paso's International Airport in Texas. The un-named witness was a 35 year-old border inspector who was driving his car when its lights dimmed and went out, and the engine stalled. He stopped the car and got out to investigate.

He saw an egg-shaped object with a bluish glow pass over his vehicle at an altitude of 100 feet (30.5m), moving in a westerly direction. He also heard a whirring sound 'similar to an artillery shell'.

After the Blue Egg flew over the airport towards the nearby Franklin Mountains, it lifted vertically.

2. Group see Giant Flying Football

"It was oval in shape, half the size of a railway carriage"

The Argus newspaper — the primary source of information in this chapter — reported a somewhat bizarre group UFO sighting at the end of May, 1954:

'FLYING FOOTBALL' DIVES ON MALVERN

It was a 'flying saucer' ... it looked like a giant football. This is what one of six people who saw an object in the sky at East Malvern on Saturday night claims.

All are certain they saw a flying saucer.

They wrote down their impressions immediately the saucer disappeared.

The people comprised a woman school teacher, a policeman from Russell Street [Police HQ], a radio announcer, an A.B.C. (Australian Broadcasting Corporation) official, a Postal Department technician, and a clerk. [*The Argus*, May 31, 1954, p.7]

The story continued with short descriptions by the participants of what they saw:

THE SCHOOL TEACHER: (It was) pear-shaped, with a beam of light extending from the blunt end. A noise, too hard to describe its density. Traveling low and fast in the direction of south-east.

THE POLICEMAN: At approximately 12.24 I saw an oval-shaped machine speed from the sky and hover low (about 60ft) [18-meters] above the ground. Scarlet flames were shooting out of it. Shadows of some people, I think, could be seen for several seconds. It disappeared with a tremendous roaring sound.

THE CLERK: A whirring noise that frightened me. A yellow flame spurted from the rear like a Buck Rogers rocket ship. There seemed to be vague people shadowed in the strange light emitted from the oval-shaped ship.

THE POSTAL TECHNICIAN: At 12.25 a large circular object, about the shape of a plate appeared about 40ft or 50ft. [12-15-meters] above the ground. It would be hard to judge the distance. It was just above the trees, traveling fast. There was a possibility of seeing people. Yellowish flames. [*The Argus*, May 31, 1954, p.7]

The A.B.C. official, David Reece, had been farewelling friends outside his East Malvern home when the sighting occurred:

I was saying goodbye to some friends when I heard a noise. It was a sort of Brrrrr — like the dial tone of a telephone. [The object] traveled at a fantastic speed yet appeared to be moving slowly, as if time and speed had become distorted. When it reached the lowest point, shapes — like human figures — could definitely be seen. [David Reece in *The Argus*, May 31, 1954, p.7]

The radio announcer, Christopher Muir, was interviewed the following day. He said: 'Whatever it was we saw, it was oval in shape, like a giant football, about half to three quarters the size of a railway carriage. I could not say if there were people in it, but through what looked like portholes, or windows, there were reflections of some sort that could have resembled people.'

East Malvern is 12 kilometers (7.5 miles) from Melbourne's CBD and the Princes Highway runs through it — although this portion is locally known as Dandenong Road.

*

Five days later, at about 6.20pm on Saturday, June 5, 1954, two teenage girls had a frightening UFO experience, but were too scared to tell anyone except their parents about it for the next three days.

Both girls, according to *The Argus* (Melbourne) four days later, had 'little sleep since' and were 'frightened and nervous'.

The elder of them, Janette Brown, 16, even asked her mother if the family could move to another suburb in case the saucer tried to destroy her home and family.

Here is Janette's account:

> I was standing on Princes Highway, opposite the 21 mile (34kms) post (from Melbourne), waiting for Jeanette [Johnston, 13] about 6.20 p.m. I heard a loud drumming noise, something like a motor-cycle, but there were no cars or cycles around at the time.
>
> Then a large, dark shape appeared over the partly-built H. J. Heinz factory, and whirled towards me when I shone my torch. Just above the house where the caretaker lives, it burst into light — a gleaming, bluish, silvery-gray light.
>
> It hovered about twenty yards [18-meters] away on the top of the factory gate, as if it deliberately wanted me to look at it — or it wanted to look at me.
>
> It was a cylindrical shape, about 30ft long and 15ft high (9m x 4.5m), with a canopy and window on top and a window on each end.
>
> Then Jeanette arrived. I told her to watch the house." [*The Argus* (Melbourne), June 9, 1954, p.3]

Jeanette Johnston then described what she saw:

> A silvery colored cylinder rose above the house then swept away in a wide circle to the International Harvester factory a few hundred yards [c.275meters] away. It stayed on top of the factory for about one minute then disappeared behind the trees. [*The Argus* (Melbourne), June 9, 1954, p.3]

Both girls lived with their parents at Dandenong, then an outer south-eastern suburb of Melbourne, which experienced a post-war boom with new housing and high employment in the 1950s.

In his 1965 book, author James Holledge includes this rather dramatic reference in his account of the Dandenong sighting — no names were used, but it appears certain he was referring to Janette Brown:

> It [the UFO] got closer to her and she shone a torch at it. When it was about thirty feet [9-meters] above her she panicked and flung herself down on the ground. A car then approached and the object moved away and disappeared over the factory building. Hysterical, the girl ran home and told her parents. [*Flying Saucers Over Australia*, James Holledge, (Horwitz, 1965), p. 53]

Holledge made no reference at all to the second witness, Jeanette Johnston (perhaps he was confused by the similarity of their given names). He does, though, introduce two further parties who were closely interested in Janette Brown's experience. Holledge quotes an un-named flying saucer investigator from a Melbourne UFO society:

> She was genuinely upset. She had obviously seen something that had scared the daylights out of her. She was cross-examined in front of her parents by an Air Force man on one side of her and myself on other. I regard hers as a genuine report. [*Flying Saucers Over Australia*, James Holledge, (Horwitz, 1965), p.53]

Within ten days of the young ladies' Dandenong sighting, two further UFO reports from suburban Melbourne appeared in *The Argus*, one at St Kilda ('bright orange and emitting sparks') and the second at West Heidelberg ('strange object in the sky').

Sensing increased reader interest, *The Argus* offered a £1,000 prize for a photograph of a genuine flying saucer.

Meanwhile, on June 15 the newspaper sent a reporter and photographer to the site of Janette and Jeanette's sighting at Dandenong where an investigation was underway.

EXPERT TESTS CLUES AT SAUCER SITE

Using a Geiger counter and a highly sensitive compass, a Victorian Mines Department geologist yesterday searched an area at Dandenong for magnetic traces of a flying saucer.

Mr. John Brown, 22 [Janette's brother] ...had claimed that last week a flying saucer appeared near his home and magnetized various objects. [The Brown's home was on a street that ran parallel to Princes Highway, just one street away]...

Yesterday, Mr. Brown said the saucer's cosmic power had stopped Janette's wrist watch at 6.23 p.m., drained her torch battery of power, magnetized her handbag and belt clasps, and the iron fencing over which it hovered.

He guided Mr. Peter Kenley, Government geologist, and *The Argus* to the magnetized fencing...

The Geiger counter gave no tell-tale sounds of movement. Asked whether there were any hints of a magnetized visitation, Mr. Kenley said — with a look towards the Heinz factory: 'You might expect to see a flying soup plate around here.'

'Neighbors complained that their radio reception were affected,' said Mr. Brown.

'Storms!' said Mr. Kenley...

Mr. Kenley suggested a test on a similar fence some miles away, around the Westminster Carpet factory. The needle reaction was the same as at the Heinz fence. 'Now don't tell me that was caused by a flying carpet,' said Mr. Kenley.

But Mr. Brown is still unshaken in the belief that the flying saucer did shed powerful cosmic influence. [*The Argus*, June 16, 1954, p.9]

The following day, The *Argus* advised its readers that the first entry received in their quest for a photograph of a flying saucer was unsuccessful.

'Exhaustive tests of negative and print have been made by our own photographic experts and an independent scientist,' *The Argus* said, 'These prove to our satisfaction that the picture can be explained by natural causes ...the phenomenon is something known technically as halation. Most experienced photographers will recognize it as such.'

It may have seemed to some readers that *The Argus* was wavering a little in its support of flying saucer sightings.

But it was not so — far from it.

In their lift-out Weekender on Saturday June 26, 1954, *The Argus* featured a front-page banner headline:

SAUCERS DO EXIST — AND WHY!

According to *The Argus*, the following article was written by an 'eminent Australian nuclear physicist' whose name was withheld 'because of his link with high level research.' As if to re-assure it readers, *The Argus* pointed out that the article's author 'has investigated saucer reports since 1948' and that his article 'explains scientifically what could be behind the sightings'.

His wide-ranging story spreads across the newspaper's full 8-column width, taking about two-thirds of the total page, and was topped with a drawing of a large, airborne UFO with a planet in the background. The UFO issue has probably not received such extensive coverage in an Australia daily newspaper either before or since (with the possible exception of Frederick Valentich). [see Chapter 5]

Giant Flying Football

Of particular interest is the writer's specific attention paid to the two sightings retold from *The Argus* reports earlier in this chapter:

> During the last few weeks there have been two interesting reports from the Melbourne area.
>
> At Malvern a group of six people, attracted by a noise like a motorbike, observed the sudden appearance out of a moonless sky of a luminous, dark blue 'football, the size of a tram,' sweeping downwards in an arc only about 80 yards [240 feet / 73 meters] distant. Emitting a 'ball of orange flame,' the object continued on an upward curve and vanished. The glow from the emitted cloud of vapor or smoke was sufficient to briefly bathe both the ship and the observers in a yellow-orange light.
>
> A week later an observer at East Dandenong heard a noise like a motorbike from a dark object silhouetted against an evening sky. As it came nearer, with but a single yellowish orange headlight glowing, it suddenly burst into luminescent silver-gray, with additional yellowish-orange lights at the rear and on one side.
>
> The drumming noise ceased, but a ticking sound continued. It began to revolve with a period of three to four seconds. When compared with the size of a house over which it passed, its diameter appeared to be about 35 — 40 feet [9 — 12 meters]. About 35 yards [32 meters] from the observer it stopped its forward movement, but its revolution rate increased until the period was only about a second.
>
> It was seen to have three wheels, which formed the corners of an equilateral triangle and were suspended from a circular base. The base curved over to meet a canopy that had two sets of windows in it. The surface was smooth, without any visible seams, rivets, or bolts. Like the 'flying football,' this description agrees fairly well with a type of saucer described in overseas reports...
>
> Because of the proximity of the observers in both cases, these two events alone provide good evidence for the existence of unusual flying craft. In interviews, the integrity and conviction of these witnesses was impressive.
>
> In the second case the light available and duration of observation were sufficient to discern details of structure which could not possibly be confused with any phenomena other than a machine that is capable of hovering, rotating, and moving in virtual silence without any obvious method of propulsion. [*The Argus*, June 26, 1954, p.7]

The eminent physicist's story — five times longer than this

extract — concludes with three hypotheses: (1) that some UFO reports can only be explained by the assumption the objects are controlled by some intelligence; (2) that these are not earth-made, but extraterrestrial; and (3) that they originate from the planet Mars.

As Bill Chalker wrote in his 1996 book:

'The last of these hypotheses seems decidedly naïve. However, for the period [1954] such speculation was not totally out of step with the thinking of some members of the scientific community.' [*The Oz Files, the Australian UFO story*, p.82.]

* *

Let's pause for a moment to consider what we have just read.

Starting with East Malvern incident: Does the 'eminent physicist's' account tally with the witnesses written descriptions in *The Argus* report of May 31, 1954?

Did you notice the variations in shape, noise and color described by the witnesses? Further, four of them inferred the possible sighting of people/human figures in the craft; this is not given the slightest credence by the 'eminent physicist'.

Why not? Was it, do you think, because he thought it wasn't true? Or was too confrontational for lay readers? Or for any one of a myriad of other reasons?

Now, let's reconsider the Dandenong 'Janette & Jeanette' encounter. The 'eminent physicist' overlooks the presence of the second witness, Jeanette, and introduces new evidence ('ticking noise', 'size of a house', 'revolution rate', 'three wheels', and 'virtual silence') not mentioned in *The Argus* report.

So what?

It becomes obvious the 'eminent physicist' interviewed Janette (maybe he was the 'Air Force man' mentioned by James Holledge — see earlier), and knew from experience what questions to ask the experiencers.

Journalists, on the other hand, are usually concerned with newsworthiness and deadlines — factors less inductive to in-depth questioning on esoteric subjects; and their writing is subjected to sub-editing to eliminate irrelevancies, and/or cut to fit available space, and meet daily publishing deadlines.

Reports written of an incident tend to bring the writer's understanding and motives clearly to the fore in interpreting it.

Then it becomes the readers' turn, and each reader brings their own life experience to the interpretation of what they read. It was always thus.

Next, somewhat unexpectedly, we find the following:

> 'This particular sighting [Dandenong] has an extremely high probability of being a UFO without any provisos', wrote the author of a classified report for the Air Force. [Bill Chalker, *The OZ Files, the Australian UFO story*, (Sydney, 1996), p.80]

This short extract, as Bill Chalker later went on to reveal, was written in 1954 by the same person described as the 'eminent Australian nuclear physicist' behind *The Argus* UFO feature article, *'Saucers' do Exist — and Why!'* published June 26, 1954.

We also learn from Bill Chalker that 'the eminent physicist' was Professor Harry Turner who, at the time, was attached to Melbourne University's Physics Department, and that the Department of Air Force Intelligence (DAFI) had asked Professor Turner to undertake a 'scientific appreciation' of the official UFO reports held in the Royal Australian Air Forces (RAAF) files.

> Turner recommended greater official interest and specific interest in radar-visual reports. His most profound conclusion was: 'The evidence presented by the reports held by RAAF tend to support the ...conclusion... that certain strange aircraft have been observed to behave in a manner suggestive of extra-terrestrial origin.' [Bill Chalker, in *UFOs and Government: A Historical Inquiry* by Michael Swords et al. (Anomalist Books, San Antonio, 2012) p.370]

'Strange aircraft' indeed!

3. Lt. O'Farrell's night-time Encounter

"Our first sighting authenticated by radar"

On the evening of August 31, 1954, Lieutenant J A 'Shamus' O'Farrell undertook a solo night-time, cross-country navigation exercise in his naval Sea Fury plane, numbered 921.

He flew 630kms (224 miles) over Young, Temora, and Yass in central New South Wales, then back to his Nowra base, 160 kilometers (100 miles) south of Sydney.

This flight wrote him into the world's UFO history books, and was described in one Australian newspaper as 'the first authenticated information in the world of the existence of flying saucers'.

While Kenneth Arnold had made the first modern flying saucer sighting seven years earlier near Mt. Rainier, Washington, O'Farrell's sighting near Goulburn was significant because it was also confirmed on ground radar.

One report attributes the young pilot as saying:

> It was a fine dark night. The stars were all out, with no moon, no clouds, no bad weather and good visibility. A pleasant night for night flying...When I left Nowra, the radar there was not working, but they were hoping to get it on line by the time I returned. The operators asked me to call so they could do a check-tune on me as I came in. [Shamus O'Farrell, in Ken Llewelyn, *Flight Into the Ages*, (Sydney, 1991) p.137]

Night-time Encounter

The Royal Australian Navy's Fleet Air Arm is headquartered at H.M.A.S. Albatross, a land-based airfield near coastal Nowra, in New South Wales.

At two minutes to 7pm. (18.58 hours) O'Farrell reported his position to Canberra Air Traffic Control, and was acknowledged. Before 7.10p.m. (19.10 hours) and southwest of Goulburn, he switched his radio from civil air radio (Canberra) to his Squadron exercise frequency and contacted his Nowra base.

Very shortly afterwards, Lieutenant O'Farrell observed:

... a very bright light closing fast from 'one o'clock'. This bright light crossed ahead of me and continued to a position on my port beam [the left-hand side], where it appeared to orbit. At the same time, I noticed a second and similar light at 'nine o'clock' which made a pass about a mile ahead of me, and then turned in the position where the first light was sighted. [from Shamus O'Farrell's signed report, dated September 2, 1954, in National Archives of Australia]

Such a dramatic, close intrusion into the Sea Fury's flight path would rattle a lesser flyer. How did O'Farrell react?

I became concerned at the presence of these objects and began to think about the situation again. 'If I say too much, they [the base] will think I'm seeing objects that aren't there, and they will get worried; the best thing to do is to say nothing and just call up Nowra.' [Shamus O'Farrell, in Ken Llewelyn, *Flight Into the Ages*, (Sydney, 1991) p.138]

So Shamus O'Farrell held his nerve, and called his base:

I asked if they had me on radar, hoping they would confirm that other aircraft were in the vicinity. They replied that they had three echoes, and advised me to turn 180 degrees to be identified if I required a homing.

At this stage the two bright lights reformed at 'nine o'clock' from me, and disappeared on a north-easterly heading. I saw no other lights and was only able to make out a vague shape with the white light situated centrally on top. Their apparent crossing speed was the fastest I have ever experienced, and at the time I was indicating 220 knots. [from Shamus O'Farrell's official signed report, dated September 2, 1954, in National Archives of Australia]

Now you see them, now you don't! Pilot O'Farrell saw them, and Nowra had them briefly on ground radar!

The duty radar operator at Nowra base on this occasion was Petty Officer Keith Jessop. He, too, wrote a brief report of the incident for his superiors.

A copy of it was included in the Navy Office files:

At 7.07pm. [19.07hours] aircraft 921 [O'Farrell's Sea Fury] called up and asked if we had him on radar. After checking G.C.I. remote display, we found that two paints appeared on the display, approximately 280 degrees, 32 miles (52km).

After about 15 seconds another paint appeared in the same vicinity. One appeared to be tracking towards base, the others in a north-easterly direction.

About two minutes later we told 921 to fly 180 degrees if he wanted a bearing, so we could identify him. His reply was 'Negative', so we did not track the paints any further. [from Keith Jessop's signed, official report, undated, in National Archives of Australia]

Sea Fury 921 landed back at Nowra at 7.30pm (19.30 hours), and Shamus O'Farrell found he had a small welcoming party. 'They asked,' he said, 'are you sure you had aircraft out there?' and I said 'Yes.'

The Surgeon Commander came over and spoke to me. He asked if I felt sick, or was I upset. I said 'No'. He ran his hand over my head to see whether I had any bumps. He had a look at me and decided I was okay.

Then he said, 'Perhaps you'd like to come to the Sick Bay after you've changed and we'll do an examination.' After I was finished, I went up to the Sick Bay and he gave me a more thorough medical [examination]. He said I 'appeared to be alright.'

I found out later that, at the same time, they checked to make sure I hadn't been drinking before I took off, and all that sort of thing. [Shamus O'Farrell, in Bill Chalker, *The 'Sea Fury Incident,'* auforn.com]

Two independent witnesses were subsequently located.

The first of these was an un-named technician who was repairing an out-of-service aircraft navigational aid, known as a Non Directional Beacon (NDB), at Marulan in New South Wales. He had observed the two bright lights flying overhead. Marulan is located on the Hume Highway, the main road link between Sydney and Melbourne, and twice crossed by O'Farrell's flight path.

The other was an un-named air traffic controller at Sydney's Kingsford Smith airport — Australia's busiest terminal. He logged two unidentified lights at a time that linked them to O'Farrell's incident.

Night-time Encounter

So these are the bare bones of this sighting.

But this encounter grew over the intervening years with additional information, further interviews, and a dramatized reconstruction that blurred or extended the edges of the known details.

One contribution to this dilemma was published in the book *Flight Into The Ages* by Ken Llewelyn (1991), a former senior public relations officer for the Royal Australian Air Force (RAAF).

Llewelyn's book includes an interview with pilot O'Farrell which commenced with the words 'From memory' — which is fair enough when one considers it was published 37 years after the event, although the date of the interview itself is not provided.

O'Farrell's account includes his 360° turn of the Sea Fury and the side-by-side formation flying of the 'two aircraft' with his plane — which is unusual because neither situation is included in the official reports written by the participants soon after the event.

Many later accounts of the Sea Fury incident include these aspects of the incident as part of O'Farrell's experience.

Lt. O'Farrell's description of the unexpected aircraft in Llewelyn's book is interesting, too:

I was surprised when I spotted two aircraft, one on either side of me, each with a single bright light above it, but with no navigation lights.

Then I thought about it for some time to make sure I wasn't seeing things that weren't there. But, sure enough, I could see two dark, cigar-shaped objects, not very long — about the size of a Dakota — but their central bright lights made their outlines quite distinct. I could see not other detail, no other lights, just the one bright light centrally placed over the top of each mass. [Shamus O'Farrell in *Flight Into the Ages*, (Sydney, 1991) p.137]

O'Farrell's recollections above seem to be in conflict with his original written report in which he wrote: *I saw no other lights and was only able to make out a vague shape.*

Even the reporting that brought the Nowra Sea Fury incident to public notice is mired in errors.

Four months after the incident (on December 15, 1954) the then Melbourne afternoon newspaper, *The Herald*, published the following report by E.H.Cox under a headline:

NAVY RADAR PICKS UP TWO SAUCERS:

Two objects — believed to be flying saucers — have been recorded by radar at the Nowra naval air station. This was revealed today when the Minister for the Navy, Mr. Francis, visited the station.

A naval pilot flying a single-seater fighter from Canberra to Nowra just after dark a few days ago was joined in the air by two strange aircraft resembling saucers. He called Nowra air control to trace him by radar.

Nowra reported that the radar screen showed three aircraft flying together. The naval pilot identified himself by executing movements in accordance with directions from Nowra.

He later reported two unidentified objects which flew in company with him for some time were much faster than his Sea Fury fighter....

The identity of the mysterious machines has not been identified.

The following day's edition of *The Herald* ran a non by-lined, follow-up story that read, in part:

THOSE SAUCERS: THE MYSTERY DEEPENS

The Naval pilot who was buzzed by two flying saucers is believed to be Lieutenant R. O'Farrell of Sydney. But the authorities have not officially released the pilot's name. This is part of the hush-hush surrounding the three-months-old saucer incident. [*The Herald*, December 16, 1954]

The *Sydney Morning Herald* on December 16, 1954 had a very different approach:

THOSE SAUCERS BAFFLE NAVY EXPERTS

Sydney, Today — Naval authorities admitted today that they cannot find any human source for the flying saucers recorded on a radar screen at Nowra. At the same time saucers were seen on the screen, a Sea Fury pilot reported saucer shapes flashing past him.

Authorities confirm that the pilot was 'a man of experience'. They said they had investigated 'every human source' but could not logically explain the shapes. The mystery of the shapes is locked away in Naval files.

Melbourne's morning tabloid, *The Argus*, broke the UFO incident to their readers on December 16, 1954. (they'd been scooped by *The Herald's* afternoon edition on the previous day):

The Navy report is the first authenticated information in the world of the existence of flying saucers. But officials revealed yesterday that the incident occurred three months ago... many pilots at Nowra and senior Navy men declare they are puzzled by the report.

The pilots, many of them with combat experience in Korea, discount the possibility that the two objects could have been unauthorized aircraft... In talk among themselves they refer to the flying saucer incident but, because of the top secret classification of the incident, news of the occurrence has been kept from the public.

In their following day's paper, *The Argus* both congratulated itself and suggests the source of this top-secret news leak. It infers rather than categorically stating that Minister for the Navy, Mr Francis, was the source of their story:

Radar report confirmed

MINISTER SAYS SAUCERS WERE REAL

Canberra, Thursday. Mr. Francis, Navy Minister, tonight confirmed the sensational flying saucers report by a Royal Australian Navy pilot in the Argus yesterday.

Mr. Francis said the pilot, in a Sea Fury, observed 'two lights on his radar with vague shapes underneath' as he flew 13,000 feet (4km) above Goulburn, New South Wales.

Official secrecy, which has surrounded the sighting for three months, was broken when Mr. Francis and a group of Pressmen visited the Nowra (New South Wales) naval station — H.M.A.S. Albatross. [*The Argus* (Melbourne) December 17, 1954]

How did all this publicity affect pilot Shamus O'Farrell?

During an 11-minute segment on the Warwick Moss 1993 TV program *The Alien Files,* O'Farrell described how he felt:

It was generally regarded as a bit of a joke by the rest of the aircrew. People would have a few drinks, and say to you 'Have another drink, O'Farrell, and tell us a bit more about those flying saucers!'...

As the years went by, I became more embarrassed, and wiped it out of my memory, and never worried about it again ... I didn't see any need to tell anybody else about it, or talk about it.

As if O'Farrell's close encounter with two unidentified flying objects in 1954 was insufficient, an Australian television program re-introduced the 360° turn aspect with the apparent approval of both individuals directly involved.

To some, this additional detail made the validity of O'Farrell's sighting more persuasive, and certainly more dramatic in its visual presentation.

The presenter/anchorman of *The Alien Files* was Warwick Moss, who has also presented a similar TV series, *The Extraordinary*, which deals with a myriad of paranormal events.

Just under three minutes into the 'Sea Fury' segment, Warwick Moss addressed his audience directly:

> The actual tapes of the radio transmissions between the Sea Fury and Nowra base have been erased by the Defense Department, but the conversations you will [now] hear are as close as we can get to the real thing.
>
> They are the recollections of the pilot, Shamus O'Farrell, and his link with Nowra base radio operator, Petty Officer Keith Jessop.

Both men participated in the overall segment, and UFO researcher Bill Chalker was also present.

In the reconstruction of the radio transmissions between O'Farrell and Jessop, both spoke over radio static background noise to simulate actual conditions.

Extracted from this reconstruction are the following exchanges:

Keith Jessop: Nowra base to 921. We have you on screen with two other echoes, can you confirm? Over.

Shamus O'Farrell: Contacting Nowra base, yes, I'm at 13,000 feet in close formation with two other aircraft.

Keith Jessop: Nowra base to 921. Can you identify aircraft for us please?

Shamus O'Farrell: 921. Negative.

Keith Jessop: Nowra base to 921. Could you execute a 180-degree turn, so we can identify your position?

Shamus O'Farrell: 921. Commencing a 180-degree turn.

Keith Jessop: Nowra base to 921. Complete 360 [degrees] and return to track. Over.

Shamus O'Farrell: 921. Roger.

The TV show had another surprise to reveal, too. Shamus O'Farrell confirmed the unknown lights flew in formation with him, one on each side:

> They were formatting on me, and holding their station with me. They were about the same distance out on either side.

Warwick Moss re-stated this point, more directly:

> Suddenly he (O'Farrell) was confronted with the impossible. Two unidentified craft — two brilliant white lights — flying in formation with the Sea Fury. One was about thirty meters [100 feet] on his port side, the other thirty meters to starboard.

Why such pertinent information about the encounter — the Sea Fury's 360° turn and the objects flying in formation with O'Farrell's plane — was not included in the participant's official Navy accounts has never been explained.

Nineteen years after his Sea Fury encounter, Shamus O'Farrell was still actively engaged in the Royal Australian Navy's Fleet Air Arm.

In 1973 O'Farrell received a telephone call from Sir Arthur Tange, Secretary of the Department of Defense, announcing that Dr J Allen Hynek, former consultant to the US Air Force, was coming to Australia and 'he (Tange) would like me to meet him (Hynek).'

O'Farrell later repeated to Bill Chalker his response the Minister was:

> I haven't got all the facts; they're all a bit hazy. So he [Tange] sent me the two Defense Department files over to read, to refresh it all.

O'Farrell later discussed his time with Hynek:

> He was a very interesting chap, and he made the comment that there were about 13 or 15 sightings, I don't remember which, that he was aware of over the years that were like mine and could not be explained away.

> The interesting thing, he said, was that all these sightings had been made by professional people in aviation. By that he meant they were military pilots, military aircrew, civil aviation operators, air traffic controllers, airline pilots and the like.

They were the ones he [Hynek] was now [in 1973] going around meeting the people themselves and investigating.

All the others [sightings by non aviation people] he had written off and had been able to explain down to some other phenomena.

It came to the point where he said [to O'Farrell] 'Your sighting cannot be explained away' and he left it at that. To this day I wouldn't know where it came from or where it went. [Bill Chalker, *The 'Sea Fury' Incident*, ufocasebook.com/seafury.html]

Despite his initial doubts, Shamus O'Farrell's naval career does not appear to have suffered as a result of his UFO sightings. Among his several subsequent postings he has been Commander Air and Fleet Aviation on H.M.A.S. *Melbourne*, and Australian Naval Attache in Washington.

In 1984 the R.A.N. newspaper *Navy News* published a resume of Shamus O'Farrell's career, commencing with:

OLDEST PILOT TOUCHES DOWN

The RAN's oldest pilot, **Commodore J. A. O'Farrell**, retired recently after a career of 37 years [*Navy News*, 9 March 1984, p.4.]

4. Merger in Skies over Zanthus

"The smaller objects merged with the larger one"

'Walter abruptly woke me up in great excitement and asked me to come into the cockpit quickly. I did so, and he asked me if I could see what he was looking at. At first I didn't because I was still suffering from the effect of sleep, however after about 30-seconds I could see what he was excited about ...' [Captain Gordon Smith]

So began what became known as the Zanthus Aircraft Encounter of 1968.

Captain Gordon Smith and Captain Walter Gardin, 34, were flying an empty, eight-seater Piper Navajo (VH-RTO) to Perth after a charter flight to Adelaide.

At the time of Capt. Smith's abrupt awakening, they were cruising at 8,000-feet (2½ miles) over Zanthus, a remote Western Australian outpost on the Trans Australian railway – about 210kms (130 miles) east of Kalgoorlie. It was 5.40pm local time.

Why was Captain Walter Gardin so excited? Capt. Smith explained:

> Some distance ahead, at the same level and about 50° to my right (I was in the right seat) I saw a formation of aircraft. In the middle was a larger aircraft, and formatted to the right and left and above were four or five smaller aircraft. We were on a track of 270° magnetic, and these aircraft appeared to be maintaining station with us. [extract from Capt. G. Smith's official report of incident]

Because he hadn't been notified of other air traffic sharing an almost identical track, Smith radioed Kalgoorlie communications center and asked about other traffic in his flight area.

He was told there was none!

He informed Kalgoorlie of the formation he had in sight, and they in turn notified other eastbound traffic of the 'danger of unidentified traffic 203km (126miles) east of Kalgoorlie'.

Then the Piper Navajo lost all radio communications with Kalgoorlie, on all frequencies. They were receiving the carrier wave without voice propagation — 'only a hash and static' were heard in the plane.

Both pilots sent several transmissions to Kalgoorlie without receiving a response. Capt. Smith said 'I transmitted about 7 times, and Walter [Capt. Gardin] about 6 times with no results.'

During this period of radio black out, Captain. Walter Gardin was required to make a position report to Kalgoorlie. He had tried, but couldn't contact them. Because of their failure to make this report, the Dept. of Civil Aviation (DCA) Kalgoorlie, became concerned the aircraft may have crashed.

Meanwhile things were changing with the aircraft formation they were closely observing:

> Also at about this time we noticed that the main ship split into two sections while maintaining the same level, and the smaller craft then flew out left and right, but staying at the same level, and coming back to the two main halves of the bigger ship.
>
> At this time there appeared to be about 6 smaller aircraft taking turns of going out and coming back and formatting on the two halves. Sometimes the two halves joined and split, and the whole cycle continued for ten minutes. [extract from Capt. G. Smith's official report of incident.]

The trained eyes of Capt. Gordon Smith also noted other peculiarities:

> The shape of the main ship seemed to have the ability to change, not dramatically, but a change from say, spherical to a slightly elongated form, with the color maintaining a constant dark gray or black.
>
> However, the smaller craft had a constant cigar shape, and were of a very dark color. Their travel out and back had a peculiarity not associated with normal aircraft — in fact they appeared to travel out and come back without actually turning like a normal aeroplane would have to. [from Capt. G. Smith's official report.]

Merger in the Skies

This dazzling aerial display was about to end:

At 0950GMT [5.50pm local time] the whole formation joined together as if at a single command, then departed at a tremendous speed. Not disappeared as, say, gas would but departed in about 3 or 4 seconds, diminishing in size till out of sight.

The weather at the time of sighting was fine, with no haze above 6,000' and about 2/8 altostratus cloud to the south of us and the other aircraft. [from Capt. G. Smith's official report.]

At the conclusion of his written report on this incident, Capt. Smith added a further four points of clarification, as follows:

Notes on UFO:

1.The distance from our aircraft of the UFO would be impossible to gauge, because the prerequisite of establishing distance is to know size, and the size of these objects are unknown. However, for comparison size, the main ship compared to that of a Boeing 707 from about 10 miles [16kms].

2.Immediately after the departure of the UFO, radio communications were restored.

3.Neither Walter or myself had the presence of mind to check if any deviation existed in our magnetic compass or automatic direction finding equipment whilst in the presence of the UFOs.

4.The whole formation maintained the same distance and bearing from our aircraft during the whole time of the sighting.

Captains Smith and Gardin discussed the sighting at length, both during the sighting and afterwards, trying to account for what they saw. They considered the possibility of balloons, gases, tricks of lights, and aircraft.

The first two alternatives were dismissed because they had flown a distance of 30 miles [48kms] between the Captain. Smith's first sighting to its disappearance (and you wouldn't see a balloon at 30 miles).

If it had been a trick of light, they fathomed, the color of the UFO should have changed because the sun had a considerable traverse, coupled with their westward travel during the time. Then they reached the only conclusion that would satisfy their understanding:

We concluded that the UFOs were in fact aircraft, with the solidarity of aircraft – except for the fact of the larger UFO's ability to split and change shape slightly. [Captain Gordon Smith]

When the Piper Navajo (VH-RTO) landed at Kalgoorlie at 6.38pm on the 22 August 1968, there were police in attendance because of the prospect the plane may have crashed.

Smith and Gardin were officially asked to confirm their UFO sighting, which they did, but they did not discuss any conclusions they'd reached about the possible source of the 'flying formation' they had both seen.

On departing for Perth an hour later, they were advised to make a full report to the RAAF base at Pearce.

Now our story moves into the murky field of newspaper reporting.

The first published news report of the Zanthus incident appeared in the *Daily News* (Perth) on the day following the sighting:

PILOT TELLS OF STRANGE UFO

An unidentified flying object was seen by two commercial pilots about 130 miles east of Kalgoorlie yesterday was so vivid that they immediately notified the Civil Aviation Department to safeguard any other aircraft in the area ... [they] were also concerned about the safety of their own aircraft.

Mr. Smith said he was resting in the rear of the cabin at 5.40pm when Mr. Gardin called him forward to look at a strange object about ten mile ahead of them. Mr. Gardin had followed the path of the object for about 10 minutes. It first appeared as a white glow and traveled at the same time and speed as their aircraft.

Mr. Smith said it was hard to distinguish the shape and size of the object but he likened it to the size of a Boeing 707 at 10 miles (16km).

The main object continued to split into two halves and small cigar-shaped objects continually left what he called the mother ship. The smaller objects, about six of them, flew out 3 or 4 miles (c.5.6km) and then merged back on to the two main parts of the mother ship.

After about 20 minutes the main object took off with the speed of a rocket. Mr. Smith, who had been flying for about 13 years, had never seen a UFO before. [*Daily News* (Perth), August 23, 1968]

Two days after the incident, Saturday 24 August 1968, another Perth newspaper ran a short report on the Zanthus sighting:

CHECK ON SIGHTING

The sighting of an unidentified flying object by two commercial pilots near Kalgoorlie on Thursday will be investigated by the R.A.A.F. Mr. Gordon Smith of Tuart Hill and Mr. Walter Gardin of South Perth, made full reports of the sighting to Department of Aviation officials at Kalgoorlie.

Mr. Smith said ... he was sure it was not an aircraft or a satellite. He said that a big white object had flown on a collision course with their Piper Navajo aircraft for twenty minutes before speeding out of sight.

It appeared to emit several big dish-like objects which kept within a few miles of the main object then merged with it again. [*West Australian*, August 24, 1968 p.13]

The central information in this account of the Zanthus Aircraft Encounter draws almost exclusively on Keith Basterfield's re-examination of the case published on-line on September 25, 2011, in his Project 1947 blog. Keith found Captain. Smith's written report in an RAAF Department of Defense file at the National Archives of Australia.

He also announced a research break-through in his quest for a fuller understanding of the Zanthus case:

I was fortunate enough the other day [15 September 2011] to be able to locate and interview, by phone, one of the pilots involved in this event. Walter Gardin is now [in 2011] aged 77, being 34 when the event transpired. He was kind enough to... provide some interesting new details, which have not seen light of day in 43 years.

In answer to one of Basterfield's questions about the merging of the formation to become a single object, Walter Gardin said:

Yes, they all merged. The smaller objects merged with the larger one by going in to it from underneath. The one object then departed by going upwards at a 45 degree angle from the aircraft's horizon. It diminished in size as if receding. [Walter Gardin, telephone interview with K. Basterfield, 2011]

So, after a silence exceeding four decades, we learn that the cigar-shaped smaller craft merged with the larger 'mothership' by entering it from below.

Gardin also confirmed that the sun was above the horizon at the time; that there was a clear blue sky in the direction of the formation; that the angular size of both the larger and smaller objects remained constant, and that there was no air turbulence at the time of the sighting.

Keith Basterfield found 'one potential explanation for the event' — it was a mirage.

> Martin Shough suggested this 'possible answer' in an article about the BOAC Stratocruiser flight, New York-London, with Captain James Howard on June 29, 1954 (see: caelestia.be/BOAC-appc.html]

Expressed briefly, Captain Howard, and his crew and some passengers, saw some strange objects moving at the same speed on a parallel course at about 3 or 4 miles (5½kms] to their north-west. 'There was one large object and six smaller globular things,' Capt. Howard reported:

> The small ones were strung out in a line, sometimes three ahead and three behind the large one, sometimes two ahead and four behind, and so on, but always at the same level. The larger object was continually, slowly, changing shape, in the way that a swarm of bees might alter its appearance. They appeared to be opaque and hard-edged, gray in color, no lights or flames visible. [Captain James Howard, in Timothy Good's *Beyond Top Secret*, (London, 1996) p.191]

Several email exchanges between Keith Basterfield and Martin Shough followed, swapping data, seeking further details and explanations, and comparing arguments.

Martin Shough's argument was complex. He commented:

> As with the BOAC Ladrador case, the lateral movements of the smaller objects occurred in a very narrow band ('without actually turning like a normal aeroplane would have to'). Interestingly, this happened at the same time the "main ship split into two sections" which might suggest that the inversion layer became thicker at that point allowing more objects to enter the mirage duct.

In the end, Keith Basterfield drew his own conclusion:

> I don't believe that the mirage hypothesis (for Zanthus) is valid. In my opinion, this event represents an excellent example of a 'core' UFO phenomenon, and deserved a scientific investigation at the time (1968).

In Timothy Good's 1996 book, *Beyond Top Secret*, Good concludes his short mention of the Zanthus incident with the following intriguing paragraph:

Merger in the Skies

When the American atmospheric physicist Dr James McDonald attempted to make further enquiries about the (Zanthus) incident, the pilots refused to respond. Years later, a pilot member of the Victorian UFO Research Society who was personally acquainted with Gardin and Smith confirmed that the pilots had been ordered not to discuss the encounter. [*Beyond Top Secret*, p.166].

Timothy Good drew on Paul Norman's article 'Countdown to Reality' in *Flying Saucer Review* [Vol. 31, No 2, 1986, p.17] for this information.

* *

In October 2011, Keith Basterfield posted online another cold case investigation in which he pointed out some remarkably similar parallels to the Zanthus Aircraft Encounter of 1968.

The incident happened on January 10, 1954, fourteen years before Zanthus, and involved an Australian National Airlines (ANA) DC3 flight from Broken Hill, New South Wales to Adelaide, South Australia.

When this flight was just north of Morgan (on the Great South Bend of the Murray River) Captain W Booth said the object appeared on and off for about six minutes:

> His co-pilot, First Officer Furness said the object seemed to move back and forth across their line of flight as though circling, but they could not catch up with it. Both the men said the object must have been an optical illusion but could not explain how it occurred ... [Adelaide *Advertiser*, January 11, 1954, p.1]

Keith Basterfield pointed out the DC3 was flying at 8,000ft – as with Zanthus. An official check revealed there were no other aircraft in the area at the time – as with Zanthus. The sun had just set – as with Zanthus. And finally, the object appeared to be at the same altitude as the DC3 – as with Zanthus.

> First Officer Furness said the object ...appeared to be circling slowly and resembled the silhouette of an aircraft at a distance of 40-50 miles [64–80kms]. Captain Booth said he had been flying for 14 years and had never seen a similar sight before. [Adelaide) *Advertiser*, Jan.11, 1954, p.1]

5. Valentich vanishes over Bass Strait

"I think he encountered a UFO."

This was Frederick Valentich's big day ...a solo flight, partly over ocean waters, and at night.

On the young pilot's flight plan he nominated an hour and nine minutes to reach his destination, King Island, which is halfway across the western entrance of treacherous Bass Strait. Once there, he would pick up a few friends and return to his base at Moorabbin, one of Melbourne's general aviation airports.

The date was Saturday, October 21,1978 — five months after Frederick obtained his class-four instrument rating permitting him to fly in these conditions — and he was keen to add some more flying hours in his Log Book. He had flown this route before, but not at night.

It was a trip he never completed.

Valentich hired a blue and white Cessna 182, call sign Delta Sierra Juliet, for the flight, and had sufficient fuel to stay airborne for five hours. Having completed the necessary paperwork, he took off from Moorabbin at 6.19pm. and headed towards Cape Otway.

Once in the air, Valentich established radio communication with Melbourne Flight Control (M.F.C.), located at Melbourne's major airport, Tullamarine. Duty officer for the sector covering this flight that evening was Steve Robey, a pilot himself.

Valentich Vanishes

At 7pm., precisely on schedule, Valentich reported being over Cape Otway.

The next message received from Valentich's 'Delta Sierra Juliet' was at 7.06:14p.m. The following communications were recorded from this time — words in brackets are open to other interpretations; M.F.C.stands for 'Melbourne Flight Control':

Adapted from the official Aircraft Accident Investigation Summary Report

7.06:14pm Pilot: MELBOURNE this is DELTA SIERRA JULIET is there any known traffic below five thousand

7.06:23pm M.F.C: DELTA SIERRA JULIET no known traffic

7.06:26pm Pilot: DELTA SIERRA JULIET I am seems (to) be a large aircraft below five thousand

7.06:46pm M.F.C: D DELTA SIERRA JULIET what type of aircraft is it?

7.06:50pm.Pilot: DELTA SIERRA JULIET I cannot affirm it is four bright it seems to me like landing lights

7.07:04pm M.F.C: DELTA SIERRA JULIET

7.07:32pm Pilot: MELBOURNE this (is) DELTA SIERRA JULIET the aircraft has just passed over me at least a thousand feet above

7.07:43pm M.F.C: DELTA SIERRA JULIET roger and it is a large aircraft confirm

7.07:47pm Pilot: er unknown due to the speed it's traveling is there any air force aircraft in the vicinity

7.07.57pm M.F.C: DELTA SIERRA JULIET no known aircraft in the vicinity

7.08:18pm. Pilot: MELBOURNE it's approaching now from due east towards me

7.08:28pm M.F.C: DELTA SIERRA JULIET

7.08:42pm /open microphone for two seconds/

7.08:49pm Pilot: DELTA SIERRA JULIET it seems to me that he's playing some sort of game he's flying over me two three times at a time at speeds I could not identify.

7.09:02pm **M.F.C:** DELTA SIERRA JULIET roger what is your actual level

7.09:06pm **Pilot:** my level is four and a half thousand four five zero zero [feet]

7.09:11 p.m. **M.F.C:** DELTA SIERRA JULIET and confirm you cannot identify the aircraft

7.09:14pm **Pilot:** affirmative

7.09:18 pm **M.F.C:** DELTA SIERRA JULIET roger standby

7.09:28 pm **Pilot:** MELBOURNE DELTA SIERRA JULIET it's not an aircraft it is… /open microphone for two seconds/

7.09:46pm **M.F.C:** DELTA SIERRA JULIET MELBOURNE can you describe the er aircraft

7.09:52pm **Pilot:** DELTA SIERRA JULIET as it's flying past it's a long shape /open mike 3 seconds/ (cannot) identify more than (that) it has such speed /open mike 3 seconds/ before me right now Melbourne

7.10:07pm **M.F.C:** DELTA SIERRA JULIET roger and how large would the er object be

7.10:20pm **Pilot:** DELTA SIERRA JULIET MELBOURNE it seems like its stationary.* What I'm doing right now is orbiting and the thing is just orbiting on top of me also it's got a green light and sort of metallic (like) it's all shiny (on) the outside

* This word has been interpreted by some who have listened to the actual tape as 'chasing me' not 'stationary'.

7.10:43pm **M.F.C:** DELTA SIERRA JULIET

7.10:48pm **Pilot:** DELTA SIERRA JULIET /open microphone for 5 seconds/ it's just vanished

7.10:57pm **M.F.C:** DELTA SIERRA JULIET

7.11:03pm **Pilot:** MELBOURNE would you know what kind of aircraft I've got is it (a type) military aircraft

7.11:08pm **M.F.C:** DELTA SIERRA JULIET confirm the er aircraft just vanished

Valentich Vanishes

7.11:14pm Pilot: Say again

7.11:17pm M.F.C: DELTA SIERRA JULIET is the aircraft still with you

7.11:23pm Pilot: DELTA SIERRA JULIET (it's ah nor) / open microphone for 2 seconds / (now) approaching from the southwest

7.11:37pm M.F.C: DELTA SIERRA JULIET

7.11:52pm Pilot: DELTA SIERRA JULIET the engine is rough idling I've got it set at twenty three twenty four and the thing is (coughing)

7.12:04pm M.F.C: DELTA SIERRA JULIET roger what are your intentions

7.12:09pm Pilot: my intentions are ah to go to King Island ah Melbourne that strange aircraft is hovering on top of me again / two seconds open microphone / it is hovering and it's not an aircraft

7.12:22pm M.F.C: DELTA SIERRA JULIET

7.12.28 pm Pilot: DELTA SIERRA JULIET MELBOURNE /17 seconds open microphone/

7.12:49pm M.F.C: DELTA SIERRA JULIET MELBOURNE

That was the end of the recorded transmissions. No words were spoken during the final 17 seconds when Valentich's 'open microphone' was recorded at 7.12.28pm, but crackling from a 'strong electromagnetic interference' was detected.

Nothing further was heard from Frederick Valentich.

His fate, and the identity of the unidentified 'non-aircraft' he encountered over Bass Strait, has been the basis of continual investigation and speculation.

Among the speculation is the claim that the official transcript of the flight tapes were 'censored' – that eighty words describing the flying object which harassed Valentich were removed from the end of the tape. As recently as 2012 this claim re-surfaced in the *Ufologist* magazine – but there important differences between claims and proof.

Immediately following the cessation of the two-way radio communication, Melbourne Flight Control sent an alert to all airports, aeroplanes, light stations, police stations, fishing co-ops and shipping in the area, advising them of the situation.

'I'd been playing golf,' the flight service supervisor at King Island, Brian Jones, recalled, 'and got a call to say that an aircraft was missing across Bass Strait.'

Jones went to the airport, turned on the runway lights, and began calling 'Delta Sierra Juliet' — without response.

At 7.33pm, when the Cessna failed to arrive at King Island, the 'Distress Phase' of Search and Rescue procedures was declared.

An air, land and sea search began involving fishing vessels, the Melbourne-Launceston vehicular ferry, other ocean-going ships, a Royal Australian Air Force P-3 Orion aircraft fitted with special metal-tracking sensors, and eight civilian planes. The media were also notified of the missing Cessna.

Brian Jones from King Island joined the search almost immediately.

'It was an unreal night,' he recalled, 'there was no wind, and when we got out to sea you could actually see the reflection of the stars in the water' — a most uncommon phenomena in Bass Strait.

At Fredrick's home in suburban Melbourne, confusion reigned. 'When at first he didn't come,' his father, Guido, recalled, 'we thought he'd had an accident. At around 11pm. some journalist mentioned to me that he heard it was to do with some strange object surrounding him. This was the first hint we heard about some UFO.'

The following morning Frederick's girlfriend, Rhonda Rushton, heard the 6am radio news report of a missing Cessna over Bass Strait, and rang Moorabbin airport immediately. 'They said to me 'How are you related? Why are you inquiring?' and I said 'I'm Frederick's girlfriend, if it's Frederick.' They said, 'Yes it is.'

The thrust of the story had changed overnight. 'In a matter of 24-hours it turned into a major UFO mystery because the ground-to-air conversation had been 'leaked', Australian UFO researcher Bill Chalker recalled on the US late-night radio show Coast to Coast AM in 2005, 'It was literally a front page story right around the world, and caused quite a sensation but, sadly, the reality of it is: Valentich disappeared, and hasn't been found since.'

The search for the aeroplane, or its wreckage or debris from a crash, continued for several days, covering an area greater than 1,000 square miles (around 2,500 square kilometers).

Valentich Vanishes

An article in Melbourne's *Age* newspaper on the third day of the search read:

> The father of missing pilot Frederick Valentich said yesterday he hoped an unidentified flying object had been involved in his son's disappearance.
>
> 'I would rather that than finding wreckage of the plane.' The second day of the land and sea search failed to find any trace of the 182 Cessna yesterday. Mr. Guido Valentich said he was forced to believe that something unusual had happened to his son. 'The fact they have found no trace of him really verifies the fact that UFOs could have been there,' he said.

The search was called off on October 25, 1978, four days after the incident. Nothing associated with the Cessna 182 or pilot Valentich were discovered ... no wreckage, no plane parts, nor floating life preservers, fuel tanks or oil slicks. Zilch.

Some fascinating evidence emerged over two months later.

Ken Llewelyn, former Royal Australian Air Force public relations officer, details it in his 1991 book *'Flight Into the Ages'*:

> ...amateur photographer, Roy Manifold, took a series of sunset shots off Cape Otway twenty minutes before Valentich made the first transmission to the Melbourne Flight Service Unit. Using a 35-mm Olympus camera set on a tripod, Manifold took a series of six photographs, about twenty seconds apart. At the time, all he saw through the viewfinder was a perfect sunset. [Ken Llewelwyn, *Flight Into the Ages*, Felspin, 1991, p.140]

Roy Manifold later admitted to a TV crew shooting for *The Unexplained Files:* 'It wasn't until I went down to the rocks next morning, and saw the Orion aircraft flying very low over the coastline, I asked the guys fishing on the river what the fuss was about? They said the Orion was looking for the plane that went missing last night.'

'I had heard a plane (overhead) the previous night, but didn't see it,' Roy Manifold told George Simpson, researcher for the *Unexplained Files* filmmaker.

Three weeks later, the [Manifold's photo] prints were collected from Kodak and Roy's wife, Brenda, noticed a smudge on one of the photos.

The couple were well aware of Valentich's disappearance because of the media coverage and their proximity to the last known position of the aircraft.

Brenda joked that it could be a UFO but her skeptical husband rejected the suggestion and gave the negatives back to Kodak to search for a more plausible explanation. No faults could be found on the negatives or prints. [Ken Llewelyn, *Flight Into the Ages*, p.141]

'The anomalies appeared in the fourth and sixth photographs,' declared UFO researcher Bill Chalker in his *'The Oz Files: the Australian UFO Story'* (1996):

> The fourth photo shows what looked like a dense 'black lump' in the water, giving the impression of something rising from the water. The fifth photo appeared normal. The sixth shows a strange mass situated in the sky directly over the position of the anomaly in the fourth photo. It looks like an object caught in flight with a possible exhaust or trail of material.

The late Paul Norman, then President of the Victorian UFO Research Society [VUFORS] in Melbourne, was acutely aware of the increasing UFO speculation, and offered support:

> Paul Norman had them [the photographs] computer-analyzed by Ground Saucer Watch of Phoenix, Arizona. The results concluded that 'the images represent a bona fide unknown object of moderate dimension, apparently surrounded by a cloud-like vapor or exhaust residue.' The results also showed that the object was about one kilometer [a little over half a mile] off-shore and measured eight meters [around 26ft.] in diameter. [Ken Llewelyn, *Flight Into the Ages* (Felspin, 1991) p.141]

Paul Norman's organization had been extremely busy with reports of strange phenomena in the skies leading up to the Valentich incident. He told an ABC Radio National program, first broadcast on May 21, 2000 — 22 years after the event:

> Six weeks prior to the Valentich disappearance, we [VUFORS] were receiving increasing numbers [of reports] of objects and erratic moving lights all around the area, and they reached a peak that very weekend that he disappeared ...all around Bass Strait they were seen by people along the Great Ocean Road, and on the Geelong Highway, and out at Cape Otway. [Paul Norman, *Radio National*, 21 May 2000]

Melbourne's daily newspapers, and other media outlets, received many other reports of unusual aerial sightings and wild speculations in the days and weeks that followed Valentich's disappearance:

> *The Age, Melbourne, October, 24, 1978* — Bank manager Mr. Col Morgan says he saw this star shaped glowing object hovering over the Melbourne-Geelong Road on Saturday night. He said he and his wife were driving to Geelong. The object appeared as they were passing

Valentich Vanishes

through Brooklyn at 7.10pm. ...it was only when they reached Geelong [61kms / 38 miles] that the object disappeared from view.

The Age, Melbourne, October 24, 1978 — Hundreds of sightings of UFOs were reported yesterday from Geelong, Frankston, Cape Otway and Brighton.

'A woman from Queenscliff said she saw what appeared to be a ferris wheel spinning in the sky less than two hours after Mr. Valentich's plane disappeared,' the *Sunday Age* reminded its readers in 2008 in a thirty-year review of the case

Another interesting comment comes from Llewelyn's 1991 book:

> One of the most intriguing sightings was one by a Port Phillip ship pilot, Captain Frank Jolley ...he said the object was conical in shape, about eighteen meters [60ft.] in diameter and traveling at between 100 and 200 knots at a height of about 900 meters [approx. 3,000ft]. This sixty-second observation by a professional who is well versed in unusual meteorological phenomena is particularly important to the Valentich case. It was over the same stretch of water that Frederick Valentich disappeared, and just twenty-two days after his disappearance. [Ken Llewelyn, *Flight Into the Ages*, p.122]

Paul Norman published an article in the VUFORS magazine disclosing perhaps the most important evidence to date about the Valentich disappearance. It was based on interviews he conducted with an un-named man with his two nieces and son. Norman revealed to his readers that three new eyewitnesses had come forward with an account of both 'the aircraft and a green light flying just above the aeroplane.'

The observations took place from a hill two kilometers [1¼ miles] west of Apollo Bay [16kms/10 miles directly north-east of Cape Otway], where a party of four were rabbit shooting. One of the ladies noted a green light to the south-west and called to the others to look. Her uncle looked up and saw the lights of an aircraft and thought she was referring to those lights.

> She said: 'No, look above the aircraft.' The uncle then saw the green light flying above. He suggested both aircraft and green light were about ten to twenty miles distant [from him]. [Paul Norman, *VUFORS Newsletter,* March 1991 issue]

The following day, when the uncle mentioned the green light after realizing that the pilot and aircraft were missing, his wife laughed at him and so did his workmates. Paul Norman asked him why he did not report the sighting earlier and he said, 'There was so much ridicule at that time that no one believed me.'

In the year 2000, Dr Richard Haines and Paul Norman co-wrote a 14-page article published in the *Journal of Scientific Exploration* (Vol.14, No.1) called *Valentich Disappearance: New Evidence and a New Conclusion.*

The new evidence in the article's title refers to the reports obtained from 20 eyewitnesses in the Apollo Bay — Cape Otway area describing an erratically moving green light in the sky at the same time of evening as Valentich's flight.

Bill Chalker, Australian UFO researcher, received permission in November 1982 to examine the Department of Aviation UFO files, but was specifically denied access to the Valentich files on the grounds they were Air Accident Investigation files and not UFO files.

Chalker knew a large file on the Valentich Affair existed within the Department of Transport bureaucracy:

> I last saw this file back in late 1982, while sitting in front of Mr. A. Woodward at the Melbourne office of the Bureau of Air Safety Investigation. He had the file opened in front of him while answering my questions. I was trying not to be too obviously seen reading the file in its upside down perspective. [Bill Chalker, *The Oz Files* website, June 28, 2012]

Access to this file, which later became known as 'DSJ-Cape Otway to King Island 21 October 1978 — Aircraft missing (Valentich) 1978 – 1992', was denied to UFO researchers. It subsequently became 'lost or mislaid' between government departments, or had been 'destroyed by fire'.

*

As the years passed, researchers looked for other examples that might parallel the Valentich mystery and provide some clues towards its solution.

Several cases came immediately to mind. The first occurred in December 1969 – nine years before Valentich's Bass Strait disappearance — and involved a 29-year-old pilot Peter Phillips flying from King Island [Bass Strait] to Moorabbin (Melbourne) in a low-wing Fuji aircraft. Department of Aviation officials said his final radio transmission stated he was eight kilometers from Cape Otway, flying at 1,000 feet (300 meters), when his engine began to run roughly. It appears likely the aircraft crashed into the sea, — however no trace of Peter Phillips or his plane were ever found.

Valentich Vanishes

The next incident happened almost three years later, in September 1972. Max Price, a very experienced owner-pilot, was flying a Tiger Moth between Hobart, Tasmania's largest city, to Flinders Island in Bass Strait to refuel, then on to Australia's capital, Canberra.

Despite carrying a high-frequency radio survival beacon, and being seen multiple times as it flew along Tasmania's east coast, the Tiger Moth and its two occupants disappeared without trace before reaching Flinders Island (350kms / 217 km) east of King Island).

A earlier unusual incident occurred during World War Two: an RAAF Beaufort bomber was flying at 4,500 feet/1370meters over Bass Strait one night in February, 1944 when an unexpected escort was seen by the crew keeping pace with their Beaufort at about 150 feet/46meters distance. It was described as a 'dark shadow' with flames erupting from its rearmost edge.

The Beaufort's navigational equipment and radio failed to operate during the twenty minutes the visitor retained its station. Then, suddenly, the escort departed at a speed three times greater than the Beaufort's capability. On landing, the incident was reported to superior officers, but the pilot claimed he was laughed at.

Interesting though they are, these cases didn't assist in the resolution of the main question: what caused pilot Valentich and his plane to vanish?

*

One 'extraordinarily bizarre and unbelievable claim' linked to the missing Valentich plane emerged on Bill Chalker's *The Oz Files* website.

In 1995, while investigating several UFO sightings in rural north-west New South Wales with his friend Robb Tilley, they became aware through a Coonabarabran hardware store owner, Laurie, who had been told a story of a South Australian farmer's experience on the day following the disappearance of Frederick Valentich:

> The farmer said he was harvesting lucerne when he heard a loud screeching sound coming from the harvester. He thought it might have been a bearing, so he uncoupled the harvester from the tractor's power drive, and jumped off and went back to have a look. The farmer was trying to work out the source of the continuing noise, when he became aware that he was in shadow.

He looked up and saw he was directly underneath a large saucer-shaped object, and going by the size of his harvester, he estimated it to be about 30 meters across (approx. 100 ft.). The loud screeching sound continued ... the farmer began to think there was something horribly wrong with this huge object. So he ran to get out from under it. He got the impression that one of the object's engines had stopped working.

He then told Laurie the most unusual thing was that he saw the massive object had a Cessna stuck to the outside of it – 'the whole aircraft.' It was flat up against the side of the object with its tail hanging down ... According to Laurie, the farmer said the object – 'the saucer' — still accompanied by the screeching sound then flew away over a ridge in the direction of a nearby Army range. [abbreviated from: Bill Chalker, *The Oz Files* website, October 18, 2013]

Chalker and Tilley have not yet found the South Australian farmer, and their informant Laurie has since died. While they have not abandoned their investigation of 'a number of different names and clues' their time and resources are limited.

George Simpson retold this story at the 2014 VUFOA conference in Melbourne hoping to attract other researchers to join the search for this mystery farmer/witness. The extent of his success, if any, is not publicly known.

*

In 2012, South Australian researcher Keith Basterfield submitted a Freedom of Information request trying to track the main Valentich file down. Keith said 'I submitted a request for access to the file, reasoning that [after more than thirty years] the papers on the file dated 1978-1981 should now be publicly available.'

His Freedom of Information request paid off, and Basterfield gained access to the 315-page central file on Valentich.

This file contained aviation data (flight plan, meteorological information, etc.), reports by Department investigators (conversations with fifteen individuals ranging from cray fishermen, flight instructors, and plane refueller, to Valentich's father, girlfriend, and close friends), and sixteen documents relating to radar plots, radio coverage, a single UFO report, and other information pertinent to the missing aircraft and pilot investigation. It also clearly stated 'The Region does not intend to take any further action on this matter unless positive factual evidence is obtained.'

During 2013, a documentary production team visited Bass Strait to review the Valentich story for America's cable TV service Discovery Channel as part of a series named *The Unexplained Files*.

Melbourne ufologist George Simpson became the local link in setting up the interviews with key people involved, and eventually appeared in the 25-minute episode himself, conducting several interviews. The program included comments by air traffic controller Steve Robey, American aircraft accident investigator Dr Richard Haines, King Island flight service officer Brian Jones, and clips of Frederick's father Guido Valentich, along with other contributors.

The Valentich family and friends erected a memorial plaque to Frederick in the grounds of the Cape Otway lighthouse in 1998. It displays a photograph of the pilot and airplane, and a touching account of his final radio transmission.

Guido Valentich paid an annual pilgrimage to this site until his death in May 2000. Rhonda Rushton, Frederick's former girlfriend, said, 'I didn't go there every year like Guido — it was too hard emotionally. I always went every five years — 5th, 10th, 15th, 20th, 25th and 30th. I missed the 35th year though [she now lives several thousand miles away in Queensland].'

Pilot Steve Robey from Melbourne Flight Control, the last person to speak with Frederick Valentich, unveiled the memorial plaque. What did Steve Robey think caused the plane and pilot to vanish?

'Well, it wasn't another aeroplane', he said. 'Another aeroplane wouldn't have traveled through the air like this thing did … at speed and changing direction so rapidly, disappearing at one point, orbiting on top of him while he was also orbiting.'

Then he added 'I think he encountered a UFO.'

6. Cressy Minister changes His Tune

"Out of the clouds above came six small discs"

The Rev. Lionel Browning had been skeptical about Unidentified Flying Objects for most of his life. He had read reports of them but they all seemed a little fanciful, and lacked any resonating truths that he believed would be necessary to alter his opinion.

Then, on October 4, 1960, an amazing thing happened:

Like most other people I got a big laugh out of these spaceship and flying saucer reports. But last Tuesday my wife and myself changed our tune. [Rev. Lionel Browning in *Flying Saucers Over Australia*, Stephen Holledge, (Horwitz, Sydney — 1965). p.77]

Rev. Browning, an Anglican minister at Cressy, Tasmania, was standing with his wife in the dining room of their home looking through a window at a distant rainbow during a rain squall:

As they were looking at the scene, his wife drew his attention to a long cigar-shaped object which was emerging from a rain squall. The object was a dull, greyish color and at regular intervals along its length had what looked like a short aerial array which projected outwards and upward from the north-facing end of the object. [Keith Roberts, Tasmanian UFO Investigation Centre (TUFOIC) in *Ufologist*, Vol.12, No.4, 2008., p.23]

At first I thought it must have been refracted light, but the thing had too much substance. It was traveling below fifty miles per hour and was certainly no normal aircraft because it was moving below stalling speed. [Rev. Lionel Browning in *Flying Saucers Over Australia*, Stephen Holledge,. P.77]

Rev. Browning calculated that the object 'seemed slightly longer than a Viscount aircraft' which he saw frequently flying in the area, so he estimated the object's length as one hundred feet (32 meters). He also reckoned, from landmarks below the object, that it was some 3 to 4 miles away [5 – 6½ kms].

The object was not stationary but moving north on an even keel and maintained a constant height of about 400 feet (120m.). Then it stopped.

Then the watching couple witnessed an amazing scene:

> It hovered about three miles from us. Then out of the clouds above and behind, came shooting five or six small discs. They moved at terrific speed towards the big ship. They came like stones skipping on water. They looked like real saucers — flat underneath with a dome on top. [Rev. Lionel Browning in *Flying Saucers Over Australia*, Stephen Holledge,. pps.77-78]

UFO investigator Keith Roberts describes the final moments of the sighting:

> The small objects stationed themselves at positions around the cigar at a radius of 800 meters. After an interval of several seconds, the cigar-shaped object, accompanied by the smaller objects, reversed [back towards and then] into the rain squall from which it had emerged. In all, the sighting had lasted about two minutes. [Keith Roberts, TUFOIC, in *Ufologist*, Vol.12, No. 4, 2008, p.23]

The couple watched and waited for a few minutes longer, hoping for a further appearance, but there was none. No unusual noises had been heard by the Brownings during their sighting.

'There was something ominous about the precision with which the homing took place around the mother ship,' Mr Browning commented.

Another eye-witness, Mrs D. Bransden said:

> 'It was a fantastic sight – like a lot of little ships flocking around a bigger one.' [Michael Hervey, *UFOs Over the Southern Hemisphere* (Robert Hale, London) 1975, p.208]

Cressy is a small country town of a thousand residents located about 30kms directly south of Launceston, Tasmania's second largest city after Hobart. It is a thriving rural community and highly regarded by trout fishermen.

Soon after his sighting, the Rev. Browning telephoned Launceston's Airport Control Tower at Western Junction — about

20kms/12.5 miles north-east of Cressy — and reported his experience.

According to Ben Hurle, director of Victorian UFO Action (VUFOA) who made a 'cold-case' video of *'The Cressy UFO Incident'* in 2014, 'they told him that they hadn't seen anything at that particular time.' They also confirmed that there had been no air traffic in the area. But they did file a report of Rev. Browning's sighting to the Civil Aviation Department's headquarters.

Two hours after the Browning's sighting, several residents in outlying districts heard a loud explosion that was followed by mild earth tremors.

'I could hear the earth shake' — Mrs J. Robson

'It was followed by rumbling vibrations' — Mr B. Spencer

Some suggested the noise came from the direction of the Rev. Browning's sighting.

Eighteen kilometers/11 miles south-west of Cressy, the Poatina underground power station was under construction at this time. Cressy residents were accustomed to hearing blasting coming from these works, but Ben Hurle emphasized 'there was definitely no work going on at that location at that time' [approximately 8 p.m. on Tuesday 4 October, 1960].

On October 6 — five days after their sighting – Rev. Browning provided a full report of the incident to his local newspaper, the Launceston *Examiner*.

As veteran Australian ufologist Bill Chalker later wrote:

> A succession of media stories followed, elevating the sighting in to national prominence. Again, because of the undeniable credibility of the witness, the RAAF [Royal Australian Air Force] were in a difficult position in their efforts to contain the rapidly escalating public clamor.
> [Bill Chalker, *UFOs Sub Rosa Down Under*, part 5, 1996]

The following day the *Examiner*'s front page announced:

FLYING SAUCER SEEN AT CRESSY.

Mysterious ships in the sky

The *Examiner* included a photograph looking out from the Browning's dining room, with Rev. Browning (wearing his clerical collar) pointing with outstretched arm in the direction he and his wife had seen the craft. Superimposed on the photograph was a drawing of the mothership and its surrounding discs.

There were a few errors in this Launceston *Examiner* story, according to TUFOIC's Keith Roberts:

> Apart from giving the length of the object as 300 instead of 100 feet/30m and having stated that he [Rev. Browning] knew of other witnesses, the published report was accurate. He [Rev. Browning] also stated the artist's impression depicted fairly accurately the shape, size and appearance of the objects but they should have been shown as being below and not above the skyline.

It was a scene impossible to photographically reproduce today. The Browning's Rectory had only been built the year before (1959), on a hill with commanding 180° views from north to south right across the valley. Now, after more than half a century, it is surrounded with high, mature trees and gardens which obliterate these views almost entirely.

Video presenter Ben Hurle of VUFOA mentioned other unexplained local aerial phenomena in the days and weeks following the Browning's encounter, including:

> 1. Ten days after the Browning's sighting (on 14th October) a woman and her daughter saw a cigar-shaped object 300 feet up, at 4.30p.m. in the Cressy area.
>
> 2. 17th October, a couple and their son saw a strange object emitting an eerie light south of Launceston near the airport. It was flying towards Cressy, and approached at a 'terrific speed'.
>
> 3. 18th October a father and his two sons, Mr R J Bretnall and Robin (13) and Terry (10), were fishing at Longford [10kms/6 miles north of Cressy]. The time was between 7.00p.m. and 8.00p.m. An object swooped down over them, made a whizzing noise, while an orange light flicked on and off. They described it as an 'aeroplane without wings.' It stayed for a short time, and then shot off towards Western Junction. [Ben Hurle, VUFOA video *'The Cressy UFO Incident'*, 2014]

Another incident happened on 18 October 1960, one later commented upon by South Australian researcher Keith Basterfield. Mrs D A Webster and her daughter of Delmont, Tasmania reported seeing a moving aerial object which began hovering at 4.30 p.m.. It was cigar-shaped, had a round nose and a sloping tail. Delmont is an area south-east of Cressy and shares the same postcode (7302).

Two days later, October 20, 1960, the topic of UFOs and the Cressy sighting were raised in Australia's Federal Parliament by their local Member, Mr Duthie, who asked during Question Time:

Has the Minister for Air read the reports of unidentified flying objects sighted in Australia in the last two years, especially the detailed description of such an object at Cressy in my electorate by the Reverend Lionel Browning and his wife two weeks ago, and twice last weekend? Does the Minister accept responsibility for investigating these sightings? Has the Minister any information about them that may be of interest to the people of Australia?

The Minister for Air, Mr Osborne, responded:

I have read the press reports of these sightings in Tasmania, and in accordance with the usual practice, all the information that is available concerning them has been furnished to my department and is now being examined. The Department of Air does obtain information about all well reported cases of unidentified flying objects.

Of all these reports, only 3%, or 4%, cannot be explained on the basis of some natural phenomenon, and nothing that has arisen from that 3% or 4% of unexplained cases gives any firm support to the belief that interlopers from other places in this world, or outside it, have been visiting us. [*Hansard Parliamentary Record*, October 20, 1960]

A week later, on October 27, 1960, Rev. Browning heard a loud explosion at 9.30 in the evening. His opinion, reported by Keith Roberts of TUFOIC, was that it was 'too close and loud' to originate from the hydro-electric construction zone ten miles away. It was, in Rev. Browning's words, 'associated in some way with the flying objects seen by him and his wife'.

On November 11 – almost six weeks after the initial event – the RAAF sent Wing Commander Gordon Waller to Cressy to interview the Rev. and Mrs Browning at the Cressy Rectory. Waller was the senior RAAF officer in Tasmania and in charge of the RAAF's University Training Squadron.

[Waller] had received a request from the Minister of Air to investigate a UFO sighting at Cressy. He was stationed in Hobart, so he went to the local aero club and hired an aircraft, flew it to Launceston, where he landed the aircraft in a paddock near to the Browning's residence.

Gordon [Waller] said that he was:

'...struck by the ordinariness of these two people' [referring to the Brownings]. He was impressed by the fact that the observation was 'not a fleeting observation'... (he) completed his official report on the case and sent it off to higher authority. [Keith Basterfield, *UFOs Scientific Research* blogspot, July 6, 2012]

His visit to Cressy lasted an hour and a half. One of the things Wing Commander Waller took away was a detailed plan drawing of the Browning's sighting, indicating 'trees', 'rain', 'heavy rain', the movement direction of the mothership and small discs, and distances marked in nautical miles.

Bill Chalker, quoting from a document he saw while searching official government files ('RAAF UFO Sightings file series 580/1/1, Part 2'), explains the interpretation placed on the Waller report:

> In a memorandum dated November 14, 1960, the Director of DAFI (Department of Air Force Intelligence) operations reported to the Australian government's Minister of Air's staff officer that 'a preliminary analysis of the available information indicates that this sighting was some form of natural phenomena associated with unsettled weather conditions.'
> [Bill Chalker in *UFOs and Government, A Historical Inquiry*, (Anomalist Books, San Antonio, 2012), p.386]

Was this an official attempt to discredit the sighting?

Bill Chalker, again:

> The Air Force Intelligence statement released a few days after Wing Commander Waller's interviews ... dismissed the [Browning's] observation as 'a phenomena (caused by) a moon rise associated with meteorological conditions at the time.' The intelligence report further stated, 'The presence of 'scud' type clouds, moving in varying directions due to turbulence in and around a rain squall near where the objects were sighted, and the position of the moon or its reflections, produced the impression of flying objects.' [Bill Chalker in *UFOs and Government, A Historical Inquiry*, p.386]

The Rev. Lionel Browning was none-too-pleased with the RAAF's explanation. At no time during his interview with the RAAF investigator, he said, was he asked about clouds. Keith Roberts of TUFOIC elaborates:

> The moon, he (Browning) said, would have been competing with a glorious sunset, whilst the easterly sky was not visible due to rain covering the Ben Lomond area.

A check reveals that the sun was indeed about to set in the western sky, and would have been the more likely of the two astronomical bodies to light up the sky. Rev. Browning told Professor McDonald [internationally acknowledged expert in meteorology and atmospheric physics] that the sun was illuminating the objects, there being a distinct difference between the dull grey of the larger object and the shiny, metallic luster of the smaller disc-like objects.

The moon was just rising, but at the time of the sighting would have been a mere 6 degrees to the east. In fact it may have had trouble at that time in being visible over mountains to the east. [Keith Roberts, Tasmanian UFO Investigation Centre (TUFOIC)].

Prof. James E McDonald interviewed Rev. Browning during an Australian visit in 1967. In March the following year, McDonald presented a paper titled 'UFOs – An International Problem' at an Astronautics Symposium held in Montreal, Canada. He quoted his interview with Rev. and Mrs. Browning and drew his own conclusions about the sighting:

> From my own viewpoint, as one interested in atmospheric optics and in unusual refractive anomalies, the official suggestion that "scud" subject to turbulent motions could be optically distorted into anything remotely resembling the phenomena reported by the Brownings seems entirely out of the question.
>
> In asserting such a meteorological explanation as was issued by the RAAF intelligence office, little evidence of scientific knowledge was exhibited, unless that office felt that the essential features of the Brownings' account had to be simply disregarded as unreliable. Yet the interrogating RAAF officer, Wg. Cdr. Waller, evidently had no such inclination to disregard these witnesses' description of their observations, nor do I. [extract from transcript of James E McDonald paper, *Astronautics Symposium*, Montreal (1968)]

*

On November 15, 1960, just four days after Rev. and Mrs Browning were interviewed by the RAAF, a United States Air Force JB-57 aircraft operating from the RAAF base at East Sale, Victoria had a UFO encounter while flying just north of Launceston, Tasmania.

When the pilot read the report of the Browning's sighting in the Melbourne press of November 18th, he decided to lodge an official report of his own encounter which had taken place a few days earlier.

Nothing was publicly known of this encounter until Bill Chalker disclosed the pilot's sighting report 'buried in the Department of Air Force Intelligence UFO files'. It read in part:

> I spotted the object and immediately commented to [the navigator] that it was not an aircraft, but looked more like a balloon. We judged its altitude to be approximately 35,000 feet/9140m., heading 140 degrees and its speed extremely high...

We observed this object for five or seven seconds before it disappeared under the left wing. Since it was unusual in appearance, I immediately banked to the left for another look, but neither of us could locate it.

The color of the object was nearly translucent, somewhat like that of a 'poached egg.' There was no sharp edges but rather fuzzy and undefined. The size was approximately 70 feet/21.3m in diameter and it did not appear to have any depth.

Nothing appears to have been done by RAAF personnel to appraise this sighting, assign it an alternative explanation, or disregard the experiencer's provided information in a public forum.

*

The Rev. Lionel Browning traveled to Melbourne soon after it had happened and spoke to a VUFORS meeting about his sighting. He became the patron of the Tasmanian Unidentified Flying Objects Investigation Center when it was started in 1965, and gave them many of his papers.

7. Moreland Story Hidden from Public

"I was bathed in green light"

Mrs Eileen Moreland's close encounter one misty New Zealand morning in 1959 remains only partly revealed more than half-a-century later.

Between then and now lies a new marriage, 'Top Secret' government documents and a fair bit of robust speculation – with American experts J Allen Hyneck and Prof. James E McDonald separately finding her case worthy of a visit to the South Island to gain her personal account of the incident.

Her story is set at Blenheim, site of the Royal New Zealand Air Force (RNZAF) Woodbourne base — which 18 years later featured in the 'Kiakoura Lights' episode [see next Chapter] — and was where her husband, Frederick, worked.

The Morelands lived on a 9 acre/3.6ha. dairy farm on the Old Renwick Road, Blenheim, and it was Eileen Moreland's task to milk their eight cows each morning.

On Monday, 13 July 1959, Mrs Moreland rose as usual before 5.30am:

> The morning was cold, with a blanket of cloud at a height estimated to be 2000 feet (600 meters). Mrs. Moreland had first gone and turned the light on in the milking shed, then with torch in hand, set off over the paddock to round up the cows.

Moreland Story

However, whilst only halfway across the paddock, some 150feet (45m) from the shed, she noticed a green glow emanating from the cloud above and bathing the ground below in a 'ghostly green light.' [from Paul Messenger's machinery4change.org/counter1.html]

She stopped and looked upwards, knowing it could not come from the moon as it was in a different direction:

> Then suddenly, two green lights, 'like eyes', appeared through the clouds, circled by a band of orange lights. All about her the ground was illuminated by the sickly-green light, and, looking at herself and her hands, she saw that she too was bathed in this green glow.
>
> Feeling that she did not want to stay put, she bolted for the pinus radiata trees bordering the paddock.
>
> The cows could be seen plainly in the light and she ran among them and stood against the trunk of one of the pine trees. [F & P Dickeson, on *ofocusnz.org.nz*]

Here's Mrs. Moreland's account of what happened next, taken from an interview published in the *Nelson Evening Mail* on July 22, nine days later:

> I stood and watched. A saucer-shaped glow with two indented green lights in the bottom descended. The air became very warm. Two rows of jets around the middle shot out orange-colored flames. They appeared to revolve in opposite directions. The thing was about 20 to 30 feet / 7 –8 m. in diameter. It hovered at about roof height.
>
> The jets stopped and a light was switched on in what appeared to be a perspex or glass roof or dome, which glowed. There was a faint hum in the air as it hovered. [*Nelson Evening Mail*, July 22 1959, p.8]

A more-detailed description of the craft is provided in this extract from a different source:

> The object stopped its descent smoothly at approximately 10 meters/33ft above the ground and at approximately 5 meters/16ft above a group of peach trees of 3 to 5 meters/13ft in height
>
> The jets were of a brilliant orange color, with greenish centers, and weakened on the outside, passing from orange to the yellow. They made a weak whistling noise. When the descent stopped, the jets were immediately cut, then reappeared at an angle. Each band of the jets started to enter in rotation in opposite directions at high speed, the higher band from right to left, and the lower band from left to right, turning at such speed that the bands of lights became continuous, 'like halos.'

A light started in what seemed to be a vitreous cap or a dome of glass; which shone, while the object hovered near the center of the meadow above the group of peach trees, approximately 40 meters from where she stood. [*ufologie.patrickgross.org/ce3/*]

Mrs Moreland said she could see two seated figures in the 'dome', sitting one behind the other and facing the same direction, away from her. They were "dressed in fairly close-fitting suits of shiny material – the only thing I can think of to describe it is 'aluminum foil'.

Opaque helmets rose from their shoulders." Some reports suggest these suits creased at every movement and reflected the light.

As she watched one of the figures stood and, as he looked ahead, put his two hands out and leaned forward, as if to see something between himself and the other figure. Then he sat down again.

After a minute or two, the jets started off again and, tilting slightly at first, the thing shot off vertically at great speed and disappeared into the clouds. When it did this it made a soft but high-pitched sound.

I was so dumfounded that I stood in the trees for a moment not knowing what to do. There was a smell of something which resembled pepper in the air. At last I decided to getting in and milking the cows. [Eileen Moreland, interview in *Nelson Evening Mail*, 22 July 1959, p.8]

According to the UFOCUSNZ website, 'the cows had been little affected by the episode' (one or two did stand up), [so she] drove them to the yard.

At this point she heard the town clock striking a quarter to six, 'so the visit could not have lasted longer than two or three minutes, though it seemed ages.'

When the milking had been concluded, the same website says:

She felt a little shaken and embarrassed, not knowing at all what to make of what she had seen. She then entered the house and woke her husband, who had worked night shift, and who did not make fun of her as she had feared, but asked whether she had phoned the police force of the Air Department.

She told him she had not, and though she thought nobody would believe her, she then phoned the police, who seemed interested. Her husband phoned the Air Force at Woodbourne.

'The Police and an Air Force representative came to the farm and questioned me,' Mrs. Moreland told the *Nelson Evening Mail* reporter, 'they appeared to believe me.'

She also told the reporter a young Air Force officer had visited her yesterday [probably on Tuesday, July 21st] to draw an artist's impression of the craft. She was able to give him a detailed description, she said.

The reporter said he had already seen a drawing made by Mr Doug Thynne, an aircraft engineer employed by Straits Air Freight Express, who had previously obtained details from Mrs. Moreland. Mr Thynne had told the reporter that 'he was willing to believe there might be something to it.'

> Mrs. Moreland's case created such interest that their farm was plagued by hordes of inquisitive sight-seers, with people wandering all over the property, uninvited, leaving gates open, upsetting the cows and generally creating such a nuisance that the Morelands said that if it should happen again them would no tell about it. [*ufologie.patrickgross.org/ce3/*]

Eileen Moreland suffered from her close encounter:

> Mrs. Moreland's hands began swelling several days after her incident, and her wedding ring had to be cut off as it had become painfully tight-fitting.
>
> She also consulted her doctor regarding the development of brown pigmented areas on her face. The pigmentation lasted long after the swelling of her hands subsided.
>
> Not until six years later was the last blotch of brown skin gone. This was a brown patch over her right eyebrow that just seemed to suddenly disappear. [from Paul Messenger's *machinery4change.org* website]

The peach trees over which the craft hovered died and were later pulled out.

The RNZAF arranged for Mrs Moreland to undergo some 'audiotone' readings in order to establish the noise levels she heard during her encounter. Apparently she identified the craft's hovering noise at 25,000 cycles, and the high-pitched ascending sound was even higher.

The Director of the Carter Observatory in Wellington, Mr I L Thomsen, told the *Nelson Evening Mail* that the RNZAF had sent him a report of what he called the 'Blenheim Incident,' but he hadn't yet had time to study it.

'It is certainly an unusual report, and different from the ordinary run of reports of strange objects seen in the sky,' he added 'I would like to have interviewed the person concerned,' Mr Thomsen said, 'preferably as soon as possible after the happening she described.'

Mr Thomsen said he had an open mind on the subject.

In June 1967 the distinguished American physicist, Professor James E McDonald visited Mrs Moreland to hear the details of her encounter face-to-face.

Six years later, Dr. J. Allen Hynek, American astronomer, similarly spent time with her. Both scientists then went on to Australia as part of their journeys 'Down Under,' and expressed their satisfaction with Eileen Moreland's account.

Back in New Zealand, though, as the years passed a growing unease began to develop.

> Challenges had been made to the NZ Minister of Defense, Mr Gill, to release the official files held on the Moreland case. The Minister was reported in the *Christchurch Star*, July 10, 1979, as having offered to release the files if Mrs Moreland consented.
>
> This she was not happy to comply with, as it had been over twenty years since the event, and she has now remarried, and wishes to live her retirement out in peace. [from Paul Messenger's *machinery4change.org* website]

There had been several indicators that certain aspects of the 'Moreland Case' had been withheld from public scrutiny:

1. An August 1959 report that Mrs Moreland had again detected a further 'pepper' smell at the farm (weeks after her initial contact).

2. An apparent corroborative report of another UFO sighting early in the morning of the same initial date, from just three miles from the Moreland's.

3. An accusation that a senior RNZAF officer's wife had heard a 'jet engine-type sound' at the same time, despite no official flight being recorded.

Now we move forward over 30-years: With the December 2010 New Zealand government UFO file release there were file holdings on the Moreland case, along with quite a number of blanked pages with the typed explanation: 'This document has been withheld from release to the public to preserve personal privacy in accordance with the Official Information Act, Section 9 (2)a.'

Moreland Story

In fact, as the 1959 investigation progressed, the CONFIDENTIAL classification had been changed to TOP SECRET. A close reading of the folios and material showed the case was drawing renewed media and researcher attention which highlighted fascinating dimensions to the case. [Bill Chalker, *theozflies*, September 27, 2011]

Amongst the files released in 2010 was this drawing:

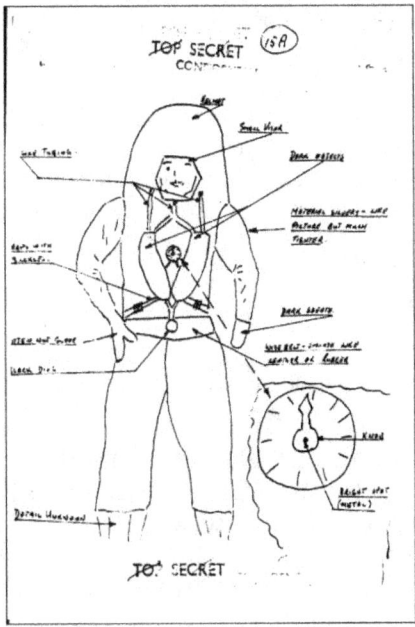

If this was drawn by Mrs. Moreland, or by someone following her instructions, how was she aware of the detail on the front view of someone she saw only from behind, and only from the waist up, at a distance of 45m/150ft?

And what is the circular device worn on the figure's chest, a device of sufficient significance that a dotted line in the drawing leads to an expanded view of the device? Note, too, the figure has an amputated left hand.

It appears that Mrs. Moreland's public statement (to the *Nelson Evening Mail*], was incomplete.

This answer can be surmised from a briefing summary written by the Chief of Defense Staff (Air Marshall R B Bolt) for the Minister of Defense, a copy of which was included in the released government files, and includes some previously suppressed details:

UFOs DOWN UNDER

On 13 July a woman living near Blenheim reported that between 5-6a.m. that morning she had seen an oval-shaped object, measuring 20 yards/18m. across and 4 or 5ft./1.4m. through, descend before her.

She was caught in a green light produced by two beams shining from beneath the vehicle and was unable to move.

The vehicle was manned by two men, wearing silvery suits and helmets, one of whom descended from it and came over to her. He shouted at her in a foreign language.

In a fright she hit out with her torch and ran for nearby trees. The man re-boarded the vehicle, which was hovering some 10-12ft./3½m. from the ground. It then ascended straight up into the sky emitting a high-pitched whistle and leaving a patch of hot air and a smell like that of burnt pepper.

Another witness later reported seeing an unidentified light at about the same time.

So, where does that leave us? There's still 'quite a number' of pages remaining unrevealed.

What will they tell us? Was Mrs Moreland abducted? Did she go on board the craft? Did Mrs Moreland receive any bodily marks she didn't mention? What was the duration of the event – remember, 'it seemed ages.' Is there any explanation of the circular device shown in the drawing, or of the amputated left hand?

We may have to wait until the year 2040 when the files are due to be fully released.

8. New Zealand's 'Kiakoura Lights'

"We've stumbled on a UFO playground!"

The bond between Australians and New Zealanders — or 'Aussies' and 'Kiwis' as they call one another — is a curious one. On the sporting field, they are fierce opponents; in the Arts, the 'Aussies' claim many 'Kiwi' stars as their own; on the battlefield, they are trustworthy brothers-in-arms — and have been for well over a century.

In the case of the 'Kaikoura Lights', it took a Kiwi working for an Aussie television channel to bring international focus to the aerial phenomenon that surprised New Zealanders during the Christmas holiday period in 1978.

It became the best-documented civilian UFO sighting worldwide — and remains so to this very day!

TV news journalist Quentin Fogarty, together with his wife and two young sons arrived in Auckland, New Zealand around midnight on 20 December 1978 after a delayed flight from Melbourne. The family collected a hire car and headed off to a waterfront motel.

They intended to spend the first part of their three-week holiday on the North Island staying with family members and then, on 30 December, fly to Christchurch on the South Island to say with journalist friends and visit Quentin's mother.

On Boxing Day, December 26th, they were in Martinborough, east of Wellington, staying with Mrs Fogarty's parents when a telephone call from Quentin's employer — the Channel O newsroom in Melbourne — came through.

Stories of unusual aerial objects seen in the New Zealand skies five days earlier had appeared in the Australian media, Quentin was told, and Channel O was interested in a follow-up story. Quentin Fogarty was asked to check the scene out and see if there was sufficient material for a further television news item.

The story centered around several unidentified, color-changing 'orbs' seen off the east coast of New Zealand's South Island by the crew of an Argosy freight plane in the very early morning of December 21- objects which had appeared on air traffic control radar as well as the aircraft's own radar!

Quentin agreed to see what he could do. He needed to contact the principal witnesses, seek interviews, arrange a film crew, and get his proposed storyboard straight in his mind. All this while he was on holiday!

First, he made arrangements for freelance cameraman David Crockett, and his sound recordist wife, Ngaire, to be available over the next few days. Then he telephoned the Argosy captain, Vern Powell, who agreed to a television interview.

Next, to his surprise, the key government employees in the air traffic control center during the night in question were available and keen to contribute their experiences.

Finally, and fully aware he was pushing his luck, Quentin Fogarty approached Safe Air Ltd., the airfreight contractors, to see if they would permit the film crew to travel on the following weekend's evening flight from Wellington to Christchurch retracing the route of Vern Powell's flight. They, too, agreed.

Safe Air Ltd. is based at Woodbourne aerodrome, near Blenheim on the northeast shoulder on New Zealand's South Island, just 44miles across Cook Strait from Wellington. Safe Air had two Bristol 170 freighters and two more-modern Argosy 222 freighters, one of which was involved in the UFO sightings on December 21.

Woodburne aerodrome was used as a military base during World War II and in the 1960s housed a secret United States facility rumored to be involved in extra low frequency (ELF) radio communications.

At the time of the UFO sightings the Woodbourne aerodrome was also a domestic airport and an operational base for the Royal New Zealand Air Force.

Kiakoura Lights

On Friday, the day before flying to Blenheim, Fogarty and cameraman David Crockett visited the Wellington air traffic control center to interview John Cordy, the senior controller. He and Andrew Herd were the duty team on the night of the sightings.

> 'We had people on the ground seeing things,' John Cordy said, 'pilots in the air seeing things, and we had returns on radar.' Quentin felt that both John and his colleague Andy were a little annoyed with the local media who had largely ignored the controllers' side of the story.

> 'We tracked one of the targets for approximately two and a half hours,' Andy Herd said, 'It moved in and paralleled the Argosy piloted by Captain Powell and First Officer Pirie. They observed it as a brilliant white light — and I can offer no explanation.'

On the following day, Quentin Fogarty farewelled his wife and children and flew to Blenheim with Ngaire and David Crockett late in the afternoon to interview with Captain Vern Powell.

The interview went smoothly. Quentin later wrote: 'He told me he had come to the conclusion that UFOs did exist and that if they were going to harm anyone they would have done so a long time ago.'

Vern drove the TV trio to the airport, and introduced them to their Argosy aircrew — Captain Bill Startup and First Officer Bob Guard — for the freight run to Christchurch.

Captain Startup explained the importance of quietness on the flight deck and said he'd try to make their trip as comfortable as possible. One of the film crew could occupy the 'dickie' seat on the flight deck, but for take-off and landing the other two would be strapped into seats built into the rear-loading door of the cargo hold. Cameraman David was the logical choice for the spare flight deck seat.

Quentin and Ngaire were overwhelmed with noise during take-off as the Argosy's four Rolls Royce turboprop engines thrust the aircraft down the runway. Speech was impossible. They were sitting in a cramped, window-less environment, facing a metal bulkhead, fifteen feet/4½m. lower than the flight deck at the rear of the plane, eyes glued to a seat belt sign, anxiously waiting for it to blink off so they could join the others.

Their salvation was short-lived. Within fifteen minutes of their 'release' they were back again for the descent and landing at Wellington where their newspaper cargo was loaded.

During the last minutes of 1977, the Argosy departed Wellington for Christchurch. After the seat belt sign was switched off, the TV crew filmed a short introductory segment in the cargo hold.

Quentin addressed the camera: 'We're at an altitude of 14,000ft (4,267m) and we're on exactly the same route taken by Captain Powell when he encountered those mysterious objects. It's a beautiful clear night outside and naturally we'll be looking out for anything unusual.'

The aviation 'track' between Wellington and Christchurch is a dog-leg course from Wellington running to a reporting point twenty-five miles/40km. due east of the coastal to town of Kaikoura [i.e. the reporting point is out to sea, and known as Kaikoura East], then to Christchurch. Aircraft flying between Wellington and Christchurch (and vice versa) change air traffic control jurisdiction once they pass Kaikoura East and are required to report their identity, altitude and directional bearing on reaching that point.

Several minutes after midnight, First Officer Bob Guard drew Capt. Bill Startup's attention to something — a group of unusual lights were moving up, down, and sideways, and pulsating on and off randomly.

Capt. Bill climbed part of the way down the rear access ladder and signaled the film crew to the flight deck.

Quentin Fogarty arrived first, to find Bill and Bob looking towards the front right hand side of the aircraft.

'They pointed out the lights of Kaikoura township in the distance,' Quentin recalled, 'There, apparently hovering above the town, was a row of bright, pulsating lights. My heart skipped a beat!'

Captain Startup queried Wellington air traffic control (ATC) by radio: 'Have you got any returns in the vicinity of the Kaikoura peninsula?'

Seven seconds later Geoff Causer, duty controller, replied 'There were targets in your one o'clock position at a range of 13 miles/21km., that have been appearing and disappearing, and were visible up to about a minute ago.'

Geoff Causer had been watching the anomalous radar images for thirty minutes before Startup's question but, because he concluded they were not solid objects, he hadn't warned the Argosy crew. Bill Startup asked Geoff to keep his eye on them.

It was a squeeze to have five people together on the flight deck. David Crockett was in the 'dickie' seat with his camera, midway behind the flight crew; Ngaire crouched behind Captain Startup on the left with her recording equipment; and Quentin stood behind Bob Guard's seat holding a microphone.

David found it most difficult to do his job — he had to crouch down and maneuver his hand-held camera between the flight crew — with the camera magazine sometimes bumping switches on the control panels overhead. Even in such a cramped position, he managed to capture some of the action on film as the distant lights changed color, position and blinked out.

Bill Startup later wrote:

'First one of these bright lights would come on, then it would put out a beam like a searchlight down towards the sea. The beam would show for about four or five seconds, then the beam and light would both go out. A little while later another light would come on and send a beam down... with no fixed rhythm or pattern.'

Quentin decided to record some commentary on tape: 'It's fairly hard to describe my feelings at the moment, but we've probably seen six or seven, or even more, bright lights over Kaikoura and a number of these have been picked up by Wellington radar.'

Later, he told a BBC reporter that 'it was as though we had stumbled upon a UFO playground.'

His observations were recorded separately on tape, not on the film sound track. Fortunately he made occasional references to information from Wellington ATC and because all ATC tapes are automatically overprinted with the time, synchronizing the images on film with Quentin's commentary later helped researchers to gain a clearer picture of the phenomena.

At about 12.20 am, Captain Startup told Wellington ATC he was going to make a left orbit (a 360 degree turn) and rejoin his former southbound track, either to satisfy his own curiosity but most likely to provide David Crockett the opportunity to again capture the distant flashing orbs.

Geoff Causer at Wellington ATC acknowledged Bill Startup's message and advised him of another 'target' that just appeared on Bill's left side, about one mile/1.6km. away, briefly, and then disappeared again'.

The Argosy completed its turn without anyone on board seeing this mysterious visitor.

Bill Startup continues the story:

We had been back on track for only a couple of minutes after the orbit when Geoff Causer reported a target at 12 o'clock at a range of three miles (4.8km). And there dead ahead of us were a couple of very bright blue-white lights, flashing regularly at a very rapid rate ... the lights were very close, far closer, it seemed to me, than Geoff Causer's estimate of three miles. The gap was closing very quickly. They were so close that taking avoiding action was out of the question ... I am not sure whether the object passed over us or under us, but I think it was over the top. This all happened fast, in about three to five seconds.

The Christchurch-bound Argosy was almost at the Kiakoura East reporting point. Geoff Causer in Wellington spoke to the Christchurch ATC and explained the Argosy 'will be a couple of minutes late at Kiakoura East – he's been UFO hunting.'

The ATC at Christchurch laconically responded: 'Oh well, I suppose we'll get him when he's bagged his limit!'

The Argosy reached Kiakoura East at 0028, (twenty-eight minutes past midnight) banked gently and altered its course towards Christchurch, 90 miles/150km distant. Bill switched the VHF radio to the Christchurch frequency and exchanged basic information and received clearance for his approach and landing.

Then the unexpected happened.

Bill Startup again:

'We had been in Christchurch airspace just over a minute when the Christchurch controller radioed to say Geoff Causer had telephoned through a report that he had a target a mile (1.6km) behind the Argosy ... this thing, whatever it was, was right behind us, in the one place where we could not see it ... I became convinced that it must be something under intelligent control.'

[About 0030] Geoff reported that he now had a further target at three o'clock to the aircraft at a range of four miles (6.4km) ... looking out from the flight deck, I did not see any lights to correspond with the radar reports.

[45 seconds later] Geoff Causer called again to say: 'There's a strong target right in formation with you, could be to the left or right. Your target has doubled in size.' Now it is getting a little scary ... [Geoff Causer in Wellington] could see and we could not and I had to accept that his report was precise and accurate.'

Kiakoura Lights

A further 45 seconds passed before the Argosy aircrew heard again from Geoff: 'The target has now reduced to normal size.'

Next, it was First Officer Bob Guard's turn to see a white light at three o'clock to the aircraft apparently keeping station with it. This object held its position out slightly behind the starboard wingtip for several minutes before dropping back to 4 o'clock, then 5 o'clock, and finally 6 o'clock (as seen by Wellington ATC).

Geoff Causer confirmed this final position, and added a further surprise: 'It's now six o'clock to you at about fifteen miles (24km), and its been joined by two other targets.'

Much of these communications were of little value to the TV crew filming from the flight deck — David Crockett could not film what he could not see — but on Quentin's audio tape he repeated some of the ATC radar reports which later proved significant in substantiating the sequence of events on board.

At 36½ minutes into the New Year, Geoff Causer advised that the three objects behind the plane had merged into a single image, and that its radar blip was larger than the one of the Argosy!

After reflection, Captain Startup considered the lights posed no threat to his aircraft. 'They were not trying to attack us,' he said, 'but merely looking at us.' He decided to carry out another 360-degree orbit in an attempt, as Quentin Fogarty put it, 'to spot our mysterious companions.'

Startup received air traffic clearance for the orbit. A quarter of the way through the turn nothing unusual was observed; half way through there was still nothing exceptional abroad, finally the turn was completed without anything abnormal being seen. The Argosy continued towards Christchurch, 60 miles (97km) away. A sense of relief was apparent on the flight deck.

The TV crew started packing up their gear in preparation for the descent and landing. Bill Startup told them they were welcome to join the return flight to Blenheim in just over an hour's time if they wished. Quentin said they'd think about it and decide once they had landed; but the Captain got the impression 'they might have had enough thrills for one night.'

About 18 miles/29km from the Christchurch runway, First Officer Bob Guard saw another flashing light about four or five miles (7km) off the Argosy's starboard [right] side, keeping pace with the aircraft. Christchurch ATC was asked if their radar had a target showing in that position; shortly afterwards it was confirmed, but the light suddenly accelerated away to the south-west at a seemingly low altitude.

Meanwhile Quentin and Ngaire were settling into their seats in the rear of the cargo hold. Ngaire was adamant that nothing was going to drag her back on board the Argosy. She was saying a firm 'No' to Bill's offer. She had simply had enough, and who could blame her?

The Argosy landed at Christchurch at a minute passed 1.00am David had remained in the third cockpit seat and filmed the landing. His film showed a very bright light in the sky, just beyond the south-west end of the airport.

The TV crew joined the air-crew in the Christchurch radar room for a coffee and chat. There was still a decision to be made about joining the return flight to Blenheim. Ngaire made it clear she wasn't participating; Quentin was ambivalent, and David was keen to go.

> 'I still had not made up my mind about the return trip, although my curiosity was starting to get the better of me,' Quentin later wrote, 'David, on the other hand, was extremely keen to go back. He knew he had very little footage and he wanted more. Gradually I came around to his way of thinking. There was also the fact that I was supposed to be in charge of the assignment. I could hardly crawl off to the security of my bed and leave the cameraman on his own.'

> 'Also, the light-show on the way down had been a compelling spectacle. The chance of an encore finally became too hard to resist,' he added.

Quentin was shortly on the telephone to his wife. She and the children had arrived in Christchurch eight hours earlier and were staying with TV news journalist Dennis Grant, an old friend of the Fogartys, who were expecting Quentin there to stay for several days. Quentin asked his friend if he could get some faster film for David's camera, and rush it out to the airport. Then Quentin described what he'd seen during the flight.

Dennis initially thought he was joking but, after being convinced, he agreed to drive to the airport immediately — with some new film.

Arrangements were hurriedly made: the film from the southbound flight was given to Ngaire for safekeeping. With Captain Startup's permission, Dennis Grant joined the film crew in Ngaire's stead; and Quentin had a 'crash course' in operating the sound equipment.

Meanwhile, Geoff Causer from Wellington ATC contacted Christchurch to report on-going radar returns 'which could be of interest on the northbound leg.'

The cargo-less Argosy departed Christchurch at 0216 for what turned out to be an-anything-but-routine flight.

Just three minutes after departure, a large, very bright orb was seen from the flight deck slightly above and to the right of them. Bill Startup confirmed the target on the aircraft's radar.

> 'The bright object is still with us just off our starboard side,' Quentin recorded in his taped commentary, 'According to our cameraman, David Crocket, who is filming it for the past few moments, it appears to have a brightly lit bottom and a transparent sort of sphere on top, so it appears to be ... well, like a ... flying saucer!'

Newcomer Dennis Grant said it reminded him of a ping-pong ball in a dark room and illuminated by a spotlight: 'At times the object seemed spherical as it kept pace with the aircraft,' he said.

Captain Startup switched the aircraft's radar to mapping mode, and there it was — a big, clear target within the 20-mile/32km ring, precisely in the direction of the object. The blip was strong and clear. Bill could see a distinct trail of after-images, glowing less brightly than the latest to appear, a clear indication of movement. It certainly was not a planet.

By the time the Argosy reached the top of its climb — about 13,000 feet/3,962m — the glowing orb had, more-or-less, held station with the aircraft for nine minutes.

The aircrew held a brief discussion about making a small course deviation to take a closer look at the visitor, but not a full orbit. It was agreed between them. After Bill Startup told the TV film team of his intentions, he switched off the radio beam and used the turn control on the autopilot to make the Argosy head left towards the object. At 0229 the Argosy banked, and the starboard wing dipped providing Bob Guard with an unobscured view of the object. Bob said it looked like a squashed orange!

The object was then directly ahead and Bob thought the aircraft gained about half a mile/804m on it before it moved to their starboard side. 'After it moved out to starboard it was below us and I was looking down on it. It stayed in that position for a while, not very long,' Bob said, 'and then it suddenly fell away below and behind us.'

Captain Startup notified Christchurch of his 'track correction to the east' and headed back towards the Kaikoura East reporting point. There was a lull in 'visitor' activity and Bill hoped for an uneventful remainder of the flight to his Blenheim base.

Quentin echoed this sentiment. On his taped commentary he said 'I, for one, am hoping that the rest of the journey will be uneventful. I think I've just about had enough of UFOs for one night.'

Alas, it was not to be.

The Argosy turned the Kaikoura East corner at 0246. Geoff Causer at Wellington ATC, whose jurisdiction the aircraft had just entered, had been watching several radar 'targets' in the area. He passed this information on to Bill Startup, who possibly identified them on the Argosy's radar as well, but because they couldn't be seen visually from the flight deck, Bill did not make any comments to the others.

At 0251 Geoff Causer reported 'a strong target at 12 o'clock to you [that's directly ahead of the Argosy] at 20 miles/32km' The aircraft responded with 'We have that one also and quite a good visual display at the moment.'

> 'These lights were very much like the first ones we had seen on the southbound leg around Kaikoura,' First Officer Bob Guard recalled, 'they were flashing on and off at a fairly slow rate — a short flash followed by a shorter spell of darkness and then another short flash.'

> 'From memory I believe they were bobbing up and down a little, like the ones we had seen earlier, and flashing on and off as they did so, with some sort of brilliance,' he said, 'I think this was what was in my mind when I told Wellington they were giving a good visual display.'

By this time the Argosy was descending from 13,000 feet/4km; it was just over 30 miles/48km to reach Blenheim. The strong light mentioned by Geoff Causer was very close to the Cape Campbell lighthouse with its rotating light sweeping out to sea. Bob Guard pointed this difference out to the film crew, although the beam from the lighthouse was not seen from the flight deck. The flashing light disappeared long before the Argosy got close to the area.

Quentin's tape recorded account and the recollections of the aircrew vary significantly for this final stage of the flight. Quentin spoke of an 'extremely bright' light that 'dropped at incredible speed' and seemed to be 'rolling and turning'. 'There appears to be a whole cluster of them. You can see orange and red among the lights. There's one particular one that keeps flashing to the right of ... [unfinished]. You can see three distinct lights.'

Kiakoura Lights

Captain Startup later wrote:

> 'It is possible — although by no means certain — that the bright flashing light in the pattern of three distinct lights Quentin Fogarty referred to was in fact the beacon at the Woodbourne airport [Blenheim].'

A bright orange light was seen some 75 miles/120km away, over Tasman Bay, across the northern tip of the South Island. It was impossible to tell if it was on water or in the air — Bill Startup felt it may have been the powerful lights strung around the decks of a squid boat to attract squid. But it moved north-east at a rapid pace (covering 35 miles/56km in two minutes), and as Bill said, in his usual understated way, 'That is fast for a squid boat!'

The Argosy needed to lose a little height for its descent into Woodbourne, and undertook a 360 degree orbit during which it lost around 2,000 feet/0·6km. During this orbit, at about 0256, Bill Startup saw 'pinpoints of light' all over the sea in Cook Strait, just south of Wellington.

'They were scattered over a fairly large area in no particular pattern,' Bill said, 'It appeared that either there was a massive fishing fleet on its way through the strait, or else there was something like phosphorescence on the water.'

Nothing else of significance was seen during the remaining minutes of the descent.

> 'Seldom do I record in my flight logbook any comments about a particular flight,' Captain Bill Startup said, 'but after I landed at Blenheim about 3.10am on December 31, I felt some comment was justified about the flight I had just completed.' It reads: 'What a flight ... UFOs?'

In high excitement, the group gathered in the operations room of Safe Air for a chat without the need to shout over the roar of the Argosy's engines and to sort a few things out. What happens if there's nothing on David's film? An understandable feeling of nervousness fused with their excitement. Quentin knew he had a world scoop on his hands. His journalist friend, Dennis Grant, telephoned his own boss (it was after 3.30am) and told him his news. Bill Startup rang his wife, asking her to make up a couple of beds for Quentin and David. Dennis had arranged to stay at the home of Paul Leslie of Safe Air.

> 'By 4.30 am David and I were sitting in Bill's living room tucking into a couple of brandies,' Quentin recalled, 'and trying to come to terms with our incredible experience.'

Then he decided to telephone his chief-of-staff in Melbourne to tell him what had transpired. 'It took me quite a while to convince him I was not pulling his leg.'

Quentin agreed to return to Melbourne, with the film, that very day, New Year's Day. Ever the investigative journalist, he decided to go to Christchurch via the town of Kaikoura to see if there were any eye-witnesses who saw the lights and could be interviewed.

He arranged for Ngaire to drive a hire car from Christchurch to Kaikoura, where he and David would meet her at midday at the post office. His hostess, Bill Startup's wife Shirley, agreed to drive them 81 miles/130kms down the coast to Kaikoura from Blenheim.

Dennis decided to stay in Blenheim; he had arranged for another film crew to fly in later and join him for his own interview with Bill Startup about the flight.

At daybreak, Bill drove to his local police station. 'Whatever it was that had happened off the Kaikoura coast could be some sort of threat to the country,' he thought, 'It had to be significant one way or another.' Their response? 'Thank you and good morning.' So began for Bill the feeling that nobody was really interested.

After breakfast, Quentin convinced Bill Startup to give him one final television interview, down at the aerodrome, standing in front of the Argosy, recounting the night's experiences and explaining why the planet Venus played no part in what was seen. Bill readily agreed.

Then, after a quick round of farewells, it was time to leave for Kaikoura with Shirley Startup at the wheel.

They listened to the radio as they traveled, hoping to hear a news report of 'UFOs in the sky'. During the first hour heading south, not one reference was heard. Then, as they neared journey's end, one Christchurch station, Radio Avon where Quentin Fogarty had once worked, broadcast the 'amazing UFO sighting' news. Quentin then phoned them and explained exactly what he'd seen the previous night.

Nobody in Kaikouri had seen anything unusual in the sky overnight. There had been no reports to the police, nothing seen by holiday campers, no callers to the telephone exchange.

Ngaire arrived at the rendezvous and Quentin and David transferred to the hire car with their film and gear, then headed south to Christchurch, 112miles/180kms away, with Ngaire, and sleep-deprived Fogarty driving.

Radio Avon repeated their up-dated UFO story during the team's drive south along the coastal highway. It was picked up by the national radio network, Radio New Zealand, and within the hour the incident became international news.

Arriving in Christchurch around 4.30pm, Fogarty received a message to call his boss in Melbourne. Neil Miller wanted Quentin, and the film, back in Melbourne on the first available flight. (Air New Zealand, Christchurch to Melbourne, departing at 10.15pm.)

So much for Quentin enjoying a holiday with his family!

Back in Blenheim, Captain Bill Startup began being bombarded by media inquiries from around the world. Most callers didn't appear to take the UFO sightings very seriously. After all, they occurred during the 'silly season' between Christmas and New Year, a time for relaxation and frivolity, and talk of 'little green men from Mars' and 'space travelers' suited the mood. Captain Startup was even addressed (perhaps deliberately) by one interviewer as 'Captain Startrek'. This unfortunate attitude persisted and Bill was not impressed.

On arrival at Channel 0 studios close to 1.00am, Quentin Fogarty handed the films over for laboratory processing. When that was completed, a few key personnel gathered in the editing room to see what precisely had been caught on film.

It wasn't until the editor played the second roll frame-by-frame that Quentin realized David Crockett had captured some fascinating footage. They saw a light quickly grow to 'a huge beach-ball shaped object' and, suddenly, shrink into a smaller object 'that looked remarkably like an acorn'. There were plenty of other bright blinking lights, but the huge, shrinking beach-ball caught everyone's attention.

Quentin was then faced with preparing material for three TV packages — one for the Channel 0 news in Australia, another for a BBC newsman who wanted an on-the-spot interview and some visual clips, and finally another for CBS in America to be sent via satellite.

Quentin completed his three reports before almost fading to black himself. By this time, he had been awake for fifty hours.

It was 8.00am before he could rest — in two office couches pulled together to form a bed. After a short snooze, Quentin had to prepare a half-hour UFO documentary that aired straight after the Channel 0 news that evening.

Captain Startup was confused when he first saw the material in an New Zealand television studio on January 2, 'To me, some of the shots attributed to the main sighting out of Christchurch (on the return journey) where there were these lights darting around, certainly weren't what I saw. I think they got the sequence slightly out.'

Di Billing, Television One News journalist, suggested to Bill Startup that some who saw the TV program reckoned it was either Jupiter or Venus on film.

Startup replied, 'I still feel quite strongly that was not the case.' He was supported by cameraman David Crockett who reacted 'It's not possible it was Venus,' he said, 'Venus was just a very small dot in the lens — nowhere near the size of the other object — and rather dull.'

Bill Startup felt the television people were not taking the UFO sightings very seriously. 'They were looking more for entertainment than information,' he said.

One interested New Zealander was Prime Minister Robert Muldoon. He specifically asked to be informed of the conclusions of the Defense Department's study into the reported UFO sightings.

Three weeks later, in a public relations department two-and-a-half-page press release, the Royal New Zealand Air Force said:

> The unidentified radar and visual sightings reported by aircraft and the air traffic control radars off the north-east coast of the South Island recently, are the result of natural but unusual atmospheric phenomena.

The report also mentioned 'the planet Venus', 'spurious returns on Wellington air traffic control radar', 'lights from squid boats', 'lights of trains or vehicles traveling along the coast', and 'lights from surface or planetary sources affected by atmospheric reflection, refraction, and distortion'.

'Although I did not really think the authorities would say that UFOs existed,' Quentin Fogarty said in commenting on this report, 'I had hoped that just for once they would have the courage to admit they were baffled.'

'It's a strangely vague and obscure document,' Captain Bill Startup wrote, 'It makes me wonder why they bothered to hold the inquiry at all.'

* * *

Kiakoura Postscript:

Dr Bruce Macabee, American physicist and N.I.C.A.P. consultant, having visited 'Down Under' to interview witnesses of the 'Kiakoura Lights', declared it 'one of the most complicated civilian UFO episodes in history.'

Captain Bill Startup's book, *The Kiakoura UFOs*, was published in 1980; Quentin Fogarty's book, *Let's Hope They're Friendly!* was published in 1982.

9. Headache Brewing at 'Willow Grove'

"I wished it would come again; it was beautiful"

On Friday 15 February 1963, dairy-farmers Charles Brew and his 20-year-old son Trevor were halfway through the morning milking when a remarkable event occurred.

At 7.10am. Charles was standing at the open end of the milking shed when, through the rain clouds overhead, he saw an object he first thought was a helicopter descending towards their cattle holding yards.

> I looked out and saw the object coming down fairly slowly and steeply to a height of about 75 to 100 feet [27 m]. The object was about 25 ft [7.6m] wide and looked like a thick disc. It was battleship-gray in color and appeared to have a band of glass or plastic around the circumference and a number of protrusions which looked like scoops.

> I thought it was going to land, but it suddenly shot off in a westerly direction at two or three times the speed of a jet and disappeared into a cloud. [Charles Brew, *Sun News Pictorial* (Melbourne) February 16, 1963, p.5]

Charles estimated the lowest point of the object's flight path against the height of adjacent gum trees. It hovered on an even keel for just a few seconds, giving Charles time to get a very good look at his unexpected visitor.

His son, Trevor, didn't see a thing – but he certainly heard it.

Willow Grove

Fifty-two years later he recalled the incident for VUFOA-TV's Ben Hurle:

'I was up at the far end, milking a heifer. I heard this noise and thought oh, no. Not another pulley belt's come off the drive wheel! Then all the cows bolted forward and nearly went through the end of the shed!' [Trevor Brew, interview with Ben Hurle, VUFOA-TV, published April 25, 2015]

'The noise,' Trevor explained, 'sounded like an Aboriginal didgeridoo – a percussion type of sound. The power of it was really phenomenal.'

The farm animals reacted instantly:

'The stock went crazy – anything strange spooks them. The cows surged forward twenty to thirty feet. The dogs went quiet. The horse – I'd ridden her bareback earlier in the morning to bring the cows in – she was tied up in the yard, I saw her rear up.' [Trevor Brew, VUFOA-TV, April 25, 2015]

Half a century after the event, Trevor couldn't remember whether his father discussed the event with him that morning or not, but he knew his father had been stressed over it, and had telephoned the Melbourne *Sun* (News Pictorial) newspaper which sent a reporter 85 miles [136kms] to interview him.

The Brews lived at Willow Grove, just north of Moe in the lush farming countryside of Gippsland, Victoria.

The following morning the Melbourne *Sun*'s page five headline read:

JUMPING COWS! IT'S A 'SAUCER'

MOE, Friday — A dairy farmer has reported seeing a "flying saucer or something" which sent a horse and his herd of cows into a panic early today.

The farmer, Mr. Charlie Brew, of Old Sale Rd, Willow Grove, north-west of Moe, said the object was about 25 feet (7.6m) wide and looked like a thick disc. [extract from *Sun News Pictorial* (Melbourne, February 16, 1963,. p.5]

The local *Moe Advocate's* subsequent headline demonstrated more restraint:

FLYING SAUCER SENDS CATTLE INTO PANIC

A 'flying saucer' – or something – sent a horse and a herd of cows into a panic at Mr. Charlie Brew's farm at Willow Grove on Friday morning. [extract from *Moe Advocate*, February 20,1963,. P.3]

In this news item we learn from Mr. Charles Brew:

'There was no engine noise, but a kind of pulsating, whooshing sound, as might be made by the scoops' and that 'the whole visit lasted only about the time it would take to turn your head.'

Three independent investigations of the 'Willow Glen-UFO incident' followed:

- The RAAF (Royal Australian Air Force) sent a team of two airmen, a Flight Lieutenant and a Squadron Leader on 4th March, to investigate and report on the Brew sighting.
- The VFSRS (Victorian Flying Saucer Research Society) was represented by its president, Mr. Peter Norris. He recorded a long interview with Charles Brew, and obtained a sketch of the object and the location.
- Noted American researcher, James E McDonald interviewed the Brews during a 1967 visit to Australia. He cited the Brew case during an address to an international symposium in 1968.

Let us look at each of these interviews in turn, and record any significant differences or advances the investigations provide.

**

The RAAF report revealed more details about the object from Charles Brew:

The structure of the object appeared to be man made ... the lower portion, about 3ft (.9m) high, was rotating in an anti-clockwise direction and was of a blue-ish appearance. The upper portion appeared to be stationary ... Protruding out of this dome was something which resembled a broom handle. No figures were visible in the dome. Then Mr. Brew stated 'It looked like a flying merry-go-round. There was a swishing and burbling-type sound.'

Mr. Brew stated that it was raining heavily and continuously ... He did not observe any thunder or lightning. [extract from RAAF investigation report, National Archives of Australia]

The RAAF investigators interviewed Dr Berson of CSIRO Division of Meteorological Physics section to see if clouds could create the type of phenomenon witnessed by Mr. Brew.

'They agreed that a tornado condition could give this effect.' [*Keith Basterfield's blog,. January 29, 2015*]

The conclusion reached by the RAAF team stated:

There is little doubt that Brew did witness something and it is most likely that it was a natural phenomenon. The phenomenon was probably a tornado. There was no reported damage along its path, therefore one would assume that it was weak in nature. [*extract from RAAF investigation report*]

* *

Peter Norris, in his VFSRS interview with Charles Brew, asked if he saw anybody in the transparent dome section of the object. Brew's response was: 'It was raining heavy, and no, I can't honestly say I did see anybody, although I was looking hard enough.'

Brew also mentioned an 'aerial sort of thing' protruding from the top of the dome, 'I'd say it was about 5 or 6 feet (1.7m) long, of either chrome or some lightish metal thing.'

Further, Charles Brew confirmed there was no light coming from 'the dome' or 'underneath' the craft.

Norris also established that two CSIRO (Commonwealth Scientific and Industrial Research Organization) visitors came to Willow Grove and spoke with Charles Brew at least three days before the RAAF team arrived. Surprisingly, their 'number one question' put to Brew was 'Did he get a headache?' He replied:

> I thought it was too ridiculous [to mention]. But I did get an awful headache just behind the eyes. I never suffer from headaches normally and I took a [proprietary tablet], but it didn't seem to have any effect. [*Keith Basterfield's blog,* January 29, 2015]

'That ties in with our theory,' Brew was told, and he gained the impression from the CSIRO men that his headache was more-than-likely caused by the 'electromagnetic effect' from the flying object.

Norris also learnt that the CSIRO were very interested in a 'sort of ironstone' rock reef which runs through the property and district. They 'took away rock samples' because the reef 'may have some attraction for it [the airborne object].'

When the RAAF team arrived, Peter Norris was told, 'they photographed the surrounding countryside using long distance cameras' and 'took particular notice of the rock formations.' They told Brew his sighting 'tallied exactly with what's been seen in other countries' …and, to the best of their knowledge, his was 'the lowest and best sighting [reported]'

**

American UFO researcher James E. McDonald of the Institute of Atmospheric Physics at the University of Arizona, visited Australia in 1967 and among several local incidents he investigated was Charles Brew's Willow Grove sighting (his interview with the Brews was conducted in the same milking shed from which the sighting was made).

While we don't have McDonald's investigation report, the internet provides a downloadable, 41-page pdf of an address given by him at an international symposium during which he quoted aspects of the Willow Grove case.

On March 12,1968 – roughly 5 years after the sighting — James McDonald spoke at the Canadian Aeronautics and Space Institute's Astronautics Symposium held in Montreal, Canada.

His paper was called '*UFOs–An International Scientific Problem.*'

During his introductory remarks, McDonald said:

> The UFO problem has not received anything that can be called scientifically adequate study. It is my strong impression that Air Force officials and public information officers sincerely believe that the UFO problem is a nonsense problem, one involving nothing more than misidentified natural phenomena ...

To support his contention, McDonald quoted ten unsatisfactory explanations attached to several investigations, drawing on incidents from Canada, Japan, United States, Spain, Peru and Australia – his tenth and final case being Willow Grove, Moe.

He repeated step-by-step the details previously known, and added one further anecdote:

> It took some time to recover the animals that had bolted; and those already inside the fenced area were strongly disturbed for some time. Brew stated to me that it was many days before any of his cattle would walk over the part of the hillside pasture over which the object had momentarily hovered ...

McDonald also added:

> The object is similar in its general features and size as that seen by a witness I interviewed in New Zealand, Mrs. Eileen Moreland (*see Chapter 7*). Her July 13, 1959 observation, like Brew's, and like that of many other UFO witnesses, is extremely difficult to explain in present-day scientific or technological terms.

Among his concluding remarks, James E. McDonald said:

The above ten illustrative cases are only intended to convey a general impression of the puzzlement that inheres in so many UFO reports, to suggest that possibly we do have here a problem of considerable scientific interest. In my own opinion, the UFO problem may be the greatest scientific problem of our times; but I do not expect ten cases to convince doubters.

* *

In his book, *Flying Saucers Over Australia*, James Holledge concluded his brief account of the Willow Grove incident with:

Mr. Brew was another one of those people who refused to believe in UFOs until "he saw one himself."

'I wished it would come again,' he said wistfully. 'It was beautiful. I could feel the life pulsating from it.' He is satisfied, now, that they do exist. [*Flying Saucers Over Australia*, (Horwitz, Sydney) 1965. p.88]

10. A Rude Awakening at Childers

'The family witnessed 3 spacemen from the craft'

George Vas and his family were roused from their sleep in the early hours of January 14, 1969 by the frenzied barking of their dog, Ica.

All the family — George, his wife Milanka, and their two daughters, Olga (14) and Maria (13) — heard the racket, and struggled to full consciousness, slightly alarmed by the insistent canine outside. The time was 4.30a.m.

The Vas family had left Western Australia about three months earlier, traveling around their new homeland by caravan and picking up odd jobs along the way. Mr. Vas, a Rumanian-born repairman, was hopeful of finding work in the Rockhampton district in Queensland.

On the evening prior to their rude awakening, George had parked his caravan on the roadside north of Childers, intending to visit Rockhampton less than 20 miles further north the next day.

Their dog Ica ensured they had an early start to the day.

George Vas said:

I heard a noise like a swarm of wasps, only much louder. I rushed around the side of the caravan, but could see nothing. Then Maria, who was sleeping near the window, yelled that she could see something above the trees. When I got to the other side of the caravan, the others were outside, too. We all saw the spaceship. [Rockhampton) *Morning Bulletin*, January 16, 1969, p.3]

Mr. Vas told the media the spaceship was shaped like a Mexican sombrero and about 25 — 30 yards [23m – 27m] in diameter. He said it 'gave off a brilliant violet color.'

As the family stood, spellbound in their night attire, they witnessed the descent of three spacemen from the craft. George Vas described them as 'roughly human in shape, but about three times larger.'

Wow! Giant spacemen.

Maria Vas described what she saw in greater detail:

> Each of the spacemen descended in a tiny craft similar in shape to the bigger spaceship. They had blocky arms and legs, and generally shapeless bodies. They gave off a violet-yellowish glow. The three spacemen did not seem to be concerned that they were being watched.
>
> They began collecting plants and sugar cane shoots from a cane patch at the edge of the road. The plant specimens were sucked up through a transparent funnel leading to the mother spacecraft. [*North Queensland Register*, January 18, 1969, p.2]

Maria's older sister, Olga, explained a moment of tension which occurred while they were watching. As one spaceman moved closer to where the girls stood, their father yelled 'Run, run!' but the visitor simply picked up several stones and turned away without menace.

Then, after ten minutes had elapsed, the spacemen returned to the mothership:

> They took off very quickly, going straight up. Even after it had gone we could still hear a faint sound, like a single wasp, Mr. Vas said. As the spaceship took off, the hair on his head and arms stood up as if affected by a form of magnetism. The girls, Olga and Maria, said this also happened to their hair. [(Rockhampton) *Morning Bulletin*, January 16, 1969, p.3]

The girls both described the spaceship as 'very beautiful.' They said they had tried to stop passing motorists to tell them what they'd seen, but no-one would stop — but who could blame them, it was about 5 a.m. after all!

George Vas was, it seems, an expert on spaceships. He claimed Childers was his third sighting. As a child in Rumania he saw one in 1918; then, in 1946 or 1947, he saw another in Belgrade.

'What my family has seen is of great importance to the rest of the world,' he said.

He also pointed out that there were many things about the spaceship which he regarded as 'too technical' to explain. He was, however, willing to explain them to scientists in Canberra, if someone paid his travel expenses.

He provided a sketch of the spaceship to the *Morning Bulletin*, which was published with his interview.

Flying Saucer Review (U.K.) reported this incident in their Issue '69, Vol. 15, No. 3 under the heading 'Giant Humanoids collect cane' (page 33).

11. Tully Farmer finds UFO 'Nest'

"A saucer-shaped object rose from the lagoon"

Back in 1947, when Albert Pennisi and his wife first considered buying a 100acre/40ha sugar-cane farm at Euramo, ten miles south of Tully, Queensland, they visited the property to check it out.

During their inspection, an amazing event took place. To their astonishment, they saw:

> ...large revolving beams of light that shone up into the sky from other parts of the property. Albert climbed on to the roof of a shed to get a better look at the lights, but couldn't find out what they were. [Lee Paqui, 'Tully Revisited,' a presentation by UFO Research Queensland, 2016]

Albert later said it was 'like a battleship sailing across the property'.

It may also have been a sign of things to come, but Albert went ahead and bought the property which included a lagoon known, due to its shape, as Horseshoe Lagoon.

> The water in the lagoon is invariably obscured by a dense growth of reeds, each about half an inch [1.27cm] thick, the stem protruding above the surface, to an average height of about two feet (61cms). The entire lagoon with its growth of reeds is completely hidden from the casual passerby by an eight to ten feet (2.4m–3m) belt of sword grass. This grows to a height of six or seven feet (2m). [Stan Seers, *UFOs: The Case for Scientific Myopia*, (Vantage Press, 1983), p.69]

The water in Horseshoe Lagoon, which is central to this chapter, was about five to six feet deep (1.5m).

Nineteen years later, on the 19th of January 1966, an incident took place on Horseshoe Lagoon that caused Albert and his family considerable distress:

> Mr. Pennisi's farm was besieged by hundreds of curious people who had come from all over Australia … [he] was caused considerable hardship and frustration, as dozens of people ambled across his property without first seeking permission.
>
> His farm tractors were in constant use pulling cars out of the mud and he was eventually forced to build a barricade across the roadway at the entrance to the property, and forbade entrance to everybody. [Murray Stott, *Aliens Over Australia*, Sydney 1984, p.147]

The cause of this entire hullabaloo became known as the Tully Saucer Nests and led to international interest and speculation.

At about 9.am that morning 28-year-old banana farmer, George Pedley was driving his tractor across the Pennisi property towards and then beside Horseshoe Lagoon:

> He thought he detected an occasional misfire in the tractor motor. He leaned forward in his seat to listen, and almost immediately heard a distinct hissing noise, which he thought momentarily was a tire leaking air.
>
> Then, to his astonishment, a large saucer shaped object rose from the lagoon, ascended slowly to the level of the tree tops, tilted a little to one side, and then, in a fantastic burst of speed vanished in a south-westerly direction. [B Denton & C A Phillips, *The Tully Report*, UFORQ]

George Pedley's much-later interview with Bill Chalker provides greater detail in George's own words:

> Suddenly, an object rose up out of the swamp. When I glanced at it, it was already 30 feet/9m above the ground, and at about tree-top level. It was a large gray, saucer-shaped object, convex on the top and bottom and measured some 25 feet/7.6m across and 9 feet/2.7m high. While I watched, it rose another 30 feet/9m, spinning very fast, and then it made a shallow dive and took off with tremendous speed. Climbing at an angle of 45 degrees, it disappeared within seconds in a south- westerly direction … I saw no portholes or antennas, and there was no sign of life either in or about the ship. [George Pedley in Bill Chalker's '*The 1966 Tully Saucer Nest: a Classic UFO Physical Trace Case*', 1997]

But this was far more than a 'Close Encounter.'

Tully Nest

George Pedley jumped from his tractor, keen to see where the object had been before it took off. He pushed through the tall sword grass to the water's edge and found a large cleared circle in the swamp reeds. The water within the circle was rotating slowly and appeared to be totally free of reeds.

George looked at it, thinking 'I have really seen something!' Then, very matter-of-factly, he rode off on his tractor about his daily work. He was, it seems, more interested in the cleared circle in the swamp than the flying saucer he'd seen at close quarters!

Around lunchtime, George returned passed the spot again. Still curious, he decided to stop and take another look. This time the circle of cleared water was a floating mass of reeds that had obviously surfaced in the few hours since he was there earlier. The reeds where pressed down by comparison with those on the circle's perimeter, and resembled a huge 'nest.'

Queensland Flying Saucer Research Bureau photograph © P. V. Fignale

And there was something else:

The reeds were radially distributed in a noticeably clockwise manner, and he was emphatic that at the time the reeds in the nest – as it came to be called – were quite green, as were all the other reeds in the lagoon. [B Denton & C A Phillips, *The Tully Report*, UFORQ]

Now keen to share what he'd seen, George Pedley told Albert Pennisi that afternoon about the floating circle of reeds. They agreed to visit the site later that day.

As many as four people were in this mid-afternoon 'inspection' group:

> Mr. Alf McDonald, a Stock Routes inspector for North Queensland, dived with Mr. Pennisi and a member of the local police into the waterhole. On inspection he gained the impression that "some force had sucked the roots up cleanly into the floating nest." He said "There was no stubble under the circle. The roots were sucked up whole and the lagoon floor was smooth," [Pinkney & Ryzman, *Alien Honeycomb: the First Solid Evidence of UFOs*, Sydney, 1980, p.26]

By this time the reeds in the circle had turned brown and appeared dead.

Fortunately for future generations, Albert Pennisi rushed home and returned with a camera. Several of these photographs recur in the numerous online accounts of the Tully Saucer Nest incident. One shows a man (named as Albert Pennisi) wading through the 'nest.'

Here's the trace evidence gathered from this mid-afternoon, lagoon-side gathering: (a) at the spot where George Pedley saw a radial circle of green reeds and grass at lunchtime (i.e. the nest) had, by mid afternoon, turned brown and appeared dead; (b) this circle or nest was not attached to the lagoon floor, that is, it was floating on the surface, and (c) the reeds making up the nest were matted in an clockwise direction.

Bill Chalker includes a further fascinating, but qualified, finding in his 'Tully Saucer Nest' overview:

> Subsequent underwater checks indicated three large holes in the muddy floor of the lagoon beneath the Pedley nest. Whether these were there at the time of the sighting could not be absolutely proven, but to some they suggested the possibility of tripod landing indentations. [Bill Chalker, '*The 1966 Tully Saucer Nest*', 1997]

The Tully Report by B Denton & C A Phillips (UFORQ) summed up 'its most incredible feature:'

> ...the amazingly clear impression of the UFO left on the surface of the nest. The outer perimeter was sharply down-thrusting, as if by a huge inverted saucer, with a perfectly circular protuberance about 6 or 8 feet/1.8m-2.4m in diameter and possibly 18 inches/46cm deep.

The photographs support this.

At 7.30 in the evening of 19 January 1966, Albert Pennisi and George Pedley reported the incident to the Tully police.

Tully Nest

The following morning at 7.00am, Sergeant First Class A. V. Moylan, officer in charge of Tully police, together with George Pedley, visited the nest site (or, as the police sergeant described it in his official report 'the depression in the swamp').

The *Townsville Daily Bulletin*, in reporting this visit in their 21 January edition, quoted the police sergeant:

> The grass in the depression was still lying flat, and had browned off but did not appear to have been burned. Mr. Pedley said that the previous day, when he saw the huge mark, the grass was quite green. Sergeant Moylan said there was no sign of any marks having been made by cattle or any other animals. There were no tracks leading in or out of the depression, and the grass had been flattened smoothly. [*Townsville Daily Bulletin*, January 21, 1966, p.1]

Sgt. Moylan, writing his official report of the visit, suggested an alternative explanation of the Pedley sighting and then expressed doubt about his idea's likelihood:

> In this matter I formed the opinion that the depressed area in the swamp grass had been caused by a small helicopter and that the observer, in the early morning bright sunlight shining on the rotor may have mistaken the shape. His [Pedley's] description of the take off lent some strength to my opinion. However there was cleared land to the east for about 200 yards [183 meters] where such an aircraft could have more safely landed instead of the position indicated by the observer, close to the trees. [part of Sgt. A. V. Moylan's official documentation after his site visit.]

In her *'Tully Revisited 50th anniversary address'* in 2016, UFORQ editor Lee Paqui mentioned:

> Before they [the police] passed the case over [to the R.A.A.F.], they found two further nests, smaller than the original, and in one of which the reeds went counter-clockwise. There were even what appeared to be burns in the small nests.

Sgt. Moylan telephoned the Royal Australian Air Force (RAAF) base at Townsville later that morning and spoke with Flight Lieutenant Wallace. He was told he would be sent a proforma questionnaire for George Pedley to complete. They obviously discussed the sighting because the next day, 21st January, Flt. Lt. Wallace asked the Tully policeman to obtain 'a sample of the grass from the scorched area' for scientific testing.

At around 3.30 that afternoon, Sgt. Moylan returned to Horseshoe Lagoon and obtained the required grass sample. Together with the completed sighting report, the sample was dispatched back to Townville RAAF base on Australia Day, January 26th 1966.

But they were not the only samples taken from the site, as we will shortly learn.

News of George Pedley's sighting had, around this time, spread into the wider community and both local and Brisbane papers soon carried the story.

The *Townville Daily Bulletin* article (already mentioned) also included a quote from George Pedley:

> On Thursday night, Mr. Pedley told a *Townsville Bulletin* reporter that when he first saw the object, he did not know what he was looking at. He said that he "could not believe his eyes at first," but after seeing the shape and size, the speed with which it flew away, and the impression made in the grass afterwards, he took it to be a 'flying saucer'. [*Townsville Daily Bulletin*, January 21, 1966, p.1]

On Friday morning the Tully Nest received a short mention in the Brisbane press and the following Sunday (23rd) the expanded story was spread over two columns with a photograph.

Judith Magee, reporting in *Flying Saucer Review*, said the Sydney *Sun-Herald* of January 23 added spice with an enormous page 1 banner headline: 'MORE FLYING SAUCER NESTS!' and announced 'there had been new discoveries in the Horseshoe Lagoon area near Tully:'

> These were by a Mr. Tom Warren, a cane farmer of Euramo, and a Mr. Hank Penning, a Tully school-master, who were taking a walk around the lagoon when they discovered the two new depressions. One appeared to be some days old, but the other, only a few feet away, seemed reasonably fresh. They were about 25 yards [23m] from the first one [Pedley's], but hidden by dense scrub. The fresher one was only 8 feet [2.4m] across, and the reeds were flattened in an clockwise direction ... all the reeds were dead, but they had not been scorched. [*Flying Saucer Review*, Vol. 12. No. 2, 1966]

Despite the variation in descriptions, it appears likely that these nest discoveries were the same pair referred to by UFORQ editor Lee Paqui earlier.

> The Brisbane paper, the *Courier Mail*, of January 25, 1966, stated, 'RAAF officials discounted the theory that nests have been made by helicopters. The RAAF said that in depressions left by helicopters the grass usually ran in an anti-clockwise direction – the main nest found at Tully ran in a clockwise direction.' [Bill Chalker, '*The 1966 Tully Saucer Nest*', 1997]

Tully Nest

Meanwhile journalists, TV news-crews and curious holidaying sightseers rushed to Euramo and sought out Pennisi's Horseshoe Lagoon, all keen to see the 'UFO Nest.' Laymen and experts freely offered their own alternative explanations for the swirled impression found in the lagoon reeds.

> All sorts of theories abounded for the nests. Helicopters, nesting birds, crocodiles, dogs, secret military devices, spaceships, reed eating grubs, willy willy and whirlwinds were among the many ideas trotted out. [Bill Chalker, *'The 1966 Tully Saucer Nest: A Classic UFO Physical Trace Case,'* 1997]

On the morning of the fifth day after George Pedley's sighting (Sunday, January 23) the president of the Queensland Flying Saucer Research Bureau, Stan Seers, telephoned Albert Pennisi and introduced himself. Stan was a laboratory assistant in the Physics Department of Queensland University.

Mr. Pennisi could be forgiven if he thought: 'At last, someone with an serious interest in the phenomenon is paying attention!'

Stan Seers sought all relevant details, including:

> ...samples of reeds from both inside and outside the nest to test for radiation. The samples were air freighted to Brisbane, approximately one thousand miles [1,610kms] south of Tully, early the following morning and I collected them at 6.00pm that evening.
>
> The tests were authorized by the head of the University physics department ... [and I was] nominated one of the staff members to do the job. [Stan Seers, *UFOs: The Case for Scientific Myopia*, (Vantage Press, 1983), p. 72]

The tests proved negative.

The University of Queensland stated that the nests could have been the result of severe turbulence, which normally accompanies line squalls and thunderstorms in North Queensland at that time of year.

> Judith Magee commented: "The fine weather conditions of the previous night (18 January) with lack of hot winds and century temperatures could not account for the dead reeds in the lagoon the following morning." The sun had been up for only a brief time. Nor could it be understood why ... there was no damage to trees, shrubs or vegetation outside the perimeter of the nest. [Pinkney & Ryzman, *Alien Honeycomb*, Sydney, 1980 p.27]

In February 1968, just over two years from the initial incident, the QFSRB installed a magnetic monitoring device fitted with self-triggering movie-camera (an 8mm Eumig) in a position covering the greater part of Horseshoe Lagoon. Later Albert Pennissi had another monitoring device, with buzzer, installed in his home 1¼ miles (2km) from the lagoon. Albert habitually checked this device daily.

> On March 2, 1968, the North Queensland radio station 4K2 broadcast a newsflash to the effect that an airliner flying from Cairns to Iron Range had been paced for some minutes by a UFO. An inspection of the [Horseshoe Lagoon] monitor found that the device had been triggered, the camera activated, and the mechanism — although all twenty-five feet/762cm of the film had been run through — was still slowly turning over with the batteries almost exhausted. [Stan Seers,ibid, p.76]

This mechanical malfunction was disappointing, but the swamp reeds were undisturbed and it became a simple matter of replace the batteries and rewind the film. Which was just as well because...

> On March 4 the device was triggered and sixty feet of 8mm film was exposed ... the film was removed from the camera in the presence of witnesses and sent to Kodak in Melbourne for [processing]. Ten days later Kodak wrote back saying the film canister had arrived empty. Somewhere between posting the canister and its arrival in Melbourne, the film had disappeared.

> But, to add even more mystery to this, on March 13 – nine days after the camera was triggered at the Pennisi farm, and probably about the time Kodak were receiving the empty canister in the mail – two RAAF helicopters were observed inspecting the lagoon for a considerable length of time. [Lee Paqui, 'Tully Revisited,' a presentation by UFO Research Queensland, 2016]

At about 5.30am on February 8, 1969 – eleven months after the previous 'triggering' – the Pennisi alarm was triggered again. Albert drove to the lagoon and discovered a new nest about twenty feet [6m] from the bank at the southern end of the lagoon. It was much larger than George Pedley's 1966 nest (and subsequently measured at 29 feet 6 inches/9m diameter). Without disturbing anything, Albert returned home and contacted Stan Seers in Brisbane.

> I caught the afternoon plane for Cairns and arrived there at 7.45pm. A further 2½-hours drive, mostly through torrential rain, with Mr. & Mrs. Pennisi brought us to the farm. In view of the inclement weather and the lateness of the hour it was decided to postpone my first inspection of the nest until the next morning.

The rain stopped overnight and we arrived at the lagoon on one of the farm tractors in fine weather at 5.45am ... Mr. Pennisi assured me that nothing had changed since his inspection the previous day. We waded out through the almost six feet/1.8m deep water ... the weeds had been extracted completely with roots from the floor of the lagoon and were floating on the surface like a huge mattress with 12-18 inches [½m] of the mass above the water... The first thing to catch the eye was the noticeably radial distribution of the reeds ... in a counter-clockwise direction. [Stan Seers, ibid, pps.81, 82]

Albert Pennisi and Stan Seers then stood together on top of the reed nest. It easily withstood their combined 25-stone [158kgs] weight. "It was possible," Stan wrote, "with care, to walk about on it." The pair then waded ashore and returned to the Pennisi home for breakfast.

On their second trip to the lagoon that day, Seers commenced taking colored photographs of the new nest and its environs. He shortly ran out of film, necessitating a return to the house for black and white film he'd left behind.

Their third trip back to the site led to a surprise finding:

> Mr. Pennisi remarked on the unusual appearance of a tree at the far distant end of the lagoon ... and [we] drove around to inspect it. Just before reaching it, possibly thirty yards [27.4m] away, we both exclaimed at another and much newer nest. This one was only twelve feet [3.6m] in diameter and closer to the lagoon bank but had most of the characteristics of the larger one. It had the appearance of having been made overnight.
>
> Twenty-five feet [7.6m] from this new nest was the tree we had come to inspect. About fifteen feet [4.5m] above ground level, extending out over dry land, was a protruding branch with an area of leaves, perhaps six or seven feet long [2m] and a depth of possibly three feet [0.9m] which had every appearance of recent scorching. [Stan Seers, ibid, p.83]

On closer inspection, the men noticed that the scorched leaves were curled, crisp and browning. All other leaves surrounding the scorched area were green and healthy. The surface area below the scorched leaves were covered in healthy, thick, green weeds and grass about two foot six inches/.7m tall.

Stan Seers made two further visits to Horseshoe Lagoon during his short stay at Euramo. Shortly after dark the pair optimistically returned for several hours, hopeful of a sighting of their own. 'The mosquitoes finally drove us home at about 10pm,' Stan wrote.

Early the following morning they returned to collect reed samples for botanical analysis at University of Queensland. They took the opportunity to check the scorched leaves again and found a 'marked deterioration' had happened overnight; the leaves were quite brown and lifeless.

Nothing of significance came from the examination of the new reed samples.

Further nests have been reported at Horseshoe Lagoon. Albert Pennisi named the dates; '1966 the first one, '69 the next, '72 the third, '75 the next one, and '80, and '82. The last marking came in 1987.'

* *

There was an intriguing side-story which emerged from the Tully UFO Nests incident.

It had fascinating ramifications, and involves several sets of very unusual footprints found nearby the Horseshoe Lagoon site soon after George Pedley's initial report.

Bill Chalker made specific reference to the footsteps in his 1997 review of the Tully Saucer Case:

> Christine Rounland ... came across some ground markings that resembled curious tracks in loose ploughed soil of an adjoining paddock between Pedley's banana palms. They led from the direction of the lagoon area and extended a short distance into the ploughed field.
>
> They were shaped like a teardrop, pointed on one end and rounded at the other. Each was about 3-4 inches [7-10cms] in length and about 2 inches [5cm] across at their widest point. They were spaced out at about 12 inch [30.5cm] intervals and in a straight line.

An article published in *Woman's Day* magazine, with the heading 'Strangers from Outer Space' attributes the following quote to George Pedley talking with their reporter:

> 'A day after I saw the saucer, a neighbor called my attention to some tracks on the soft earth between the bananas,' George told me. 'I'd say they were made by a sharp, horny foot, about 3 inches [7.5cm] long, with a soft frog* in it. (*The elastic horny center of an animal's foot — usually not weight-bearing) And I'd say they were made by something that had two feet, not four. They were straight in front of one another, about a pace apart, and in line with the flying saucer nest.' [Woman's Day, February 21 1966 issue]

Tully Nest

These mysterious footprints remain an aspect of the Tully Saucer Nest incident that is not broadly discussed, perhaps because they raise the uncomfortable idea that they may have been made by the occupants of the craft.

12. Intruder at a Rosedale Water-tank

"A domed object with a white top"

George Blackwell, 54, lived alone on a 600-acre/243ha grazing property, White Acres, at Kilmany between Rosedale and Sale in east Gippsland, Victoria.

> He was the caretaker of the property. I found him to be a down-to-earth man, fully aware of the absurd-seeming nature of his experience. [Bill Chalker, *The OZ Files; the Australian UFO Story*, Sydney 1996.]

On the evening of September 29, 1980, George Blackwell went to bed at around 10.30pm and had no trouble going off to sleep. Over the years he had become accustomed to the traffic noises from the Princes Highway which ran past his home, but on this night around 1.00am his sleep was disturbed by an unusual screeching whistle.

And something else as well:

> There were also noises of cattle bellowing and a horse running around in apparent panic... he switched on the bedroom light, noted the time, and went outside in his night attire, to see what was the matter with the stock...

> Looking outside, he noticed cattle up at one corner of an adjacent paddock and a horse running anti-clockwise in a small paddock at the back of the house. [Keith Basterfield & Bill Chalker, in *UFO Research in Australia & New Zealand*, compiled by V & P Godic, UFO Research Australia, 1989]

Rosedale Water Tank

Then George Blackwell saw something in the distance. His immediate impression was that it was an aircraft, and it was about to crash. But George was wrong.

> Immediately he observed, out of the corner of his eye, an object moving from his right to left. Its estimated height at 8-10 feet [2½-3m] above the ground.
>
> As he stood and watched it, it appeared to pass between a shed and a cyprus hedge (estimated distance about 500feet/152m) and then between a silo and a tree. When behind the shed he states that part of the object was below his line of sight...
>
> When clearly in view by the silo, he saw there were no wings and no tail, and he described it as a domed object with a white top. It had orange and blue lights on its surface and he estimated its diameter at about 26 feet [8m]. Its height was given as about 15 feet/4.5m.
>
> The object then progressed over a paddock, passed by a haystack and appeared to rest over a distant, open-topped, concrete 10,000 gallon/45,460L water-tank for an estimated minute before moving to a stationary position apparently on the ground to the left of the tank as viewed from the house. [Keith Basterfield & Bill Chalker, in *UFO Research in Australia & New Zealand*, compiled by V & P Godic, UFO Research Australia, 1989]

George Blackwell went back inside and dressed quickly; he knew he'd have to investigate this strange happening further. In the back of his mind were recent local stories of cattle rustling, and he was aware of his responsibilities as the property's caretaker.

As he went outside to get his motorbike, he could still see and hear the object on the ground in the distance.

He rode his 100cc Suzuki up the laneway towards the water-tank, and he stopped to open a gate and ride through. He was surprised to see an injured cow anxious to get through the gateway in the opposite direction. This cow had been hurt in a road accident and had broken a leg. She liked to lie down at a particular spot in the paddock, and was always resistant to efforts to move her. Now, she was a long way from her 'spot', bellowing, and frothing at the mouth. George let her through the gate, and watched her. The injured cow hid under a nearby raised shed, and remained there until 4.00pm.

It was an omen of things to come.

Further up the laneway, George opened another gate to enter the paddock where the water-tank stood. As he rode towards the glowing object, George felt a strange bodily sensation:

> The closer I got, the worse I got. It seemed to muck up my arms and I couldn't control the clutch. I just sort of went like jelly on a plate — a huge, big jelly tipped out on a plate. [George Blackwell in: Bill Chalker, *The OZ Files; the Australian UFO Story*, 1996.]

George stopped, trembling, about 50 feet/15m from the object. He sat astride his bike with both his feet on the grass; leaving the engine running and headlight switched on. For the next three minutes he remained there, with his hands covering his ears to protect his hearing from the intensity of the whistling noise, trying to rationalize what he was seeing.

Up close the object appeared to have a white dome on top, and a larger orange section underneath with circular lights (or windows) around it.

'Jeeze, it's a UFO,' is how he later explained his conclusion to Bill Chalker.

Without warning, the noise increased to 'an awful scream' as a 'black tube' appeared around the base of the object and inflated to a size greater than the object's diameter.

This was followed by a blast of hot air and an explosive 'bang' as the object lifted off. George was almost knocked to the ground by this lift-off blast, but he clung to his handlebars and stood firm.

At a height estimated at 8–10 feet/2½–3m, the object steadied itself and fell silent, and loose material (stones, cape weed and cow dung) fell away from underneath it. George says he watched by his motorbike's headlight as the black tube deflated towards the center of the object's base. He also reported seeing six evenly-spaced spokes around the rim of the base.

As George was mentally noting these points, the object rose rapidly into the sky and departed silently in an easterly direction until lost from sight.

George's motorcycle was, interestingly, unaffected by the presence of the UFO. He rode it into the spot where the UFO had stood and later confirmed he saw a ring of black flattened grass about 30-feet/9m across.

George sat astride his machine and thought back through the events he had recently witnessed.

Rosedale Water Tank

The more he thought about it, the more tired, anxious and disorientated he felt. He looked at his watch; it had stopped at 1.10am. He made his way home, took his watch off, and lay down on his bed, fully clothed. But sleep evaded him.

At 5.00am, more agitated than rested, he returned to the water-tank site, despite experiencing again the 'funny feeling' as he drew closer:

> With daylight, he found a ring standing out quite clearly in the precise spot where the object had been. The surrounding paddock was a blanket of yellow flowers, but on the ground the mark was near-black or brown, consisting of grass flattened in an anti-clockwise direction, to a width of 18inches/.5m. Inside the ring only green grass remained. The yellow flowers had been removed. Total diameter of the trace was 28 feet/8.5m. Evenly spaced within the perimeter of the ring were six 'spokes' of relatively undamaged grass. [Keith Basterfield & Bill Chalker, in *UFO Research in Australia & New Zealand*, compiled by V & P Godic, UFO Research Australia, 1989]

George also found a defined track of debris leading from the flattened area towards the east. This was made up of the stones, weed and dung shed by the craft before its final departure.

He felt unwell looking around the landing site, so he returned to house for breakfast (later, investigators suggested his queasiness may have been caused by exposure to radiation).

Around 9.00am the owner of White Acres arrived on a regular visit. He told George he looked 'as white a sheet' and inquired after his health. George replied, "Come with me, I've got something to show you." Together, they inspected the circular mark on the grass near the water-tank, as George retold his story of the strange happenings of much earlier that same morning.

They also made another discovery.

The water-tank, which had been full the day before, was dry. Ten thousand gallons/45,460L of water had vanished overnight!

On peering into the 12-foot [3.6m] high concrete tank, they could see the muddy residue from the bottom was piled up to 2-feet [61cm] high in the center of the tank in a conical shape – the water appeared to have been sucked up under a tremendous swirling pressure! Normally, emptying this tank for cleaning purposes took 72 hours just to drain the water out, via an outlet on one side.

During this inspection, George Blackwell developed an ailment he seldom experienced. It was around 11.00am when he complained of a sharp, pain across his forehead and on the top of his head, which persisted for four hours. For the next week, his headache returned daily, defying all analgesic doses to relieve it.

The cattle, too, suffered a degree of disorientation. It took about seven hours before all the cows found their own calves after their early morning, bellowing bedlam. Others, in a large paddock to the east, were still being rounded up a week later. None of the stock would go near the actual landing site circle.

Another interesting effect was found during the men's inspection of the property. A 66-foot-wide [20m] swathe of flattened grass was seen below the object's track across the paddocks – from between the shed and the hedge, between the silo and tree, and on to the water-tank area.

After he'd heard George's story and completed his inspection, the owner reported the incident to the local newspaper, the *Gippsland Times*.

It made the leading front page item on 1 October, 1980:

KILMANY MAN SEES UFO

Mr. Blackwell said yesterday what he saw was almost 'unbelievable'. The Hereford cattle in the adjacent paddock woke him at 1.00am. 'I heard a whistling sound, and got up to see what was worrying the cattle ... Then I saw this thing, about 10 to 15 feet [3-4.5m] high, with a row of lights, like portholes. It was white with a black-brown band. I actually saw it land on the ground just a little way off the highway.' [*Gippsland Times*, 1 October 1980, p.1]

Other physical discomforts plagued George for the next seven days — after his breakfast he began vomiting and experienced diarrhea. Fortunately his evening meals caused no problems.

When asked if he had any trouble sleeping he replied, 'There was no chance of sleeping, mate.' He was able to doze off from time to time, but suffered from nightmares involving helicopters and aircraft, and would wake up sweating and trembling. 'This went on for seven or eight days and I was getting really depressed, it wasn't getting any better. I thought I'd better see a doctor because it wasn't like me at all.

Then on the last night I had a frightful dream. I was down in the paddock chasing the thing with a double-barreled shotgun, one of those old guns with hammers on it. I pulled one of the hammers back and must have bounced on the bed really hard, because I woke up and almost landed on the floor. After that I came right.' [George Blackwell in: *The OZ Files*; *the Australian UFO Story*, Bill Chalker, 1996]

Rosedale Water Tank

Media attention focused on George Blackwell and the White Acres property immediately following the *Gippsland Times* article. A Melbourne television crew arrived shortly afterwards. UFO investigators were, it must be said, slower to follow up this encounter.

Paul Norman, from VUFORS and Victorian representative of the U.S. MUFON group, inspected the property two weeks later with Pat Gildea, his associate. Norman said it was "A very impressive example of a UFO landing and physical trace event." The *Gippsland Times* ran another front page article, with photograph, on Norman's investigation on October 15, 1980:

Analysis of soil Samples.

UFO TALLIES WITH OTHERS

Researchers check site

A Kilmany farmhand's description of an unidentified flying object tallies with sightings described throughout the world, according to the Victorian UFO Research Society ... members Mr. Paul Norman and Mr. Pat Gildea interviewed Mr. Blackwell on the weekend and inspected marks left by the UFO on the grazing property Whiteacres between Sale and Rosedale...

On the weekend the men met another witness. On the same night, 14-year-old Kelly Postle of Kilmany saw what she thought was a meteorite in the sky over her parent's store. Mr. Gildea reported their findings to the East Sale RAAF base on Monday. He said he was surprised that the base hadn't investigated the sighting... [*Gippsland Times*, October 15, 1980, p.1]

* *

A further investigation, conducted by Keith Basterfield, Bill Chalker and Gary Little working together, took place in December 1980, three months after the event:

Although he had received visits from all sorts of people, the witness [George Blackwell] provided an in-depth report of his experience and a six hour interview and inspection ensued. The party went through the event step-by-step and inspected the marking. When viewed three months after the event, there was present a vaguely defined area of bare earth/grass of approximately 28 feet/8.5m across ... Soil and rock samples were taken for analysis but the results were indeterminate. [Keith Basterfield & Bill Chalker, in *UFO Research in Australia & New Zealand*, compiled by V & P Godic, UFO Research Australia, 1989]

UFOs DOWN UNDER

The Rosedale Water-Tank event is a striking example of a 'Close Encounter of the Second Kind' – a J Allen Hynek classification requiring 'an illuminated craft and a visible record of its visit or encounter with human observer/s. [See J. Allen Hynek, *The UFO Experience: A Scientific Inquiry* (London, 1972), pps.110-137]

George Blackwell was less prosaic about his experience. Asked months later about how he felt about it all, he replied 'I don't know. Just something that was beautiful. I think I'd feel happier if I'd had a ride on it.'

13. Country Pub under Surveillance

"When I saw it moving towards us, I ran"

'We'd been playing cards until just before midnight,' licensee Jim Tilse recalled, 'when John Burgess went out to the front of the hotel to move my truck.'

He raced back and called out 'Come and have a look at this!'

'Eric Judin and I went straight away,' Tilse said.

What happened on that early Sunday morning in 1965 became known as the 'Retreat Hotel Affair' and the subject of local speculation and a police investigation.

The 150-years-old Retreat Hotel is located on the Peak Downs Highway, Epsom — about 65kms south-west of Mackay, Queensland – on the way to Nebo.

The Retreat has had dozens of different licensees during its long existence, but in 1965 was owned and operated by J.W. ('Jim') Tilse, a former senior pilot with Trans Australia Airlines (TAA) and Queensland Air.

In their edition published on May 27th, the *Ipswich Queensland Times* led with:

THREE REPORT SEEING A 'FLYING PLATFORM' LAND

Police are investigating a reported sighting by three men near here of a mystery flying object with spotlights above a circular platform.

The circular-shaped object, said to have some 30 lights on it, was alleged by the three men to have landed near the Retreat Hotel on the Eton Range ... on Sunday night... [*Ipswich Queensland Times*, May 27, 1965]

The full story ran across three columns.

The *Brisbane Courier Mail* and *The News*, Adelaide, picked up the news item and ran with it, too, with minor variations. The *Courier Mail's* story includes a reference to Jim Tilse: 'He said he had reported the matter to police and the Civil Aviation Department.' All articles were published on Thursday, May 27, three days after the event.

Another source of information on the Retreat Hotel Affair was published in London in 1974 – Michael Hervey's book *UFOs Over the Southern Hemisphere*. Here is his description of the object seen:

> [The witnesses] saw a black disc-like object with banks of brilliant lights underneath, hovering over tree tops and about 200 feet/61m above the ground.
>
> The upper part was a flat, elongated top, gently convex and appearing solid, metal-like. It measured possibly one foot in thickness and twenty-five to thirty feet across.
>
> The under structure, approximately fifteen feet/4.5m high, consisted of several rows of orange-yellowish lights numbering ten in the top row and then in decreasing order to six lights on the bottom.
>
> Three extremely bright lights, which pulsated, were situated slightly below and outside of the arrangement. The whole light complex cast an illumination upon the area beneath with the intensity of a floodlight beam 200 feet/61m wide on the ground. Trees and grass in the area were clearly visible...[Michael Hervey, *UFOs Over the Southern Hemisphere*, pps.137-8]

Just imagine that! Or, better still, think of it appearing in front of you just two hundred yards away at midnight!

Here's Jim Tilse's account, taken from *Panorama*, the UFOPIA magazine, of what happened next:

> But when I saw it moving towards us, I ran inside and called the [Mackay] police [by telephone].
>
> The policeman at Mackay nearly died laughing and said, 'I bet its not there!'

I went outside and had another look, and said, 'Yes, it is, and it's coming towards the hotel'...

It was about 200 yards/183m from the hotel and it was moving over the treetops.

It had a great bank of spotlights, about 20 or 30 of them, below a circular platform.

When it was coming towards us, somebody said, 'Get the rifle and shoot at it,' but I said 'No fear. They might shoot back!' [*Panorama*, Volume 4, Number 3, 1965]

We turn to *The U.F.O. Investigator* issued by NICAP (National Investigations Committee on Aerial Phenomena) in America for confirmation of the latter point:

> All three witnesses were frightened, as they later admitted, [Mr. John] Burgess, an army veteran of World War II, wanted to get a rifle and shoot at the UFO, but Tilse stopped him. "They might shoot back at us!" he told Burgess. [*U.F.O. Investigator*, Vol. III, No. 3. June-July, 1965. p.1]

That short extract is from on a report by Paul Norman who conducted an on-the-spot evaluation of the Retreat Hotel Affair. Paul Norman subsequently became known as a driving force in the Victorian UFO Research Society (VUFORS), Melbourne.

Next, the 'visitor' started to move forward again, advancing towards the hotel, and drew to a stop.

> From this distance, but seen only in profile, some additional features of the object became discernable. On the bottom of the craft, now appearing as a great, illuminated mass of 1,000-gallon tank size, three triangular leg-like structures with a brilliant, pulsating light on each, were protruding. Some orange glow emanated from the under-belly, but no exhausts could be seen...
>
> Finally, after thirty minutes, the craft rose slowly to approximately 300 feet/91m and with a sudden burst of speed, accelerated extremely rapidly under an angle of forty-five degrees and disappeared in an easterly direction. [Michael Hervey, *UFOs Over the Southern Hemisphere*, pps.138]

The object made no sound while it was hovering or moving about; but when it departed both Burgess and Judin said they heard a buzz, similar to the sound of bees swarming. Jim Tilse said, 'I was closer to the hotel generating plant and heard nothing on departure.'

Jim Tilse, an experienced pilot, made one point very clear:

> He declared that the object was not an aircraft, and he was sure of this! [*Ipswich Queensland Times*, May 27, 1965, p.1]

And he is quoted in the *Brisbane Courier Mail* as adding something further:

> If I had seen it by myself, I would have kept my mouth shut so I would not make myself a laughing-stock. I have read about these things and scoffed. [*Courier Mail,* May 27, 1975 p.1]

The *Courier Mail's* front-page news story concluded with another interesting quotation:

> In Brisbane the Regional Director of Civil Aviation (Mr. Seymour) said that so far he had not received a report on the sighting. 'But,' he said, 'if Mr. Tilse says he has seen something, then I believe him, as he is an experienced pilot,'.
>
> The sighting would probably be investigated by the Air Force, as other sightings were, Mr. Seymour said. [*Courier Mail,* May 27, 1975 p.1]

A circular impression was found on the ground close to where the craft appeared to either be hovering or had landed.

The date of this discovery is unclear; it was expressed as '2 days later', but the sighting had originally been reported as just before midnight on May 23 and revised to 'five minutes after midnight' on May 24. This hair-splitting adds to the confusion as to which day the marks were found.

Tilse's 'Personal Report' to *Panorama* reads 'A circular impression was found on the ground in the vicinity 2 days later', whereas the *UFO Investigator* report reads:

> The next day Tilse photographed a circular impression on the ground where the UFO landed or hovered. As confirmed by local police and NICAP investigator Norman, it was a perfect circle – a ring three foot two inches thick (almost a meter), its inside diameter 20 feet (over 6 meters).
>
> In addition, several treetops were scorched where the UFO had closely passed. This was confirmed by Constable B Self, Nebo Police, and by Tilse and Norman.
>
> The evidence and the reports are being evaluated by the Royal Australian Air Force. [*The UFO Investigator*, June-July, 1965., p.2]

The *Courier Mail*'s next report read:

PROBE INTO THE 'THING'

Mackay – Police Constable B Self of Nebo yesterday inquired into the reported landing of a mysterious 'thing' on Eton Ridge, 40 miles/64km from Mackay, on Sunday night. He said last night he would make no comment on his findings until his report was submitted today to Mackay District Police Chief (Inspector T Boyle). A Royal Australian Air Force spokesman last night said the RAAF had not been asked to investigate the sighting ...[*Courier Mail*, Brisbane, May 28, 1965, p.11]

The three witnesses met one night after their sighting to compare their observations. Mr. Tilse's personal report was sent to *Panorama* included the following:

'Many local people claim it was just a publicity stunt,' Jim Tilse wrote to *Panorama*, 'It was not, but I have not gone out of my way to try and persuade them otherwise.'

'Mr. Judin, Mr. Burgess and I met together last night [date not provided] for the first time since the sighting. We do not now agree on certain aspects, but taken all over, we are reasonably in accord,' he wrote.

*

Now, over half a century later, certain evidence of the Retreat Hotel Affair remains distant from public scrutiny, if indeed the evidence still exists (or ever existed):

Photographs. Where are they? Have they been scrutinized by investigators? What conclusions were drawn from them?

Physical trace evidence. We learnt of landing marks (circles) and scorched tree-tops, but were any soil samples (or bark samples) taken for radiation analysis by qualified persons? If so, what was established by their evaluation?

Police investigation. Constable Self of Nebo – the local police — appeared to confirm the existence of the circles and scorch marks in Paul Norman's NICAP report; but Self later refused to comment on his report to his superior officer. Has Self's report been seen by any UFO investigator? Does it contribute anything to assist the evaluation of the Retreat Hotel Affair?

RAAF investigation. Keith Basterfield scrutinized the RAAF's UFO records in the National Archives of Australia and located copies of the Retreat Hotel newspaper reports sent from the RAAF Base, Amberley, Queensland to the Department of Air with a covering note from RAAF HQ Operational Command stating: 'No action has been taken on the matter at this headquarters.'

It appears that pilot Jim Tilse did not bring the incident to the attention of Civil Aviation Department after all, nor (at least) complete the 'usual sighting report' which is initiated by the RAAF when such sightings are notified.

14. Teenagers Scared by Gravel-pit Lights

"They observed a large disc-shaped object"

Ten years after the Retreat Hotel Affair, and in the same area, another sighting occurred.

At 4 o'clock on the afternoon of March 23, 1975, an 18-year-old youth entered Nebo (Queensland) police station to report the sighting of an unusual group of lights he and others had witnessed on the previous evening. Sen. Const. P.L. Curley interviewed the witness, took his statement and received a drawing of the object from him.

The same young man had reported the sighting to a Police Constable at Eton (who referred him to Nebo police because it was closer) and to the Department of Transport at Mackay, the nearest large population center to where he lived. That office forwarded the information by telephone to the RAAF Base at Townsville for their consideration.

Police Sen. Const. Curley was told of five young people traveling by car on the Dingo-Mt. Flora Road at 10.30pm the previous evening. The driver, 'M' – who had reported the incident – had his two younger sisters with him, 16-year-old 'N' and 12-year-old 'O'. His mate, 18-year-old 'P' rode in the front passenger's seat, while another 16-year-old girl, 'Q', sat in the rear seat with his sisters.

> [They] were traveling in a northerly direction along Dingo-Mt Flora Road and observed an object about 30 yards/27m off the left hand side of the road.

The vehicle was turned around and they drove slowly past the object [again]. They observed a ring of lights attached around the object. The object did not appear to be round.

They also observed a large disc-shaped object above the UFO. This object had purple-colored rings within it, they decreased in size, and in the center was a black central disc about 6inches/15cm across... [extract from Senior Constable Curley's report]

M's description, included in his witness report, was more extensive:

The first set of lights were about 3 feet/91cm above ground level. These lights were flashing on and off. Their color was a very dull white, but you couldn't see anything above the lights except for the blueish-green saucer-type light. This light was not a big light, it was ring upon ring [concentric circles]. In the center of this light it was black...

The blueish-green part of the light was about 12 to 18 inches (30.5 to 46cms) across. The length of the object seemed to be about 10 feet (3 meters) long. We couldn't see all the bottom lights – they seemed to be blocked off from our view ...

It seems the object consisted of two parts: a box-like base (with flashing white yellow lights) standing on legs (which were difficult to discern); and a separate circular or spherical body overhead with dull blue-green or purple concentric lights (possibly connected by a pole, which was mentioned by one witness).

The object was situated in a roadside gravel-storage compound, a cleared area of about 100 by 50 yards (91m x 46m) with a thick covering of sandy loam. Large piles of screened gravel, and sand, were deposited here for use in road construction and maintenance purposes. The area bordering the road and was surrounded by natural trees and scrub.

What happened next piqued the lads' curiosity further:

We went back for a second look. We were only driving slow[ly]. As we almost came to a halt, there was a tremendous "Bang!" It was just like standing right beside a shotgun when it is fired. Because we weren't prepared or expecting it, we all got a fright. [extract from witness statement by the driver's sister, 'N.']

One witness, 12-year-old 'O', said the explosion '... seemed to shake the car.'

Following the loud noise, the boys wanted to get out of the car and investigate further.

Gravel Pit Lights

The girls had other ideas!

['M'] informed me that after the bang, one of the girls locked all the doors and the other one grabbed the driver around the neck so they could not get out of the vehicle. The girls were very frightened and told the driver to 'get going'... [extract from Senior Constable Curley's report]

Get going they did. They headed off south along the Dingo-Mt Flora Road to the Isaac Creek crossing sixteen kilometers/10 miles away, where there was a Main Roads Camp for a road-building crew.

[We] got somebody to come along back with us to the site, but we left the girls at the Main Roads Camp. When we arrived back at the [gravel-storage] site, there was no sign of it (the 'object'). [extract from witness 'M's statement]

Having heard the outline of this incident at the Nebo Police Station, Sen. Const. P.L. Curley 'immediately proceeded to the location' (to use his own words) with 'M' and sister 'O' and began his own investigation. He proceeded to the southern end of the storage area and noticed:

...a large round mark and three half-moon-shaped marks on the ground. The marks appeared quite fresh. The half-moon marks were not flat on the ground. The inside edge went into the ground about ¾ of an inch [say, 2cms]... I estimate the large mark to be about 18 inches/46cm long and about a foot across [30.5cms]. Each half-moon mark would have been about 15 inches/38cm long and about four inches/10cms across. [extract from Senior Constable Curley's report]

Sen. Const. Curley concluded his own written report with the following comment:

Whilst at the scene I mentioned to ['O'], aged 12 years, that if we waited for a bit the U.F.O. might return. The child became quite upset and was obviously frightened. She continued to be disturbed whilst at the location and constantly looked all around as if she expected something to return. [extract from Senior Constable Curley's report]

Flight Lieutenant P. J. Hodge of the RAAF Base at Townsville was assigned the official investigation into what has since become known as the Nebo Gravel-Pit incident. He was aware of a previous sighting just 13 months earlier at Iffley Station, only 7 miles/11km from the site of this new report. An RAAF photographer accompanied Fl. Lieut. Hodge because of the claims that unusually shaped indentations were seen where the lighted object may have landed.

Hodge's investigation was particularly thorough.

He personally interviewed the driver, 'M', and established the consistency of his account as told to several people, and established 'M's pre-conceived beliefs about aliens visitors – 'He does not belong to any UFO organization, but believes there may be other intelligence in the universe'.

Hodge inquired about 'M's background, schooling and community standing from other people, and found nothing untoward. He also gained the impression that 'M' was not 'publicity or attention seeking' and 'went to great pains to bring it [his sighting] to the attention of the authorities and the RAAF.'

Once he arrived at the gravel storage area, Flight Lieutenant Hodge got down to the nuts and bolts of his work.

He recorded the physical location – 'on the right hand side of the new Mt Flora to Dingo Beef Road, 32.5 miles/52km from the turn-off from the Peak Downs Highway' – and its approximate co-ordinates.

He drew a map of the storage area, noting the thickness of the ground-covering loam and gravel, and the extent of gravel piles and their screened sizes.

He paid particular attention to the Area of Interest – 'the area where the object is alleged to have been sighted' – at the southern end of the compound.

Flight Lieut. Hodge identified five 'unusual marks on the ground – three oval-shaped areas, one roughly circular area, and a rectangular area'. Each of these were measured, mapped and photographed (including the distance between the centers of each item).

Notes were made of the extent of impact of these marked areas into the sub-soil and included the comment that 'the impacting appeared to be very recent with no weathering.'

Crushed stone samples were removed from the impacted areas and from adjacent areas for comparison.

> A number of RAAF officers were asked to view the samples [of crushed stones] on the investigating officer's return to Townsville, and without exception all agreed that the stones appeared to be freshly broken when compared with the weathered sample from the surrounding areas. [extract from Flight Lieutenant P. J. Hodge's report]

'No test for residual radiation was conducted at the site.' Hodge wrote.

Gravel Pit Lights

He also further noted the extent of tire marks and cattle hoof-prints throughout the gravel storage compound. 'All the vehicle tracks appeared weathered and with one exception (the rectangular shaped marking) none of the unusual markings appeared to be made by vehicles,' Hodge wrote.

A mob of cattle had passed through the area but their distinctive hoof prints 'were well dried out'. In Hodge's opinion, 'none of the unusual markings, were consistent with them being made by cattle hooves.'

Flight Lieut. Hodge also checked the recent weather. Both ['M'] and the road workers independently reported that heavy rain had fallen on the 18th [March] but no rain had fallen in the district between then and the afternoon of March 25 when Hodge conducted his site inspection.

Next to be questioned were three road construction workers.

Mr. Ken Smith identified himself as the person who traveled with two of the original witnesses from the Main Roads Camp back to the gravel storage area:

> Late on the evening of March 22, he [Ken Smith] was relaxing with a few friends at the camp when a vehicle containing ['M'], another man, and three girls, drove into the camp…
>
> ['M'] and the other man asked him if he would come back with them to have a look. The girls insisted on staying at the camp. Mr. Smith said they appeared to be quite frightened and insisted that they did not want to return to the site.
>
> He returned to the [gravel storage] site with the two men but they saw nothing.… [extract from Flight Lieutenant P. J. Hodge's report]

The foreman of the road construction gang, Mr. Vic Palmer, was asked about recent truck and equipment activity in the gravel storage area. He said the only vehicle on the site had been a back-hoe about two weeks previously.

Flight Lieut. Hodge then sought out the back-hoe operator and checked his equipment, a small Massey Ferguson back-hoe/front-end loader.

This equipment was last used in the gravel storage area on 14 March, four days prior to the heavy rain of 18 March, and the driver said he did not work in the area where the object was alleged to have been. Nor did he use the stabilizing pads on the rear of the tractor at any time.

Hodge pursued the 'stabilizing pads' further, as they were rectangular and one of the unusual shaped impressions was also rectangular. On small back-hoes these two pads provide non-skid stability to the machine when lifting heavy loads or working in unstable areas. Hodge measured the pads and the distance between their centers (and possibly had them photographed).

In the end, though, he concluded 'the impacted area at the [gravel storage] site was not made as a result of back-hoe operations'.

Flight Lieut. Hodge then returned to RAAF Townsville to consider his evidence and prepare a report for his Commanding Officer.

His eventual conclusion?

The Investigating Officer is unable to explain the nature of the alleged object, or the cause of the unusual ground markings which may or may not have been associated with the sighting.

15. Ron Sullivan's Bending Headlights

"What the heck's going on here?"

In a front-page article in *The Courier*, Ballarat, on April 12, 1966, Ron Sullivan's account of his experience was preceded by this quotation from him:

> I have kept it bottled up inside me but I felt it should be known publicly. I have been reluctant until now to mention this queer set of circumstances publicly. But this phenomenal thing has actually happened to me.

What happened to Ron Sullivan that he found so difficult to talk about?

In 1966, Sullivan was an enterprising country businessman. His steel fabrication business in Maryborough, in western Victoria, had contracts all over the Western District and Wimmera for the supply and erection of structural steel-framed buildings.

Thirty-eight-year-old Ron was boss, doing all the estimating and tendering himself, as well as organizing supplies and supervising on-site erection teams.

> 'I was on the road about two days every week,' Ron says, 'particularly on the Wimmera Highway.'

This highway runs west from Bendigo over 300 kms/186 miles to the South Australian border. It links several regional towns and crosses other highways running north and south.

Ron Sullivan was driving the Wimmera Highway on the

evening of Monday, 4th April 1966. He was heading to Wycheproof, about 100 miles/161km from his home in Maryborough, intending to stay in a motel overnight to check out a building job the next morning.

About 14 kilometers (8.7 miles) out of Moliagul, heading towards St Arnaud in an area known locally as Burkes Flat, Ron Sullivan had a unique experience, one he's never been able to forget:

> It was a clear night and I was driving along and saw a light in a paddock on the right-hand side of the road — I thought 'That's the back light of a tractor working,' As I got closer to it, it sort of spread out a bit more, then flared up...[Ron Sullivan, 2013 VUFOA video documentary with Ben Hurle]

That was only the first of several surprises Ron Sullivan witnessed that night:

> Suddenly my headlights pulled hard over to the right. Instead of lighting the road [ahead], they lit up the fence [on the right] as though they were attracted by a magnet. [Ron Sullivan, *Sun News-Pictorial (Melbourne)*, Tuesday April 12, 1966, p.2]

Ron could see the right hand side of the road looming up and, believing that his car had swerved to the right, for some inexplicable reason, he tried to correct it by pulling the steering wheel to the left.

But he had been traveling in a straight line all along and as a result, nearly side-swiped a large tree on the left hand side of the road.

Only the headlight beams had 'bent' to the right as he drove past a particular point, before straightening up again.

> I braked as hard as I could and glanced over to the right. In the middle of the paddock was a column of colored light about 25 feet/ 7.6m high and shaped like an ice-cream cone. [Ron Sullivan, *Sun News-Pictorial* (Melbourne), Tuesday April 12, 1966, p.2]

At the same time as the car's headlight beams were drawn to the right, Ron Sullivan felt 'a tugging' in his chest, he later told Ben Hurle of VUFOA. He recalled thinking 'Holy Molly! What the heck's going on here?'

By this time he had slowed down considerably. He looked to his right and saw the light in the field perform a remarkable manoeuver.

> The bottom of the light, a very bright milky light, came up and met the top

— and "swoosh, straight up and out of sight at a tremendous speed, faster than the speed of sound, I'd say" Sullivan recalled.

> I noticed the light didn't cast shadows; the light was contained within this object and could not escape. It didn't light up any trees. And off it went. Very strange. What it was, I do not know. [Ron Sullivan, 2013 VUFOA video documentary with Ben Hurle]

It must be emphasized that some of the previous quotes from Sullivan were made forty-seven years after the event. He was interviewed by Ben Hurle of Victorian Unidentified Flying Object Action (VUFOA) for a video documentary in 2013, when he was 86-years-old.

Ron's earlier description of these events were considerably more-colorful when quoted in his home-town newspaper, the *Maryborough Advertiser*, back in April 1966:

> He said he looked across into the paddock, and, at what appeared to be a short distance from the fence, was a display of gaseous lights — "all the colors of the spectrum." He did not stop but glanced at the paddock as often as he could while driving, and the last he saw was the lights about 20 feet/6m from the ground. The lights appeared to move rapidly up and down in a narrow area. [*Maryborough Advertiser*, April 13,1966, p.5]

Ron Sullivan continued driving north, pausing only to check his headlights when he reached St Arnaud — 30 miles/48 km from Burkes Flat. Everything was working normally, so he drove on to Wycheproof and checked in at his motel. 'I couldn't sleep that night,' Ron said, 'just wondering 'what the heck was that?'

Initially, Ron didn't discuss his experience very widely; but he did mention it to the building site overseer at Wycheproof the day after:

> I said, 'I had a bad night last night coming up [to Wycheproof], something strange happened. I don't know what it was; it was just a strange light in a paddock. I could feel my body being tugged — like gravity or magnetic fields.' [Ron Sullivan, 2013 VUFOA video documentary with Ben Hurle]

The next day, Wednesday, he drove home to Maryborough, arriving in the late afternoon. He told his wife of his experience at Burkes Flat, and they decided not to say any more about it as Ron might be subjected to ridicule.

Fate decided differently however, and Ron soon felt obliged to reveal his story publicly.

> I heard on the radio — I think it was on the sixth or the seventh [of April] — a young boy was killed in a motor accident at Burkes Flat. I said to my wife 'That's strange, that's where I had that experience.' She said, 'Well, you'd better tell someone about it.' [Ron Sullivan, 2013 VUFOA video documentary with Ben Hurle]

Nineteen-year-old electrical engineer Gary Taylor of Carnegie, Melbourne struck a tree at Burkes Flat when he lost control of his Ford Zephyr and was killed. Following this news, Ron Sullivan felt obliged to speak to the local police.

Ron's friend Hugh Hunter worked on the *Maryborough Advertiser*, so he called Hugh and enquired about the accident. Hugh asked Ron what he knew about it. Ron admitted, 'Something strange happened that night I was there." When Ron explained what he'd seen and experienced at Burkes Flat on Monday night, Hugh said "Leave it with me, Ron, I'll check with the police.'

Later, the pair agreed to visit to site together on Good Friday (April 8, 1966). 'Do you know where it is?' Hugh asked. 'I have a pretty good idea, it'll be about 14 kms/8.6miles out of Moliagul,' Ron assured him.

They found the site of Ron's encounter without difficulty — about a mile passed a house with a dam beside it, as Ron had anticipated.

After parking their car Messrs Sullivan and Hunter decided to enter the paddock to see if there were any marks where he had seen the colored lights on the previous Monday night.

> It was only then that it was found that the car was parked 20 feet/6m from a tree against which a car had crashed. This was the tree struck by a car driven by Gary Taylor, of Carnegie, on Thursday night. Taylor was killed in the crash. [*Maryborough Advertiser*, April 13, 1966, p.5]

This was the very same tree Ron Sullivan almost struck when correcting his steering after the headlights of his car 'had been drawn to the right as though by magnet' as he drove.

> In view of coincidence the matter was reported to Bealiba police who were handling the accident investigations. [*Maryborough Advertiser*, April 13, 1966, p.5]

There was yet another surprise in store for the Maryborough men searching in the paddock on the right. "Hey, Ron," Hugh called out, 'Come over here and have a look at this!'

He had found an impression. It was 'a little over three feet [a meter] in diameter and only a few inches in depth' and 'looked odd' in the fallowed ground. 'There were no foot or paw prints around it, just a bare impression in the ploughed ground.'

The depression was scooped out of the sandy soil. Farming land described as 'fallow' has usually been ploughed and left unsown, allowing the soil fertility to recover.

Melbourne's largest-circulating daily newspaper, *The Sun News-Pictorial*, featured a photograph of the incident site on page two of their April 12, 1966 edition, with a report from a journalist, Ian Livingstone, who traveled there with Ron Sullivan at dusk the previous afternoon:

> A small dusty depression in a ploughed paddock is the only clue left in Maryborough's 'column of lights' mystery. About 3ft/.9m. in diameter, and from 2 to 5 inches/9cm deep, the saucer-shaped depression is inside a paddock 50yds from the Dunolly to St Arnuad road.

Ron's recall of this depression has grown over the intervening 47 years — he described it to Ben Hurle in 2013 as being 'about nine or ten feet [about 3 meters) in diameter and about six or eight inches deep.' Such inconsistencies are predictable considering the long period of time elapsed since the original event, and do not invalidate the significant elements of the experience.

The other Melbourne daily paper, *The Age*, ran a story on page 6 on April 12 headed:

SAUCER NOT DEATH CAUSE

> Police do not believe there is any connection between a fatal accident near Maryborough on Thursday night and a reported flying saucer sighting at the same spot four days earlier...

Then followed a précis of the 'mystery lights' story, which concluded:

> News of Mr. Sullivan's experience produced the theory that Gary Taylor might have met his death because his headlights were 'diverted' by a strange light object.

The media, both local and national, showed great interest in the 'Bent Headlight Beams' case with its colorful light display and the subsequent tragedy at the same spot. Police at nearby Castlemaine, Maryborough, Bealiba and Newstead also received reports of flying saucers seen in their areas.

One reader wrote to the editor of the *Maryborough Advertiser* suggesting Ron Sullivan's 'colored lights' might have been a meteor burning up fiercely after entering the earth's atmosphere. The editor's published response read, 'There was no sign of any burning in the immediate area where Mr. Sullivan saw the lights... the depression which has received so much publicity gave no indication of burning.' [*Maryborough Advertiser*, April 15, 1966 p.8]

Ron Sullivan had a few unexpected visitors shortly after the 'bent headlight beams' story made the national news.

'Two chaps from the Air Force came to see me in the office at work one day,' Ron recalled, 'They introduced themselves, asked a few question, made some notes, and said good bye.'

A few weeks after the sighting, two more-interesting visitors telephoned to see whether Ron would be available to speak with them:

Two chaps in suits came up [to Maryborough] one day and introduced themselves. I just took it they were from some government department, because they looked pretty official.

They had a book, a black covered book, with diagrams of flying saucers [in it]. Of course, I didn't believe in them [flying saucers] in those days, but I'm changing my mind a bit now [2013].

They turned a page over, 'Is it this one?' Another page, 'Was it shaped like that?'

'Did it look like this one?' etc. ...I asked, 'Where did these pictures come from?' 'Oh, from all around the world.' I did pinpoint the closest resemblance to the one I saw ...the ice-cream cone, but when the bottom came up to meet the top, it just looked like a saucer with the dome underneath. [Ron Sullivan, 2013 VUFOA video documentary with Ben Hurle]

At the time of the initial investigation, the property's owner said there was no 'impression/landing patch' in the ground when he ploughed and raked he area before leaving it fallow.

Twelve years after the event (March, 1978), Victorian ufologist Paul Norman located the landing patch and took photographs of it, saying it was 'precisely in line with the tree the car hit' (probably inferring it was at right angles to it in relation to the road.

The police report for the coronial inquiry into Gary Taylor's death estimates his car hit the tree at 70mph/112kph after leaving a 70ft/21m skid mark.

A makeshift plaque, recognizing both Ron Sullivan's UFO sighting and Gary Taylor's death, was attached to a roadside tree on the Wimmera Highway opposite the 263km sign in 2013.

16. Hume Highway Motorcyclist Caught

'He was startled to see two silver-clad figures'

It wasn't the prospect of a speeding fine that filled Ron Hydes' mind when he pulled to the side of the highway that late afternoon. There wasn't a policeman in sight. It was an interception of a very different kind.

On August 24, 1967, Mr. Ron Hydes of East St. Kilda, Melbourne was riding his motorcycle home from Sydney along the Hume Highway. He had passed through Wodonga, when he experienced a very strange encounter.

> The sun was low on the horizon, the sky above him was clear, with some cloud in the distance. Suddenly he was engulfed in a bluish-white light, so brilliant that it almost blinded him and forced him to stop. The source of the light was directly above him and it was so bright that he was unable to see the countryside around him. 'I took my sun glasses off," he said, "and wiped my eyes, when I opened them there was a disc-shaped object about 100 feet/30m away to my left off the road.' ['Alleged landing near Wodonga', *Australian Flying Saucer Review*, No. 8, pps.4-5.]

The disc-shaped object was in a wide grass clearing sloping down to the road and hovering a meter above the ground. Ron Hydes estimated the width of the craft to be 25-30 feet/8-9m and its overall height as 15 feet/4.5m. He thought he could see a crescent symbol about twelve inches/30cm high marking the dome, but it was on the curve blurring around to the other side and couldn't be seen clearly.

It resembled two saucers, one inverted on top of the other, separated by a three-meter band of metal. On top of the object was a small dome two meters/6.5ft tall. Yet again on top of this was a flat-topped ball, about 25cm/10inches deep. [Keith Basterfield, *A Catalogue of the More Interesting Australian UFO Reports*, February 2012]

As his eyesight returned to normal, he continued staring at object in amazement, until he thought he heard a car approaching and turned his head. When he looked back, he got his next surprise:

> He was startled to see two silver-clad figures standing beside the craft. From a distance of 100ft/30m they looked about 5ft/1.5m tall, and wore silvery overalls which covered both hands and feet.[Ron Hydes] could see no sign of pockets, seams or fastenings, and he described the overalls as being so close-fitting that they looked like silver skin.
>
> On their heads the humanoids wore helmets that resembled opaque fishbowls, through which he was unable to distinguish any features. There was no visible opening in the side of the craft facing the road, to show where they had emerged. ['*On the Road from Sydney to Melbourne*', Joanna Hugill, *Flying Saucer Review*, March/April 1968, p.3]

Ron Hydes knew they were studying him from the direction their bodies were turned. He stared right back, and then took a cautious step towards them to gauge their reactions ... and they did the same towards him.

Then one figure took two further steps forward and raised his arm in a beckoning motion.

That was enough bravado for Ron. He jumped on his motorcycle – he had left the engine running — and high-tailed it out of there! His idea was to put as great a distance as possible between the object and himself as he could.

Ron says he was traveling south at between 100 & 120 mph/ 160-193kph along the Hume Highway.

Next, above the roar of his own machine, he heard a deep humming noise and knew straight away what it was.

He looked up. The craft was trailing him at an altitude of about 100ft/30m and now it was emitting a pink glow.

> He slowed down and tried to flag a couple of passing cars and to draw their attention to the object, but the drivers neither stopped nor appeared to see the craft.

As he sped along, he looked for a house or farm where he might find witnesses to the unusual sighting, but there were none to be seen. Feeling there was no escape, he once again drew onto the side of the road and stopped his engine, intending to take another, closer look. [*'On the Road from Sydney to Melbourne'*, Joanna Hugill, *Flying Saucer Review*, March/April 1968, p.3]

By now, the object had passed him, possibly to cut him off. Ron kept an expectant eye on the airborne craft, waiting to see where it landed. But it didn't.

Instead, it tilted its base towards him and shot off into the air at a 45 degree angle, becoming so bright red in the process "it hurt your eyes to look at it; it was like looking into the sun," Hydes said.

It had simply stopped, tilted and shot off into the stratosphere and beyond.

Ron continued on his ride to his East St. Kilda home in Melbourne, some 150 miles/241km away. No doubt he pondered his recent experience along the way. Why me? What did they want? Why did I panic? Could I have learnt something important from them? Where did they come from – and go to?

Questions, questions. The flying saucer did not reappear during the remainder of Mr. Hyde's ride home.

When he later told a few friends of his strange experience, all he received was derisive comments and laughter; so he decided to do some research of his own.

He found the Victorian Flying Saucer Research Society's address, and contacted them. He agreed to be interviewed in detail by the Society's investigation officers. Indeed, he was interviewed twice by them.

Later the taped interviews were 'closely examined' for 'inherent contradictions' and found to be 'remarkably consistent' by the investigators. No corroborative evidence was uncovered in newspapers or in police reports. A check of the meteorological records clearly established that Ron Hydes accurately described the weather conditions at the time.

The VFSRS investigators Peter Norman and N Thornhill provided transcripts of the interviews to a medical psychiatrist and a lawyer experienced in Crown prosecutor work, one adept at evaluating human testimony. Both advised that Ron Hyde's accounts appeared authentic and consistent.

Highway Motorcyclist

The two investigators were convinced his story was true.

*

Another interesting Australian motorcycle encounter took place in the early morning of October 20, 1979, also in the Victorian countryside.

Bill Guest of Poowong was riding his motorcycle along the Loch Road at 2.30a.m. returning home from Wonthaggi, when he glimpsed a strange, glowing object sitting about 15 meters away inside a paddock.

> He stopped his bike and turned the headlight on to the large object. It was glowing white, and shimmering phosphorescently, in the darkness. It was about 20m/66ft long, with no markings. Guest watched the silent display for about twenty minutes, trying to get up the courage to walk up to the UFO. [John Pinkney & Leonard Ryzman, *Alien Honeycomb, the First Solid Evidence of UFOs* (Pan Books, 1980) p.83]

The object then lifted about 5m/16ft off the ground and started coming towards him.

Just then he noticed his bike's headlight began to flicker seemingly caused by from some sort of electrical interference. The object then morphed into a disc shape and was spiraling before his eyes.

Terrified, he fled the scene.

*

The difficulty with solo sightings is the lack of collaborating witnesses, frequently without site traces, and the fear of ridicule causing time delays in making the incident known to those capable of authenticating at least part of the incident. The latter point happened in the following American experience:

One Sunday morning in November 1972, eighteen-year-old Charles Coulter finished cleaning up at a restaurant where he worked near Albuquerque at 1.30a.m. He was riding his motorcycle home to his parents' place when he observed a very bright light at about at about 25 degrees elevation and 5 to 10 degrees to the right of his path.

Charles estimated its size as being that of a pea held at arm's length, and thought it was most likely an aircraft's landing light.

Following his normal route towards home, having traveled about 6 miles/10km, he noticed the object was still ahead of him in the same manner as before, but it appeared several times larger than before. He decided to follow it and see what it was.

> He followed the object east ... [until] the object turned suddenly 90 degrees and headed north. ... Suddenly the object turned toward the east again, then appeared to stop. Charles found a dirt road to turn on and continued to follow... ['*UFO-Cycle Encounter*', Cliff Booth, *The A.P.R.O. Bulletin*, Vol. 26, No. 11, May, 1978,. p.2]

Then the object slowly moved a quarter-mile/0·4km north again and stopped. Charles was riding over rough, rocky open desert mesa country.

He switched his headlight off and rode at 'creep speed' to within 150 yards/137m of the object. The moon was shining and the air felt charged with electricity. Charles was aware of a low-pitched humming noise.

The object was now hovering about forty feet/12m above the ground ... At this point, [Charles's] motorcycle engine died and he felt all the hair on his body stand on end. He took his helmet off and the hair on his head stood straight up. He tried to restart the engine, it wouldn't start. He tried his lights, and they wouldn't work.

> Then an extremely bright blue-white light beam appeared to protrude or extend with the front surface of the beam slowly approaching the ground. It would reach the ground in one spot then retract slightly and move and extend in another spot ... The beam repeated this 3 times, then it extended down on Charles and his motorcycle. ['*UFO-Cycle Encounter*', Cliff Booth, *The A.P.R.O. Bulletin*, Vol. 26, No. May,11, 1978,. p.3]

The light blinded Charles Coulter. He felt paralyzed. He couldn't let go of his motorcycle's handlebars. He couldn't see his hands, arms or even his nose.

Then the light beam drew back and receded into the UFO and a panel or door closed over the hatch, cutting the source of the beam off altogether.

Next thing, the UFO departed in an easterly direction over the Sandia Mountains.

Charles had left work at 1.30a.m., spent twenty minutes getting to the encounter area, and afterwards arrived home at 3.00a.m.. He could not account for any other period of time during his encounter.

Five years elapsed before Charles Coulter reported his experience.

17. St Helens Family Buzzed by UFO

"I thought the world was coming to an end!"

Yet another encounter on a lonely road occurred on a dark, drizzling Monday night on Tasmania's east coast in 1974. A woman and her two young daughters, one asleep on the back seat, were just twelve kilometers (around eight miles) from home after a tiring 2½ hour drive from Launceston.

Their Toyota Crown was running well, they were listening to the car radio, and on a familiar road, Anson's Bay Road. They had already crossed over the Georges River bridge. Soon they'd be home, have something to eat, and share the news of their trip with the rest of the family.

Alas, it was not to be so simple...

Mrs. Richards, the driver, and eldest daughter Janine, 8, had just crossed the Branch bridge when their car radio went crazily static – but not quite loud enough to wake the sleeping Kathleen, 5, in the rear seat.

Suddenly, the sky around them lit up brightly.

Then the car lost all power, and stopped dead. Everything electrical in the vehicle failed instantly ...ignition, headlights, radio, and dashboard instruments.

That alone was scary enough, but worse was to follow:

As Mrs. Richards tried to restart the vehicle, a deafening, vibrating noise surged through the car. She felt forced to cover her ears with her hands to block it out. 'It was like thirty or forty large jets,' Mrs. Richards said, 'I felt my head was splitting open, and thought the world was coming to an end!'

Almost simultaneously, painful electric shocks began penetrating their bodies – like electric vibrations, far worse than shock from an electric kettle. This lasted for about a minute, during which Mrs. Richards thinks she screamed! [Roger Brooks, TUFOIC (Tasmania UFO Information Centre) investigator]

Then the car filled with a penetrating, choking gas ('far stranger than commercial bottled gas,' said Mrs. Richards). They gasped for breath. Janine and her mother scrambled from the front seat, dragging half-asleep Kathleen from the car and ran a safe distance away.

Mrs. Richards said all she had wanted was for them all to have 'fresh air and to breathe properly.'

Janine, 8, later admitted that during these rapid series of events, she thought the car had actually caught fire – it hadn't.

Imagine, for a moment, the situation the trio was in. They had been subjected to deafening noise, painful electrical shocks and life-threatening gas, and were alone on a damp night on a country road.

Fortunately they knew the road well, and knew that the Chappel family lived just two miles (3¼kms) away.

They arrived at the home of Harvey & Derek Chappel at about 9.45pm, around half-an-hour after their ordeal began.

Alarmed at the story they were told by a distraught Mrs. Richards, the brothers decided to visit the abandoned car straight away and check it out for themselves (Harvey Chappel was a mechanic).

The least they could do was to ensure it wasn't a danger to other motorists, particularly at night. Mrs. Richards accompanied the Chappel brothers back to the car.

To her astonishment, it started at the first attempt. Everything electrical in the car functioned normally (lights, radio, etc.) Harvey Chappel checked it thoroughly and could find nothing wrong; he noted the engine bonnet was warm which may have indicated the radiator had boiled (which wasn't surprising considering the external electrical charges the car had recently sustained.)

Buzzed by UFO

...so Mrs. Richards and the children continued on home. Meanwhile, Mr. Richards, waiting at home, had heard a distant roar and saw some lights in the sky prior to his wife's arrival. [Keith Roberts, compiler, *Tasmania: a UFO History*, TUFOIC, 2011]

He thought the noise was his family returning along the farm road and expected them to arrive shortly. He expressed surprise at their much later arrival. Then he listened to their frightening escapade.

The following day Mrs. Richards suffered from swollen fingers and arms, and had lost feeling on the right side of her face. She also had a red mark above her right eyebrow, which she thought was caused during the massive vibrations of the previous evening. Her "nerves have been in a shocking state," she said.

A doctor who saw Mrs. Richards said she was suffering from severe emotional reaction. The children suffered no after-effects. [Keith Roberts, compiler, *Tasmania: a UFO History*, TUFOIC, 2011]

But it wasn't all over for the Richards family just yet.

Only two nights later, on September 18, 1974, Mr. Richards had an extended 'light-in-the-sky' experience of his own.

He was returning home by car in the dusk from a neighbor's place when his attention was caught by a bright light in the sky that appeared to be following him. 'It seemed to be attracted by my headlights,' Mr. Richards explained.

It paced him for thirty-five minutes, slowing down when he slowed down, surging when he surged. To test his idea about it being attracted to his headlights, Mr. Richards drove using only his parking lights; and the lighted object trailed way behind him.

At the house it zoomed in from an estimated height of 2,500ft/760m to about 80ft/24m just above some trees 100 yards/91m from the house. His wife, Janine and son Ricky, 11, watched it through a window.

At one stage Ricky went outside the house for a closer look but when the object came closer, the family dragged him inside. They described it as crescent-shaped and 'vibrant egg-yellow' in color. They watched it for five minutes.

It seemed attracted by the lights of the house. When they turned the house lights off, the object soon "faded out." The family has seen odd lights about the sky in the area for years, but had taken little notice of them. [*Saturday Evening Mercury* (Hobart), September 21, 1974, p.1]

18. The Knowles Family at Mundrabilla

"Felt like my brain was being sucked out!"

Encounters on lonely roads are frightening enough, but for one family it became nothing short of a nightmare.

When Mrs. Faye Knowles and her adult sons Patrick, Sean, and Wayne, along with their two dogs, **began their drive east across Australia from Perth, Western Australia to surprise a relative in Melbourne, they had no idea it was them who would receive the big surprise!**

Before leaving their suburban Midland home on Tuesday, January 19, 1988, the travelers strapped two suitcases to the roof of their 1984 Ford Telstar car. They planned to drive through the night, sharing the driving to save time.

Perth is the most isolated capital city on earth and is linked with Australia's eastern States by a two-lane, bitumized highway that crosses the unchanging, arid, saltbush-covered Nullabor Plain. The only township along this portion of their route is Eucla (population 80) and for their basic services like petrol, food, water and shelter travelers rely on various roadhouses/gas stations/motels which are spread several hundred kilometers apart along its length.

By 4.30 the following morning the family had covered some 1,320km/830miles of their 3,420km/2125mile trip, and were about 40km/25 miles west of the Mundrabilla roadhouse in Western Australia.

Mundrabilla

Sean was at the wheel when he saw what he assumed to be truck's lights approaching from a distance. The light 'jumped about a bit', then disappeared only to shortly become visible again as they drew closer.

'Is that a spaceship?' Sean asked his older brother Patrick, who was sitting in the front passenger seat.

'Don't be stupid!' Patrick scoffed in response. The light became brighter and larger, and then disappeared again.

Suddenly they became aware the light was behind them, and close! Startled, Sean jammed his foot on the accelerator in a bid to distance them from the dazzling object.

The next thing they knew it was in front of them again, sitting stationary on the road, but looking larger and brighter.

'As we got nearer,' Sean said later in a telephone interview, 'I had to drive on the other side of the road to miss it. We nearly hit a car towing a caravan (house trailer) going in the opposite direction. Then the light disappeared again.'

The driver towing the caravan heading west on the Nullabor at this particular hour has not been found – although the circumstances of the 'large, bright light' and near-accident would surely be memorable.

Asked later by a Canadian interviewer, Mike Campbell of Radio CJOR, Vancouver, to describe the object, Sean explained 'It was egg-shaped, with a round circle in the center, and orange-yellow in color.'

In a news item published in the Adelaide daily newspaper *The Advertiser*, on Thursday, January 21, the family is quoted as saying the object was 'shaped like an egg in an eggcup, and about a meter/3.2ft wide' and 'high enough to block their view.' Sean added 'It was a weird-looking thing, and we stopped to go back and have a look at it.'

Sean did a U-turn on the highway but, as they drew closer to the unfamiliar pulsing object, he became hesitant. The object disappeared once more, only to be seen immediately behind them, again following their car.

'It was chasing us,' the still terrified Mrs. Faye Knowles recounted during an exclusive Channel 7 television interview with the family thirty-six hours after the event, 'and all of a sudden landed on our car... pulled our car back!'

Interviewer: At what stage did the object land on your roof? How fast were you going at the time?

Sean Knowles: I got to about two hundred [kilometers per hour/124mph], I got a blowout, and once the car stopped I got blanked out, and I don't know what happened after that.

Interviewer: [Blown-out tire shown on screen] If a car has a blowout at 200kms/hr there is a danger, isn't there, it will overturn? How come you didn't?

Unidentified response [probably Patrick]: There was a weight on the roof ... explain that!

Interviewer: Was the car on the road at all times, or was it lifted off the road as reported?

Mrs. Knowles: We don't really know, but we think it was lifted off the road.

'There's something on the roof,' Mrs. Knowles had said at one stage during the encounter. She unwound her rear window and placed her left hand on the roof of the car.

She felt something spongy, and quickly pulled her hand back inside. 'Its on top of the roof,' she yelled, as the interior of the car filled with pungent smoke or dust.

'I thought I was going out of my head,' Patrick recalled, 'it felt like my brain was being sucked out!'

Interviewer: Was there any sounds or smells?

Patrick Knowles: There was a humming sound. It sounded like a 'Brrm, Brrrmm, Brrrmmm', and when it was on the roof, I wound down my window... that's when our voices started to change. All of us, our voices went very deep and strange, and we felt like we were dying.

My brother chucked the brakes on the car, and this thing just shot off [the roof].

We got out of the car 'n' hid in the bushes and waited for about ten or fifteen minutes.

We went over back to the car, took the wheel off, chucked that in the boot [trunk], got the spare [wheel] out and put that on. We didn't worry about the jack, just left it there in the bushes, and we shot off.

Mundrabilla

Melbourne UFO investigator John Auchettl gave Jamie Leonarda greater detail of this portion of the Knowles family experience:

> They all began to talk like robots, they said. Then Patrick looked over towards Sean who was driving, and Sean was unconscious at the steering wheel, his hands were off the steering wheel and his head was down. The car, in their opinion, was still moving – they all described the car doing 200kph and the feeling of being dropped out of the sky, hitting the ground, the wheel bursting, and then actually spinning off the road and stopping. [John Auchettl on ABC, Radio National's *Radio Eye* program, '*To Catch a Falling Star*']

As the group stood around waiting for the wheel to be changed, a large well-lit truck approached from the west. Two family members signaled frantically to the driver trying to flag it down for assistance, but it just roared past them on the other side of the road into the breaking dawn light.

The moment the tire was replaced, the family hurriedly climbed into the car, did a quick U-turn and sped off eastward again.

Patrick Knowles: It [the bright object] started to follow us again. It was starting to become daylight [so] we turned our headlights off and it [the object] just seemed to lose us for some reason.

Interviewer: How scared were you, Patrick?

Patrick Knowles: Ah, really scared...

Mrs. Knowles: (interrupting): Terrified!

Patrick Knowles: (continuing): ...scared as I've ever been.

Interviewer: What was your feeling while all this was happening?

Patrick Knowles: We're gunna die ... that's what I felt like... it just made me feel I was dying.

They sped along the highway towards the Mundrabilla roadhouse, the nearest point of civilization, overtaking the truck that had earlier refused to stop.

A minor sense of relief came over them when they pulled into the roadhouse — there were other people and vehicles present. Although still shaken by their experience, their ordeal appeared to be over.

When they got there, they had to refill the car because it was out of fuel. We did some measurements and discovered that half the tank was empty – they had lost 260kms (162miles) worth of fuel! ... in fact it took them two hours on a journey that shouldn't have taken them so long – so they lost an incredible amount of time, and fuel! [John Auchettl to Jamie Leonarda, ABC, Radio National's *Radio Eye* program, '*To Catch a Falling Star*']

The first person they spoke to at Mundrabilla was Melbourne trucker, Graham Henley who had arrived fifteen minutes ahead of them.

Henley estimated he had been 10 to 15kms (6 to 9miles) ahead of the Knowles' car and said he had seen a bright white light hovering over headlights in his rear-vision mirrors. He assumed, incorrectly, they were the lights of another truck further back driven by a friend, 'Porky' De Jong.

'I had only just been talking to Porky on the [CB] radio,' Graham Henley said, 'but once I saw that light, it [the radio] went dead.'

It transpired that Porky's truck was the vehicle the Knowles' hailed from the side of the road and didn't stop; and was later overtaken by them at high speed while driving with the headlights turned off. Porky was not driving during the 116kms run from Madura to Mundrabilla — he was resting in the rear cabin while his companion Anne took over the wheel.

Trucker Graham Henley spoke to the Knowles family outside the roadhouse, heard some of their story, and inspected their Ford Telstar for supporting evidence of their account.

'When I first saw the family,' Henley said, 'they were terror-stricken and in a state of shock. Even their dogs were cowering in the front seat of the car. The lady was crying uncontrollably, and one of the young blokes could barely speak. I touched the mother's hand where she said she touched the thing and it was cold like marble.'

'The whole car smelt like Bakelite, or just like as if you'd blown a fuse. A soot was all over the car, it was like powdered glass, and there were four dents [in the roof] as though the car had been picked up by a magnet.'

Mr. Henley said he had checked the tread of the burst tire and underneath the car. 'There was nothing to indicate it had swerved off the road.'

'I cannot explain it, but all I know is that I saw four very terrified people that Wednesday morning,' Henley concluded.

Shortly after this, Porky's rig pulled into the Mundrabilla roadhouse and after checking their load, he and Anne joined Graham Henley talking to the group of people around the Ford Telstar sedan. The new arrivals listened to the family's account of their UFO encounter.

'The woman was hysterical', Porky later recalled, 'and kept repeating 'Someone's got to do something' and 'Someone's going to get hurt.' She had a red blotch on the back of her hand that she was worried about. One of the boys had a very white face.'

Asked by Porky and Henley if it could have been a helicopter the family heard, one of the boys indicated it was a 'whirry' noise, not a 'chuffy' one like a chopper.

The truck drivers inspected the Knowles car closely, and Porky later told UFO researchers Keith Basterfield and Ray Brooke that he didn't see any black ash or dust, or any sign of the two suitcases. He did see the blown-out tire, and marks on each corner of the car's roof — 'similar kinds of indentations one would make with a closed fist'.

The Knowles family didn't stay long at Mundrabilla; within half-an-hour they were on their way again. They drove through Eucla, crossed the State border into South Australia and continued until they reach Ceduna at lunchtime, some 557km/345 miles from Mundrabilla.

Back at Mundrabilla truckers Graham Henley, Porky De Jong and Anne spoke to Mrs. Shirley Lundon, the manager of the roadhouse, about the Knowles' experience.

She decided to report the matter to the nearest police station — Eucla, 66kms (about 41 miles) distant. Porky also spoke to the sergeant detailing his observations.

The truckers decided to borrow a light vehicle from the roadhouse and re-visit the scene of the incident, seeking clues. At about 6.00 a.m. they identified the spot on the side of the road where the stationary Ford Telstar was seen about an hour-and-a-half earlier.

They found three pieces of evidence that supported the family's account. Firstly, a 15-20 meters (about 57ft) long skid mark on the bitumen road surface, apparently made by the left hand rear tire under hard braking pressure, bringing the car to a stop.

Secondly, they identified an impression in the ground where the car jack had stood while the wheel was being changed.

Finally, the truckers saw four sets of running footprints heading in a straight line into the scrub from the car, and four sets of full footprints (as when walking) — plus dog paw marks — in the sand alongside the road. They observed that one person was bare-footed, another had either sandals or thongs, and two people were wearing tennis shoes/runners.

What they did not see, but studiously looked for, were the car jack and handle which they'd been told had been abandoned at the scene, or any sign of the two missing suitcases or scattered clothing.

The searching truckers drove back to Mundrabilla and Porky again contacted the police at Eucla, reporting his findings.

Realizing the family would have already passed through Eucla, he suggested the police speak with their colleagues at Penong — 418km/260 miles further along the highway — as he felt the Knowles' car should be stopped and the passengers officially interviewed.

Having spent most of the morning on this unscheduled interruption, both Graham Henley and Porky De Jong climbed behind the wheel of their respective rigs and continued their journeys eastwards to Adelaide.

The Knowles family were interviewed further along their route at the Ceduna police station, South Australia around lunchtime. Sergeant Fred Longley and Sergeant Jim Furnell spoke with the family and filed a report. 'They were in a terrible state,' Sgt. Longley said later, 'even though it was five hours after the incident. Something happened out there.'

Patrick and Sean Knowles were also interviewed by Senior Constable, First Grade, Trebilcock of the Crime Scene forensic squad at about 1.00pm.

> 'I made an inspection of the damage to the hood [roof] of the vehicle which they indicated to me as having been caused by the object when on their vehicle,' Senior Constable Trebilcock wrote. 'An inspection of the complete vehicle indicated that it appeared quite well looked after and did not display any noticeable damage consistent with having been involved in an accident or collision of any kind ...'

> 'On return to the station I spoke to Mrs. Knowles in a location where we were out of earshot of the other occupants. Mrs. Knowles was visibly shaken by the ordeal and insisted upon her honesty in the belief that the police were skeptical at the report they were making.'

Mundrabilla

Around 2.30pm. the Ceduna police contacted Ray Brooke of the UFO Research (South Australia) and informed him of the Mundrabilla incident while the Knowles family were still at the station. Brooke and Keith Basterfield, both highly regarded UFO researchers, led a team of six other investigators including three from interstate. Arrangements were reached for the Knowles family to drive the 774kms to Adelaide where they would be interviewed by the UFO group and their car inspected.

The Knowles family drove a further 210km/130 miles that afternoon, staying overnight at the Eyre Highway Motel at Wudinna, by which time sketchy reports of their encounter had reached the news media across Australia and particularly in Adelaide, the South Australian capital.

It must have been early afternoon when Porky De Jong and Anne arrived at Wudinna, looking forward to some fresh coffee. They found the town buzzing with excitement — a news helicopter from Adelaide had landed and strange rumors of a UFO incident on the Nullarbor had gained local currency.

Porky asked around and soon learnt where the Knowles were staying, and the couple made their way there, hoping to speak further with the family about the items both found and missing at the site of their encounter.

There was a media scrum at the Knowles' motel, with eager newsmen jostling to interview the family and learn their story. It was announced that the Channel 7 television network had secured exclusive rights for an un-named amount — making the family 'out of bounds' to other news reporters and to the UFO research team.

Porky and Anne hung around, and were eventually permitted to talk with the Knowles family. Shortly afterwards, they drove the remaining 565km/351 miles to Adelaide where Porky gave a short interview to the opposition TV network.

Channel 7 arranged for the Knowles' car to be taken to Adelaide on a tray truck for further examination and analysis.

The Mundrabilla UFO incident attracted instant media attention. UFO researcher Ray Brooke found himself the 'go to' man for almost one hundred queries during the next two days from radio, TV and newspapers services from around the world.

On Thursday, January 21- the day after the incident near Mundrabilla — the Knowles family were subjected to extensive videotaped interviews at the Adelaide studios of Channel 7 (portions of which appeared earlier in this account). The family members seemed tired, distressed and uncomfortable in front of the bright studio lights.

The interviewer did not treat them gently (i.e. 'How do we know you're telling the truth?' followed by 'A lot of people think you're making it up. Do you realize that?').

Several people thought the Knowles were unfairly treated; one was Kelly Cahill who, in a 1996 book relating her own UFO encounter, observed:

> The way in which they were treated was absolutely dreadful, and they were helpless in the face of the roasting they received... I also remember seeing the tears in Faye Knowles' eyes as a TV interviewer turned their experience into a sideshow comedy. [Kelly Cahill, *Encounter*, HarperCollins, 1996, p.150]

Ray Brooke and Keith Basterfield, leaders of the UFO research team, attended the studios and watched the proceedings, but were not permitted to conduct interviews for their own purposes, although they were allowed to chat informally with the family.

They concluded that 'the family appeared to be down-to-earth people trying to cope with some traumatic episode. Indications of a hoax were minimal.'

The next day, January 22, the Knowles completed their journey to Melbourne. Their 'surprise visit' could no longer have been a surprise to their relatives. Their mode of transport was not publicly recorded, but they did not use their own car which was being held in storage in Adelaide. It was six weeks before they returned home.

The Adelaide vehicle analysis report, dated January 29 concluded, in summary:

> Three shallow dents were observed on the roof of the vehicle; they were consistent with an object being pressed into the roof, rather than an attempt to lift the roof.

> The investigation revealed that the damage to the tire was consistent with running on a deflated tire for an extended period. It is considered that this would account for the odor, smoke and vibration sensed during the incident.

> The material taken from around the front wheels was typical of residual dust from wearing brake pads and disks. No significant dust was observed on the vehicle as presented for inspection.

The car was made available to the UFO research team by Channel 7 Adelaide on February 2nd. They conducted a detailed review of the vehicle, paying particular attention to the damaged tire, the dented roof ('at close range it was possible to locate four indentations, small in area, shallow in depth'), electrical system, and dust deposits (which, when analyzed, failed to produce anything of special significance).

By February 4, Brooke and Basterfield had sufficient material on the 'Mundrabilla UFO' incident to compile their initial report for the American-based MUFON (Mutual UFO Network), the world's largest, civilian organization which investigates and publishes alleged UFO sightings in their monthly journal.

'The Mundrabilla Incident' appeared in the March 1988 issue, with follow-up items in subsequent editions.

On their return to Perth after six weeks, the Knowles family were subjected to ridicule by friends and acquaintances.

They were out of work, lacking funds and soon moved to another address to avoid attention. The Knowles never saw their car again due, they said, to an Adelaide promoter.

'He told us,' Faye Knowles is quoted as saying, 'it could be used in television commercials, a documentary and taken around shopping centers where people would pay to see it.'

'But we didn't get a cent; we don't even know if the car was promoted at all, and now we've lost it.'

The Knowles' 1984 Ford Telstar was under a time-payment purchase scheme at the time of the incident. The Adelaide promoter placed the vehicle in storage for several months, but neglected to maintain the storage payments.

The car was put to auction in June 1988 to recover outstanding fees. It sold for just over AUD$7,000, none of which went to the Knowles.

'We just want to get on with our lives,' Patrick Knowles said, 'we want to find jobs and settle down somewhere where people do not ridicule us in the street. We are trying to forget the sharks who promised us money from our experience — they only wanted to use us.'

*

The Knowles' experience has similarities with two further incidents, where other travelers also felt their car was being lifted off the road. However, like the Knowles, these later incidents lacked supporting evidence to corroborate their experiences.

In June 2000 a huge object suddenly appeared above a car carrying four people driving east towards Bilpin from Bell in the Blue Mountains west of Sydney early one morning.

According to veteran UFO researcher, Rex Gilroy of Katoomba, an ionized blue glow enveloped the car, as the terrified occupants continued to drive on. They felt their vehicle being lifted off the road by at least two feet (61cms) and, after being 'carried' for some few hundred feet (say, 75 meters), the glow vanished and the vehicle hit the road.

John Pinkney, retired Melbourne newspaper columnist and now author of several books on paranormal phenomena, tells of an instance involving Ken Smith of Yass, New South Wales who, in June, 1993, stopped at dusk for a meal break during a 343km/213 mile trip from Gulgong to Gunning, in central New South Wales.

'As I sat there on that deserted road,' Ken Smith told Pinkney, 'I heard a sound like wire scratching against metal. Then I felt something grip the rear of the car and lift it up. I could see nothing through the rear window — but something, whatever it was, lifted the car's rear four times before dropping it back on the road. I backed out of there and drove away as fast as I could.'

Further on during his trip, Ken Smith saw 'a bright green object, about the size of a fox's eye, hovering about 45cm/18inches off the ground, shining brilliantly in the darkness. As I drove, it kept moving to the left of the car. I felt enormous relief several kilometers on when the light abruptly vanished. I've never been able to shake off the memory of that episode — or my conviction that the green light was somehow connected to the lifting and dropping of my car.'

*

The Mundrabilla UFO incident, like the two others mentioned above, are devoid of sufficient physical evidence and independent witnesses to substantiate the participants' story.

In the Knowles case, two suitcases strapped to the top of their car have not been found, nor their abandoned car jack.

This doesn't suggest their experiences didn't happen. It simply means they cannot be fully verified.

Absence of evidence is not evidence of absence — *Dr Carl Sagan*

19. Tom Drury's UFO caught on Film?

"It was very clear-cut, sharp in front"

Tom Drury was not your ordinary UFO experiencer. He was a very experienced RAAF pilot having flown transport planes during WWII in New Guinea, the Philippines and Borneo. In 1949 he joined the staff of the Department of Civil Aviation [DCA] and later stationed in New Guinea.

By 1953, Mr. T P Drury was deputy Director of Civil Aviation in New Guinea (then an Australian Territory) when the following extraordinary incident occurred:

> I was standing on the coast road overlooking the Flying Boat Base [the former Qantas Flying Boat Base] at Port Moresby with my wife and children. It was about 11am on the 23rd August 1953. The weather was perfectly clear, which is unusual. I was taking a movie picture of a native boy spearing a fish. I was not looking at the sky.
>
> My wife noticed a wisp of a cloud suddenly appear in the blue sky from nowhere, and start to build up rapidly into a white puff. She called out to draw my attention to it. I watched it rapidly build up into a thick white mass of cumulus. There were no other clouds in the sky and there seemed nothing to account for it. [Tom Drury in Rev N E Cruttwell's report in *Flying Saucer Review*, August 1972, pp.3-4].

So, being interested in meteorological phenomena, Drury quickly decided to start filming the cloud and swung his camera on to it.

Suddenly he saw an object, 'like a silver dart', shoot out of the cloud. It was, he said, 'elongated, metallic and flashed in the sunshine.'

> It was very clear-cut, sharp in front but apparently truncated behind, though the tail may have been hidden by the vapor trail. No wings or fins were visible. It shot out of the cloud upwards at an angle of about 45 degrees.
>
> It was traveling at an immense speed, at least five times as fast as a jet plane traveling at the speed of sound. It never slackened speed or changed direction, but simply faded upwards into the blue, and its vapor faded after it. It was gone in a few seconds. The vapor trail was very clear-cut, dense, white and billowing ... there was no sound whatever. [Tom Drury in Rev N E Cruttwell's report in *Flying Saucer Review*, August 1972, pp.3-4]

Whatever it was, Tom Drury knew he had captured it on his 8mm movie camera. As he pondered his next move, he mentally checked what he had just witnessed:

> I am absolutely certain of its reality. It was photographed. My wife and children saw it. If anyone in the Territory [of Papua New Guinea] had the qualifications to identify an unknown aircraft, I had. It is my business to know what is in the air. I know all types of aircraft, and have flown 32 of them myself. [Tom Drury in Cruttwell's report in *Flying Saucer Review*, Aug.1972]

He drove immediately to Port Moresby's main airport, Jackson's, and speak with Air Traffic Control there. They reported no unusual aircraft or movements within their jurisdiction.

Tom Drury reported his sighting to the RAAF (Royal Australian Air Force), who were unable to provide him with any explanation. Next, he provided his unprocessed original 8mm film to the RAAF.

From this point forward, much of what happened to Tom Drury's film is shrouded in a clumsy web of official secrecy.

On August 31,1953, Tom Drury's report of his sighting to his immediate superior was sent to the Director-General, Civil Aviation, Melbourne. The document was marked 'Secret' and included a memo saying *'We do not know of any aircraft of the operational performance implied by this observation operating in this area...'*

Four days later, on September 5,1953, a further secret memo between the same parties includes the words: *'...herewith undeveloped film.'*

The film referred to, Tom Drury's film, was then passed to the Department of Air, Canberra, two-and-a-half weeks later under yet another secret memo titled *'Flying saucer – New Guinea.'* The memo read, in part, *'...herewith is a photographic film...'*

We know of this internal mail information thanks to the Australian UFO Research Network's 'UFO Disclosure Project' – which undertook to locate and examine Australian Government files to ascertain the extent of official Australian Government knowledge of the UFO phenomenon; then to document both this and civilian knowledge on the subject.

Four months later, January 23,1954, the Adelaide *Mail* newspaper ran a page one article quoting the Air Minister, Mr. William McMahon [later Prime Minister] headed:

SAUCER FILM FOR U.S.

The Federal Government has sent a movie film of a flying saucer-like object to America for special processing.

American Government representatives in Australia have been asked to expedite the return of the film, the Air Minister, Mr. McMahon, revealed this tonight...

Mr. McMahon said the film had been processed in Melbourne but was not clear. American processing might bring out more detail.

The film was returned on March 5,1954 via the United States Embassy in Melbourne.

A further four months later, July 12, 1954, Minister McMahon's department referred the film back to the Department of Civil Aviation, Melbourne, writing:

We have subjected the film to detailed study and processing, but have been unable to establish anything more than the fact a blur of light appears to move across the film.

Memos then show the film being returned to DCA, Port Moresby for return to Tom Drury. [*Disclosure Australia* Newsletter July 24, 2005]

The above paper chase reveals the Drury film's 10-month boomerang journey from Port Moresby to Melbourne, to Canberra, to the United States, to Melbourne and back to Port Moresby — for what?

Remember Tom Drury gave a specific description of what he'd

seen: *like a silver dart shooting out of a cloud ... immense speed ... elongated, metallic ... sharp in front but truncated behind, though the tail may have been hidden by the vapor trail. No wings or fins were seen.*

Of course, it is possible anything could have been at the end of the Drury footage... a flying saucer, a missile, a stealth fighter, (add your own speculation) ...the film was undeveloped when it left the photographer's possession. But then it ended up in the hands of a foreign power for 'further processing'.

*

Our story now moves forward eleven years to Ballarat, largest inland city in Victoria, about 116kms (72 miles) west of Melbourne.

On February 27, 1965 a conference aimed at 'removing the stigma of ridicule' attached to UFO research was held here under the auspices of the Ballarat Astronomical Society.

> Not only did representatives of most existing Australian [UFO] groups attend, but so did several witnesses to some of Australia's most famous cases, including the Reverend William Gill and Charles Brew, who spoke about their experiences. Former Air Marshall Sir George Jones attended and was outspoken in his support for serious UFO research. The RAAF was represented by Mr. B.G. Roberts, Senior Research Scientist of the Operational Research Office, Department of Air, Canberra.
>
> The presence of a scientific consultant of the RAAF, along with two RAAF officers manning a hardware display, was an unprecedented step for the Australian Government. [Bill Chalker, contributor to *UFOs and Government, A Historical Inquiry*, (Anomalist Books, San Antonio) 2012, p.391]

In his address to the conference, Mr. B. G. Roberts told participants

> '...the Department has, so far, neither received nor discovered in Australia any evidence to support the belief that the earth is being observed, visited or threatened by machines from other planets. Furthermore, there are no documents, files or dossiers held by the Department which proves the existence of flying saucers.'

Several civilian UFO researchers present were skeptical of Roberts' claim. In particular, they wanted to know about the photographic evidence held from the Drury film of 1953.

> Peter Norris, President of VFSRS [Victorian Flying Saucer Research Society), asked Roberts if he was aware of the film. Roberts said he was

not. Fred Stone [Foundation President, Australian Flying Saucer Research Society, 1955] indicated that four stills from the Drury film had been supplied to him by the RAAF in 1954. Roberts clearly was uninformed about this famous case and even remarked, 'I feel a bit like Daniel in a lion's den!'

Civilian researcher Andrew Thomas indicated he had seen the film in the hands of Edgar Jarrold, the pioneer Australian researcher and director of the Australian Flying Saucer Bureau. There is evidence that Jarrold did eventually receive prints of individual frames, some 94 prints, but not the actual film. [Bill Chalker, *UFOs and Government*, p.392]

In February 1955, Edgar Jarrold wrote in *Australian Flying Saucer Magazine* [his own publication] his interpretation of the Drury film's content. He had examined 94 frames and drew some conclusions, including that the object took not one but two right-angled turns in its flight path.

These comments disagree with the description given by the original observer Tom Drury, this present writer discounts Jarrold's appraisal completely. After all, Drury said it 'never slackened speed or changed direction...'

So where does that leave us?

* Tom Drury's description sounds like an airborne missile launch.

* Perhaps the film was tampered with after it left Tom Drury's possession ...but by whom and for what purpose?

* Could the still frames supplied to Fred Stone and Edgar Jarrold have been 'phony' substitutes as a diversion?

* Maybe all the end of the film actually showed was a white blur.

Tom Drury had died in August 1984, aged 67 years, but in September, 2000 veteran Australian UFO researcher, Bill Chalker was loaned a copy of Tom Drury's print by Bill Drury, Tom's nephew.

Here's how Bill Chalker described the film:

The color film shows the native spear fisherman, a speedboat on the harbor and then immediately cuts to about 5.8 seconds of footage, apparently the end of the filming of the UFO/contrail. This section resembles, or is, a thin contrail-like image that is continuously moving up at about a 45° angle, just as described by Tom Drury. It seems clear that this remaining footage is a composite from the original. [Bill Chalker, *The Drury UFO Film Affair* (Part 2), 2001]

Tom Drury's son Paul was present when his father filmed the initial incident. He feels certain, Bill Chalker told his readers in 2001, that his father ran the whole roll of film out during the incident. 'This suggests that there may have been a significant amount of footage present on the 'missing section.'

20. Rev. Gill's 'Remarkable Testimony'
"I waved... one figure waved back!"

Tom Drury was not the only one to have seen a strange object in the sky in Papua New Guinea. This one, however, which occurred six years later, was even more dramatic, and considerably more evidential.

In his 1981 book, *UFOs and the Limits of Science*, author Ronald D Story revealed the result of a survey he conducted among ninety leading ufologists from whom he sought their case with the strongest UFO evidence.

The overwhelming nomination was the case of Reverend Gill of the Boianai Mission, Papua-New Guinea, 1959.

Several raved about it: Jacques Vallee claimed it as 'one of the great classics in UFO history'; Dr Allen Hynek said he was impressed by the quality and number of witnesses; Jerome Clark called it 'History's best case'; and Coral and Jim Lorenzens included it in their 'Startling Evidence' book of 1966.

The episode happened well over half-a-century ago — in 1959 — at an Anglican Mission located just south of the equator in Papua New Guinea which, at the time, was an Australian territory.

A brilliant light approached the mission, hovered off the ground for a long period, and radiating a blue glow. At least four humanoids were sighted on board and responded to witness gestures.

Thirty-eight eye-witnesses signed a report describing their observations drawn up by the mission leader, 31 year-old the Reverend William Booth Gill.

To place the Boianai incident in its correct context, it should made clear that this particular area of Papua New Guinea, around the huge Goodenough Bay, was undergoing what is today called a UFO flap — although the expression 'flying saucer' rather than 'UFO' had greater currency at the time.

Jacques Vallee spoke of these 'flaps' — or 'waves' as he called them — in the 1977 documentary, *UFOs Are Here*, made by Guy Baskin:

> There have been waves of sightings, usually lasting a few weeks or months, in a very concentrated fashion, in certain areas of the world. There have been such waves in Western Europe in 1954 for example; in this country [United States] in 1947; we know of waves in the Soviet Union, in China, in Australia.
>
> And what is typical of these waves is that people from all these different cultures around the world are describing the same thing in their own terms. [Jacques Vallee, *UFOs Are Here* documentary, 1977]

The extent of the 1959 'flap' in the Milne Bay area of Papua New Guinea was detailed in the *Flying Saucer Review*, Vol.6, No. 6 (1960):

> Though there were a few isolated sightings of lights in the sky, it was not until the autumn of 1958 that they became at all frequent. During that year a number of inexplicable lights and a green flare were seen by many observers, myself among them.
>
> In April-May, 1959 there were increasing numbers of reports of white spherical lights crossing the sky and performing various maneuvers. Some appeared to be at quite low altitudes, one passing in front of a 4,000ft/1219m. mountain. Clearly they are not astronomical.
>
> Then in May the kaleidoscopic color-changing lights began and persisted till September ...finally there were a few more reports of moving lights and the wave ended in November. [the Rev. N.E.G. Cruttwell, p. 7]

Rev.William Gill of the Boianai mission was skeptical about these extraordinary sightings until, on April 5, 1959, he saw a light over Mount Pudi.

'This light,' he is quoted as saying, 'moved faster than anything I've ever seen!'

Then, ten weeks later (21st June), his assistant Stephen Moi saw an 'inverted saucer' flying above the Boianai mission station. On the 25th June Rev. Gill wrote to his friend, the Rev.David Durie at St Aidan's College, Dogura, some 90kms (55 miles) distant, about these experiences. The following is an abbreviated version of his letter:

Dear David,

I am almost convinced about the 'visitation' theory. There have been quite a number of reports over the months, from reliable witnesses...

I myself saw a stationary white light twice on the same night on April 9th, but in a different place each time ... I should think this [Moi's sighting] is the first time that the saucer has been identified as such.

I do not doubt the existence of these things (indeed I cannot now that I have seen one for myself) but my simple mind still requires scientific evidence before I can accept the from-outer-space theory. I am inclined to believe that probably many UFOs are more likely some form of electric phenomena — or perhaps something brought about by the atom bomb explosions, etc.

That Stephen [Moi] should actually make out a saucer could be the work of the unconscious mind as it is very likely... he has seen illustrations of some kind in a magazine, or it is very possible that saucers do exist, but it is only a 50/50 chance that they are not earth made, still less that they should carry men (more likely radio controlled), and it is still unproven that they are solid.

It is all too difficult to understand for me; I prefer to wait for some bright boy to catch one to be exhibited in Martin Place [a major Sydney thoroughfare]. Please return this report as I have no copy and I want Nor to have it.

Yours, Doubting William

The day after he wrote this letter, Rev.Gill was to experience, at close quarters, the first of two astonishing encounters with a flying saucer. His assistant, Stephen Moi — a fellow experiencer — was with him at the time.

Soon 38 people, including teachers Ananias Rarata and Mrs. Nessie Moi, gathered around with Rev.Gill to watch an amazing sight. Rev Gill wrote cryptic notes throughout the experience, writing down times, and actions.

UFOs DOWN UNDER

The following account draws from a transcript of a tape recorded interview with Rev. William Gill by the Victorian Flying Saucer Research Society and published in the December 1959 issue of the *Australian Flying Saucer Review* (Vol. 1, No. 1):

> I came out of the dining room after dinner and casually glanced at the sky with the purpose of seeing Venus. I also saw this object which was peculiar because it sparkled, and because it was very, very bright, and above Venus. That caused me to watch it for a while. Then I saw it descend towards us.
>
> The object came down to about 400ft/122m, perhaps less, maybe 300ft/90m — it is very difficult to judge at that time of night.
>
> As we watched, we saw what appeared to be human beings on it. The men appeared on what seemed to be a deck on top of the huge disk ... these men seemed to be working at something — they'd bend forward and appear to manipulate something on the deck, and then straighten themselves up occasionally, and turn around in our direction.
>
> Another peculiar thing about it was a shaft of blue light which emanated from the center of the deck ... this blue light — rather like a thin spotlight — pointed skywards, stayed on for a second or two, and then switched off. I recorded the times that we saw that blue light come on and off, for the rest of the night.

Rev. Gill also said the object 'appeared solid', had a 'dull yellow or pale orange color' and 'hovered and remained stationary' during most of the four-hour sighting.

When asked what the craft looked like, he said:

> Like a disk with a small round superstructure — round like the bridge on a boat. Underneath it had four legs in pairs, pointing diagonally downwards, these appeared to be fixed not retractable, and looked rather like tripods. At its base it was about thirty-five to forty feet [10-12 meters], and perhaps twenty feet [6 meters] at the top.

The four men who were seen on the deck, Rev. Gill said, were not always there together, they came and went singly. As one of the men seemed to lean over a rail and look down on the spectators an unusual scene ensued, as Rev. Gill explained:

> I waved one hand overhead and the figure did the same — as a skipper on a boat waving to someone on a wharf. I couldn't see the rail but he seemed to lean over something and I could see him from just below the waist up.

Reverend Gill

Ananais, the teacher, waved both hands overhead and the two outside figures seemed to wave back. Small mission boys called out — everyone beckoned to invite the beings down, but there was no audible response and no discernable expressions on the face of the men.

We tried to signal the beings by torchlight — when we flashed the light towards the ground, we actually thought it was going to land, but it didn't. We were all very disappointed about that.

The following morning Rev.Gill wrote again to his friend Rev. David Durie at Dogura:

Dear David,

Life is strange, isn't it? Yesterday I wrote you a letter expressing opinions re the UFOs — now, less that 24 hours later, I have changed my views somewhat. Last night we at Boianai experienced about 4 hours of UFO activity, and there is no doubt whatsoever that they are handled by beings of some kind. At times it was absolutely breathtaking.

Here is the report. Please pass it round, but great care must be taken as I have no other [copy]and this, like the one I made out re Stephen [Moi's sighting], will be sent to Nor. I would appreciate it if you could send the lot back as soon as poss.

Cheers, Convinced Bill

From 'Doubting William' one day to 'Convinced Bill' the next, indicates a swing in the Rev.William Gill's understanding of the UFO phenomenon. He knew what he saw, but he needed an explanation if he was to understand it.

At the end of each of his letters Rev.Gill asked his friend to read his 'sighting report' and send it back to him as he wanted them for 'Nor'. This was the nick-name of their mutual friend, the Rev.Norman Cruttwell of the Menapi Mission, a keen ufologist, botanist, and author of the article quoted here earlier from *Flying Saucer Review*, Vol.6, No.6 — who reappears later in this story.

A more significant reappearance was about to happen. The Reverend Gill explains:

Next day, just prior to the Evening Service at about 7.00pm., the thing was there again — it had arrived about an hour earlier — and we all decided to have the normal Evensong because the thing was out there beside the church anyway, and we thought it wouldn't go away during the service. And it didn't.

So, for another hour or two, we watched. Then, suddenly, it did go. There was this amazingly incredible speed — the whole craft disappeared to nothing across the bay in a matter of a second or so. [from Guy Baskin's 1977 documentary, *UFOs Are Here*]

As he had done on previous occasions, the Rev.Gill wrote a report on this sighting too. It was far more detailed than his spoken recollections in the documentary quoted above.

On the evening of June 27, 1959, around 6.00pm., a large UFO was seen in much the same position as on the previous evening, although this one seemed a little smaller. After he spotted the UFO, Rev.Gill gathered several locals and they stood and observed the craft for 15 minutes or so.

The clergyman considered it to be possibly the same craft he had seen on the previous evening, June 26, due to its appearance and conduct — men appeared and worked on the 'deck', its blue 'spotlight' functioned briefly, and hand waves from the ground were returned.

By the time he recorded his comments in the documentary — probably more than a decade after the event — he seems to have shifted from 'possibly' the same craft, to definitely the same craft (indicated by his expression 'the thing was there again').

Two other stationary UFOs were in sight at the time. One was seen over the hills to the west, while the other was directly overhead but much higher up.

Again, when darkness began to close in, the ground party used a torch or flashlight to signal towards the craft. Again, the UFO responded by 'making several wavering motions back and forth' like a pendulum, and 'began slowly to become bigger, apparently coming in our direction', then 'it ceased after perhaps half a minute and came no further'.

By 6.30pm., the scene remained static and the Rev.William Gill decided to go inside and have his dinner. Half-an-hour later, with the UFO still present, the mission community attended their church for Evensong. Visibility was diminished by low cloud cover by the time the church service had finished, and the group stood around hoping the clouds would lift to establish whether the flying saucer was still around.

At twenty minutes to eleven pm, a very loud, 'earsplitting' explosion rattled the mission house. Rev. Gill said it did not sound like a thunderclap, but he didn't provide any other explanation.

Reverend Gill

In his 1960 article in *Flying Saucer Review*, Rev.('Nor') Crutwell tells of other UFO sightings in the area on the evenings of Rev. Gill's first and second encounter:

> Quite unknown to Fr. Gill, on the very night of his first sighting (June 26), a trader named Ernest Evennett was staying at Giwa on the other side of Goodenough Bay, about fifteen miles [24 kilometers] from Boianai.
>
> He was astounded to see an object like a shooting star come down to within 500ft/152m of him, and reveal itself as an oval craft with a band around it and four portholes below the band.
>
> It hovered for four minutes just above him and appeared so large that he could cover only half of it with his closed hand at arm's length. He saw no men, but it was obviously a manned aircraft of some sort. When it took off again it made a curious triple sound described as 'WOOMP, WOOMP, WOOMP!' It became brilliantly luminous with a green light, and shot away over the mountains. [Flying Saucer Review, 1960, p.6]

The other sighting, on June 27, mentioned in Rev. Crutwell's article was attested by two credible Government officers at Baniara, and by the Roman Catholic Mission at Sideia:

> These objects were much further away and appeared spherical in shape, but they further corroborate the existence of strange craft in the sky. The one seen at Baniara was accompanied by a small bronze disc which seemed to hover at a fixed distance below the glowing spherical object and moved in perfect sympathy with it, as if attached by an invisible wire.
>
> Then when the main object suddenly dived as if it were about to land, and became dazzlingly bright, the disc appeared to jump upwards to meet it and vanished into it.

This rather bizarre description is not without precedent. In his book, *The Truth about Flying Saucers* — published three years prior to the Boianai encounters — French author Aimee Michel devotes several pages to the 'ex-centric patch' — an almost identical device which supposedly controls the balance and direction of UFO movement by the displacement of a force field.

He also refers to a photograph taken by 'M. Fregnale at Lac Chauvet' in which 'the patch can be seen quite clearly'. [p. 208+]

Another anecdote in the Rev.N ('Nor') E.G. Cruttwell's article includes a reference to himself. A saucer-shaped object passed over Menapi Mission School where he worked:

It missed me by about 30 seconds. On July 21, at 9.15a.m., the school children were filing across the playground into church. About half of them had entered the building, but there must have been at least a hundred outside together with seven Papuan teachers.

They suddenly noticed a 'moving star' crossing the blue sky. As it came nearer they saw that was 'like a silver plate with a dark rim' and about the size of the sun's disc. It was traveling 'faster than a plane' and wavering slightly as though affected by the wind.

Unfortunately they waited too long before calling me. I rushed out of the house, telescope in hand, just too late to see the object, but only to see everyone staring over the coconut trees where it had just disappeared.
[*The Truth about Flying Saucers* p.6]

A postscript to this story, possibly apocryphal, is included in Rowan Callick's review of the Boianai sightings published in *The Australian* newspaper on 1 January, 2010. (Callick knew Cruttwell when they both worked in Papua New Guinea):

Cruttwell famously missed out on a sighting of bright lights over his own mission station because he was ensconced in the 'smallhaus' [little house = toilet]. The following day, he had the roof replaced with a clear glass panel, just in case.

Australian ufology researcher Bill Chalker outlined the Rev. Gill's story in his *The Oz Files — the Australian UFO Story*, 1996:

Reverend Gill made notes about the experience and sent a copy of his own report — eight closely typed foolscap pages — to Rev. Cruttwell at Menapi Mission, who in turn sent a copy to Mr. D. H. Judge, a Brisbane member of the Queensland Flying Saucer Research Bureau. The report was released to the media and accounts appeared in the media during mid-August, 1959, causing a sensation.

I was privileged to have had two extended opportunities to interview Reverend Gill and discuss the events at Boianai. I was impressed with his quiet and certain manner in relating the events.

Rev.Gill was already scheduled to return to Australia at the time of his sighting, Chalker wrote, and once this happened, it gave civilian UFO groups the opportunity to assess the bonafides of Gill's reports. He gave a lecture to the Victorian Flying Saucer Research Society on 28 October, 1959 at the Nicholas Hall in Melbourne. The response was such that the VFSRS indicated that Gill's report constituted the 'most remarkable testimony of intensive UFO activity ever reported'.

The group then wrote their own evaluation, which concluded that the Boianai UFOs were advanced craft, manned by humanoid beings, and capable of fantastic aerodynamic performance. They felt that UFO researchers no longer needed to enquire as to the nature of UFOs, only their origin was to be determined.

Chalker then went on to explain how the major UFO research groups united, 'in a spirit of new found co-operation', to circulate copies of Rev.Gill's sighting report to all members of federal parliament in Canberra, accompanied by a circular letter signed by the presidents of the participating groups.

This letter urged the recipients to 'press the Minister for Air for a statement about the attitude Air Force Intelligence had of the New Guinea reports.'

Precisely six years earlier — 20 November, 1953 — the Australian Parliament had heard a Question Time exchange between Alexander Downer, who enquired whether the Royal Australian Air Force was actively investigating the UFO phenomenon, and the then Minister for Air, William McMahon (later Prime Minister), who replied that the saucers were a problem 'more for psychologists than for defense authorities.' [Hansard, p. 364]

Getting politicians to give serious consideration to such matters is fraught with evasiveness; but the new attempt proceeded:

> On November 24th, 1959, in federal parliament, Mr. E. D. Cash, a Liberal politician from Western Australia asked the Minister for Air, Mr. F.M. Osborne, whether his department (specifically Air Force Intelligence) had investigated 'reports of recent sightings of mysterious objects in the skies over Papua and New Guinea'.
>
> The Minister's reply did not address this question, but instead focused on the general situation that most sightings were explained and that 'only a very small percentage — something like 3% — of reported sightings of flying objects cannot be explained.' [Bill Chalker, *The OZ Files — the Australian UFO Story*, 1996]

After this example of political obfuscation, it took over a month before two Royal Australian Air Force officers from Canberra visited Rev. Gill in Melbourne to question him about the sighting, by then six months after the event. It was, at best, a cursory investigation. Rev.Gill is quoted as saying 'They talked about stars and planets and then left.'

The Department of Air Force Intelligence assessment concluded, in part, that:

> Although it is not possible to draw firm conclusions, an analysis of rough bearings and angles above the horizon does suggest that at least some of the lights observed were the planets Jupiter, Saturn and Mars.

Light refraction, the changing position of the planet relative to the observer and cloud movement would give the impression of size and rapid movement.

In addition varying cloud densities could account for the human shapes and their sudden appearance and disappearance.

This response seems reminiscent of Project Sign and Project Grudge evaluations in post-WWII America, when the U.S. Air Force engaged astronomer J. Allen Hynek to investigate UFO reports to determine whether there was an astronomical explanation for them or not. Many ufologists then regarded Hynek as the US government's UFO debunker.

After several years of this, 1947-1969, Hynek undertook a career somersault — his scientific training plus the caliber of many witnesses eventually convinced him 'there was something to all this' (UFOs) after all. He once said:

> As a scientist, I must be mindful of the lessons of the past; all too often it has happened that matters of great value to science were overlooked because the new phenomenon did not fit the accepted scientific outlook of the time.

Hynek started the Center for UFO Studies (CUFOS) in 1973, promoting the scientific analysis of UFO cases, and displayed a strong personal interest Rev. Gill's encounter.

Two Victorian groups invited J Allen Hynek to visit Australia, and he arrived for a lecture tour later that year. During his four-day stay in Melbourne he met and questioned Rev.Gill.

After short stays in Sydney, Canberra and Brisbane, Hynek flew to Papua New Guinea and undertook a detailed on-site investigation into the now-famous Boianai encounters, including the questioning of witnesses.

The CUFOS report concluded 'the lesser UFOs are attributed to bright stars and planets, but not the primary object.' Its size and absence of movement over three hours ruled out any astronomical explanation.

This was a view Bill Chalker shared.

Meanwhile, Rev. William Gill spent the next quarter-century teaching in distinguished Melbourne grammar schools — Essendon, Camberwell and St Michaels — and visited Magdelan College, Oxford; and North Western University, Chicago (where he lectured on his UFO encounter).

Rev.Gill said he was frequently asked why he had reverted to his usual routines — going to dinner, conducting his church service — when there was a flying saucer hovering around overhead on June 27, 1959. His reply surprised many people:

> It was partly because there was nothing eerie or other-worldly about any of this. It was all so ordinary, as ordinary as a Ford car. It looked a perfectly normal sort of object, an Earth-made object. I realize, of course, that some people might think of this as a flying saucer... The figures inside looked perfectly human. [from Rowan Callick's review in *The Australian*, 1 January, 2010]

On June 2003 — forty-four years after the event — he addressed a UFO conference in Brisbane. It was the last meeting between Rev.Gill and his long-term confidante, Bill Chalker, who recorded Gill's presentation on video. During the passage of such a long period, Rev. Gill had pondered the source of his unexpected aerial visitors at Boianai, and tentatively reached a conclusion that did not conflict with his religious disposition. As Bill Chalker phrased it:

> As far as I know, this was the closest he [Rev. Gill] came to saying maybe the Boianai visitors were angels — perhaps angels to him, aliens to others — but certainly real, and certainly visitants.

That potential explanation fits comfortably with Jacques Vallee's filmed comment quoted at the beginning of this chapter:

> And what is typical of these waves is that people from all these different cultures around the world are describing the same thing in their own terms.

Coincidently, both Jacques Vallee and the Reverend William Gill spoke on that film — the famous 1977 documentary, Guy Baskin's *UFOs Are Here*.

The Brisbane UFO conference was Gill's final public lecture. He died, aged 79, on June 13, 2007.

21. Secrecy shrouds Westall UFOs

"Together in little groups, white-eyed with fear"

Reverend Gill's account was just the beginning of mass school sightings!

It was the second-last day of Westall High School's first term in 1966. The following day, students would break-up for their Easter holidays, with no more classes or homework for two weeks. A sense of anticipation pervaded the students, and probably a few teachers as well.

But this day — Wednesday, April 6, two days before Good Friday — was to mark the largest, daylight UFO mass sighting in Australia's history.

Although only seventeen miles (27kms) southeast of Melbourne's CBD, Westall in 1966 was an outer suburb. It had areas of undeveloped bushy scrubland, market gardens and homes along the main roads, with a real 'country' feel. It was part of a broad area known as Clayton South.

The school day started normally. Two groups of Form 1 and Form 3 students, numbering about fifty, were doing Physical Education classes on the school's adjoining sports ground under the supervision of two teachers. One group was playing cricket.

At 10.15am. a student noticed a silent, low-flying, silvery-green, object overhead.

Almost immediately, other students started yelling and

pointing to the sky. Soon, everyone on the sports ground stood, open-mouthed, staring in disbelief at the hovering, round disc.

Many children screamed. Some ran to the classrooms for protection from the unknown. Teachers tried to usher them off the oval, potentially out of harm's way.

One student, Marilyn Eastwood, is quoted in the *Dandenong Journal* as describing the object as 'round, with a hump on top and round things underneath.'

One boy, Brendan Dickson, later described how the object stopped and 'descended straight down' until about 30ft/9m off the ground. Then it 'sat there for a while' before it 'lifted straight up and took off.'

It went higher, over the electricity transmission lines and pylons bordering the school's southern boundary, towards the pine trees at nearby Grange Reserve.

It is highly likely that more than one craft was seen. About 15% of witnesses interviewed later said they saw two or three.

A boy ran from outside into Mr. Andrew Greenwood's science classroom yelling: 'There's flying saucers outside!' Everyone craned their necks to see out the windows, but Mr. Greenwood said firmly 'Sit down, it's not recess yet!'

When the recess bell rang moments later however, Mr. Greenwood joined his students as they hurried outside to see what had caused the commotion.

Pandemonium had broken out on the playing field as scores of children from other classes heard the news and raced to see for themselves.

Mr. Greenwood saw the object rise into the air from behind pine trees. Later that day, he described it to a *Dandenong Journal* reporter:

> It was like a thin beam of light, about half the length of a light aircraft. It was silvery-gray and seemed to thicken at times. The thickening was similar to when a disc is turned a little to show the underside. The object was never really stationary. It seemed to move from side to side and up and down. [Andrew Greenwood, *Dandenong Journal*, 21 April 1966, p.1]

Student Geoff Holland was one of the earlier witnesses to run onto the playing field. He wrote of the experience later in a school magazine, *The Clayton Calendar* (see Note 1 at end), under the heading Eye Witness Account of a Flying Saucer:

Suddenly the school became alive with excitement and everyone began running towards where the girls were. I was among the surging mob. I had seen something that looked very unusual in the sky.

As I looked up I saw a dazzling, silvery object flying around some pine trees that grew on a ridge about a quarter of a mile [.4km] directly behind the school. It then flew across some open paddocks also behind the school and returned to the pines.

On the other side of the ridge there is a small field. This thing hovered over the pines and descended behind them and must have been directly over the field. Then I lost sight of it because of the pines. [Geoff Holland, 'Eye Witness Account of a Flying Saucer', *The Clayton Calendar*, 1966]

Westall High is only 4km/2.4miles from the Moorabbin airport and students were accustomed to seeing and hearing small aircraft overhead. Geoff Holland and teacher Andrew Greenwood both included fascinating references to the involvement of light aircraft in their accounts.

Part of Geoff Holland's article in *The Clayton Calendar* reads:

I began to notice many private aircraft, mainly Cessnas, flying towards the pines. The thing reappeared and rose to the level of the approaching aircraft. This enabled me to get a rough idea of its size. It was a silvery object as long as one of the Cessnas, but very thin.

As the aircraft approached, the thing tilted on about a 45-degree angle and started to move into the distance, gradually gaining height. The planes increased their speed and began to follow it, but the object streaked away leaving the planes far, far behind. The planes turned back, and we all stood hoping it would return but it didn't, so we all went into school, 15 minutes late.

The local *Dandenong Journal* printed a front-page article based on Mr. Greenwood's observations:

At first there was one plane apparently observing the object... Later Mr. Greenwood noticed five light aircraft circling the object and flying at a relatively low altitude. The aircraft had played a 'cat and mouse' kind of game with the object. [*Dandenong Journal*, 21 April 1966, p.1]

Another witness on that Wednesday morning was a school prefect, who had been in a chemistry class during the incident.

According to Bill Chalker in his 1996 book *The Oz Files: the Australian UFO Story*:

The prefect told [a Victorian Education Department officer] that 'the thing' had come down behind a group of pine trees, and everyone had run off in a mass evacuation of the school, all 'after the flying saucer'. A large area of flattened grass was found there, perfectly circular in shape, about 10m/33ft in diameter, with three scorch marks.

The grass was very dry, but it hadn't started a fire. A man approached the school group, and told them all to 'piss off' because it was private property. The property had been standing idle for many years.

The man walked through the area of flattened grass and seemed to 'ignore its existence', according to the prefect. When numerous screaming children told him that a flying saucer had come down there, he said 'bull shit' and various other things.

The school children eventually returned to school, accompanied by a number of teachers who had 'followed the mass exodus'. [Bill Chalker, *The Oz Files; the Australian UFO Story*, pps.118-119]. (Also see Note 2 at end)

The man who ordered everyone off The Grange may have been Shaun Matthews, whose family leased the land for horse agistment. Shaun was on holiday and spending time on the property.

While he hadn't admitted it to the children he, too, witnessed the aerial object descend among the pine trees.

In an interview in *The Sunday Age,* Melbourne, nearly forty years later, Matthews said:

> I saw the thing come across the horizon and drop down behind the pine trees and saw it leave again. I couldn't tell you how long it was there for; it went up and off very rapidly.
>
> I went over and there was a circle in the clearing. It looked like it had been cooked or boiled, not burnt – as I remember. A heap of kids from Westall primary and high school came charging through to see what happened – 'Look at this, look at that, we saw it as well!' It was a bit of a talking point for a couple of days.
>
> The way this thing moved there is no way it could have been a weather balloon or a light aircraft. [Shaun Matthews interview, *The Sunday Age,* October 2, 2005]

Another of the Westall High students, Tanya, was among the first to arrive at the site of the landed craft near the pine trees. She fainted there, and was very dazed. An ambulance was called, and Tanya was taken to hospital.

She never returned to Westall High.

Uncertainty still surrounds Tanya's outcome. Not only did she not return to school, her family moved away from the district almost simultaneously.

One female teacher at Westall High subsequently collapsed and was taken from her classroom by ambulance-men in front of her students.

Westall High School and the Westall Primary School share one large parcel of land, each fronting parallel streets. The principal of the Primary School had to go out on the morning of April 6th and missed the whole flying saucer incident.

When he returned at lunchtime, he witnessed something he had never seen before. 'The children were not playing in the playground,' he later told researcher Bill Chalker on film, 'Instead they were huddled together in little groups, white-eyed with fear as a result of the flying saucer incident. They thought they were going to be taken away by the flying saucer, and would never see their parents again.'

> They were promptly reassured that everything was fine and that their parents would come and pick them up at the usual time. [George Simpson, speaker *2014 VUFOA Conference*, Melbourne]

It is likely that one or two High School students, perhaps the more mischievous ones, sneaked down to the shops on Rosebank Avenue at lunchtime and telephoned the media about their flying saucer sighting.

Soon headmaster Frank Samblebe was fielding calls from newspaper and TV news desks. He denied that anything had been seen and, as Bill Chalker expressed it, put it down to mass hysteria.

In the midst of this frenzy, headmaster Samblebe needed to address the matter of school discipline. Dozens of children and a couple of teachers had strayed en masse from school property during morning recess and returned to the classrooms up to fifteen minutes late, chattering about flying saucers. He announced there would be general school assembly held straight after the lunch break.

Meanwhile, he spoke with the school prefect and berated him for being 'irresponsible' by following the rest of the students and teachers. Graham Simmonds, school captain in 1966, was ordered to tell the students that what they'd seen didn't exist. This seems to have set the tenor of the school assembly.

Mr. Samblebe made his attitude clear to both staff and students. 'There are no such things as flying saucers,' he told them, 'All you kids are nuts ... it was a weather balloon!' Finally he warned, 'You children are not to speak to the press, they are not permitted on school ground.' The children were also discouraged from talking about the incident amongst themselves.

Not surprisingly, the front cover of the issue of *The Clayton Calendar* carrying Geoff Holland's article (mentioned earlier) depicted three flying saucers over a group of pine trees, and a satirical caption reading 'As I was saying children, flying saucers do not exist.'

Several highly unusual things happened at Westall High that afternoon.

On the footpath outside the school grounds, a teacher and at least two students spoke to reporters from the local paper, the *Dandenong Journal*, and to a TV news team. Form 3C student Joy Tighe was telling her story to a TV newsman when a uniformed man demanded they stop filming. Pointing at Joy, he told her to 'Go back into the school ground. This interview is over!'

'So that's what I did,' Joy said years later, 'I was 12½ years old.'

However, Joy was not wholly deterred. She subsequently filled out a sighting report with Victorian Unidentified Flying Object Research Society (VUFORS) in which she described two circular discs, shaped like 'upright domes'. They were flying in 'varying directions', and 'faster than some light aircraft flying in the vicinity' and which turned on their edge and disappeared.

The other student talking to the media was Marilyn Eastwood of Form 2D. 'I got detention for appearing on the TV show,' she said, 'and then I got detention again later, when my picture and story was in the *Dandenong Journal*'.

Channel 9 telecast the clip plus some extra footage in their evening news telecast, including the abrupt ending to the interview. That was enough to convince Norm Bury, whose son had come home from school announcing 'We saw a flying saucer at school today, Dad,' that it had actually happened.

*

The day after the Westall sightings, Melbourne's daily newspapers gave little credence to the event. *The Sun News-Pictorial* published a mocking UFO cartoon; and its competitor, *The Age*, ran a small item headed 'Object Perhaps Balloon':

An unidentified flying object seen over the Clayton-Moorabbin area yesterday morning might have been a weather balloon. Hundreds of children and a number of teachers at Westall School, Clayton, watched the object during morning break... [*The Age*, April 7, 1966, p.6]

VUFORS vice-president Judith Magee visited the site two days after the event – on Good Friday – and took some photos. She wrote:

Although the school was closed, several students were present discussing the sighting. When they learned we were UFO researchers, they were eager to tell us what happened and what they saw in detail. I understand the children had been instructed to talk to no one.

In his book *A Paranormal File*, author John Pinkney tells of a letter he received in 1987 from a schoolgirl witness identified by him only as 'Mrs. B.A. of Reservoir, Victoria.' Part of her letter stated:

Next day, representatives of all three armed services called at my parents' house to ask if I could take them to the landing spot. When we got there, with my mother and brother, they told us to stay in the truck. But I heard one RAAF man say there must have been extreme heat, because the earth was burned. The cow in that paddock was in such a distressed state it had to be destroyed. [John Pinkney, *A Paranormal File* (Five Mile Press, 2000). p.79]

A further unexpected event happened within a couple of weeks of the mass sighting.

Two men in Royal Australian Air Force uniforms visited the school's science teacher Andrew Greenwood at home. He was told that if he gave any further interviews about what he saw at Westall, his teaching career would be over.

'We will let people know you are not coping with your teaching load,' they said, 'and that you are beginning to take alcohol in the morning with your breakfast, just so you can get through the day. There are no such things as flying saucers!'

The Westall science teacher is reported to have replied, 'If there is no such things as flying saucers, what does it matter to you if I say I've seen something just like one?' [Shane Ryan interview, *Podcast UFO*, December 26, 2013]

That incident introduced a whole new level of mystery to the entire event.

*

By 1988, twenty-two years had passed and the Westall sighting had slipped from public notice. It was broadly forgotten – by all but a few.

Researcher Keith Basterfield began a systematic search through various Australian Government Department files for any references to UFOs. His team project was named 'Disclosure Australia' and utilized both the Archive Act and the Freedom of Information Act to facilitate their efforts.

Keith Basterfield recalled:

> The Disclosure team had between six and nine people over the four/five year project, literally going through hundreds and hundreds of file titles, maybe thousands in the end. We were always looking for files on the Westall incident in 1966...

> The net result is we found nothing in this mammoth volume of government documentation that would even begin to hint that there was something about Westall in the government files. So, amazingly, we drew a blank. [Keith Basterfield, *Westall '66* documentary]

Fellow researcher Bill Chalker independently reached a separate but identical conclusion:

> I kept requesting more and more files, and ultimately I examined a continuity of files that satisfied me that I was seeing a comprehensive picture of the RAAF investigation at that time ... there was no Westall file. [Bill Chalker, *Westall '66* documentary]

In May 1990, however, further momentum was added to the Westall investigation.

Two new witnesses contacted UFO investigator Keith Basterfield in Adelaide with their Westall memories. Now adults, the brother and sister, Ken and Kris, had attended different local schools in 1966.

Kris, a third year student at Westall High at the time of the sighting wrote, in part:

> My friends and I raced to the far corner of the oval, and by this time there was quite a lot of other kids there... What I saw was several objects that appeared as one saucer inverted on another...

> The UFOs appeared to come down behind some trees not too far from the school ground and some of the children climbed the fence top to go over there, I didn't.

After lunch a special assembly was called where the principal informed the children that they had seen nothing and to talk to no one about it! I couldn't believe it – there were so many children that did see this event.

When I returned [home] from school I told my mother about the day's events and she mentioned that my brother, Ken, had ridden on his bike somewhere over near Westall High... [Kris in Keith Basterfield's, *Several eyewitness accounts of the Westall UFO Incident,* May 1990, ufoevidence.org]

Kris's brother Ken was 17 and attended nearby Clayton Technical College in 1966. On his way home after school, he and his classmates often passed the students walking home from Westall High school. Ken sent this testimony to Keith Basterfield:

This night the conversation on everyone's lips was the flying saucer incident. I remember it caused enough of a stir for four of us to walk about a mile across to where the Westall kids had said the saucers had gone down behind the trees earlier in the day...

The area had the grass flattened and 'tufted' in circles about 60 to 120ft (18 – 36.5m] diameter. The rest of the long grass was undisturbed. No circles overlapped.

We thought and talked of ways you could make such circles, such as walking with a rope or a tractor and a slasher. They didn't look like they were made by a method we could think of. [Ken in Keith Basterfield's *Several eyewitness accounts of the Westall UFO Incident,* May 1990, ufoevidence.org]

In her letter to Keith Basterfield, Ken's sister Kris also recalled a further observation Ken had related to her that night:

When he [Ken] returned much later he told of the flattened grass circles and of the Army and Air Force taking photos. There were lights set up and a lot of personnel. They were trying to keep onlookers away... [Kris in Keith Basterfield's, *Several eyewitness accounts of the Westall UFO Incident,* May 1990, ufoevidence.org]

*

More years passed. The Westall students of 1966 became adults, many with children and grandchildren of their own. Their memories of school days faded and a new century dawned. And yet, the memory lingered of a day long ago when they saw something they were told didn't exist. A layer of secrecy spread clumsily over the scene ... things they were not to discuss ... and who would believe them if they raised the subject?

Shane Ryan first heard about the incident when he moved from country Victoria to it's capital, Melbourne, to attend Monash University. He stayed in an outer south-eastern suburb named Mulgrave, only 6.5 kilometers (4 miles) from Westall.

At a VUFOA conference in April 2017 where eight Westall witnesses discussed their childhood UFO sighting in front of a 200-strong audience (and participated in a fascinating Question & Answer session), Shane Ryan said he first learnt of the Westall incident from a John Pinkney book – probably the one mentioned here earlier.

Shane also recalled:

> I can remember going on a short road trip out to Westall and thinking 'OK, this is where it happened.' It's a pretty unlikely place for a flying saucer event ... of course it looked a fair bit different than it did in 1966. Then I went home and proceeded to forget all about it. [Shane Ryan, interview with *VUFOA TV*, 2012]

In 2005, while searching for the subject of a childrens' book he proposed to write, the Westall story came to Shane's mind. 'I don't know why,' he said later, 'but ... I thought I'd do some initial research to see if it was going to be worthwhile as the foundation for a book.'

Although four decades had passed since the event, Shane Ryan has managed to track down 'about 60 witnesses.'

> Everyone said straight away that they knew it was not a plane, nor a weather balloon. The object was in view for up to twenty minutes, and many saw it descend. Most agreed it landed behind pine trees at the Grange Reserve. Dozens of students ran across what was then an open paddock to the reserve to investigate, but the object had lifted off and vanished.
>
> Other details are sketchier. The UFO appears to have left a circle of scorched grass; others say several circles were left in paddocks bordering the Grange Reserve. Many witnesses, not all, report seeing aircraft, up to five, trailing the UFO. Some say it made no sound, others say it did. [Shane Ryan interview, *Sunday Age*, October 2, 2005]

This *Sunday Age* interview with the budding author caught the attention of filmmaker Rosie Jones, who recognized the Westall UFO incident as 'a surreal suburban tale with a detective character on a search for truth at its core'.

She traveled to Canberra to meet Shane Ryan, who leapt at the opportunity to be involved in a documentary on the topic.

Filming began soon afterwards, commencing with the 40th anniversary Westall Reunion at the Westall Sports Club in 2006. The balance was done almost exclusively on weekends and took almost four years of Rosie and Shane's time to complete.

During filming, another key witness stepped forward.

Victor Zakruzny had been a Form 2 student at Westall in 1966 and forty-three years later (2008) recounted his own remarkable story to UFO researcher Bill Chalker. He was adamant that two objects were present.

'Victor impressed me as a compelling witness giving consistent testimony,' Chalker later wrote, adding:

> Victor indicated to me he was able to walk up close to one of the objects, while other students stood around in close proximity to the other object. A teacher and at least a dozen other students crowded along a high fence to get a view.
>
> Victor contemplated touching the object [nearest him] but thought better of it.
>
> The two objects suddenly rose up from the grass and took off, one to the west, the other flew up and orbited a small plane before flying down to the south-west Grange reserve area, with students in pursuit. [Bill Chalker, *theozfiles.blogsot.com.au/2009_01_01_archive.html*]

Victor also disclosed the reason for his previous silence – an explanation that perhaps reflects the reasoning behind headmaster Frank Samblebe's message to the school assembly in 1966.

Bill Chalker resumes his account:

> Victor later told me that he had a meeting with the school headmaster, who encouraged him not to talk of the event because it might hurt his future chances of a career in art.
>
> The headmaster gave him that advice because he himself had witnessed something similar during the war and he had experienced the pressure of being told not to talk about such things.
>
> Victor followed the headmaster's advice, but with the growing tide of witnesses coming forward since 2006, he now felt more comfortable with reporting his own experience. His artistic abilities also provided us with some striking drawings of the object he saw. [Bill Chalker, *theozfiles.blogsot.com.au/2009_01_01_archive.html*]

Victor Zakruzny and his drawings of the objects are featured on Bill Chalker's blog spot and in the 'Westall '66' documentary, which was progressing slowly but thoroughly.

*

Eventually, with Rosie Jones's documentary almost completed, Australian Foxtel's Sci-Fi Channel acquired the film property for telecasting, thus providing some much-needed money for staff and final editing.

'Westall '66: A Suburban UFO Mystery' was telecast in Australia in June 2010 and rebroadcast in 2011. Shane Ryan was delighted with the public's response:

> When the telecast happened, there was an avalanche of messages. We started receiving information from many witnesses I hadn't had contact with… people who had seen the broadcast and provided a lot of other information… but mostly an affirmation of other witness accounts.

The documentary introduced many additional witnesses and their testimonies, much of which had not been known to the wider public. Slowly a case was established that a cover-up appeared to be in play or, at least, that a blanket of official secrecy had been spread over the entire Westall High encounter.

It emerges that unknown men in dark suits had come to the school and talked to the headmaster. School captain Graham Simmonds recalls seeing a confrontation between chemistry teacher Barbara Robbins, Mr. Samblebe, and a man in uniform Graham had not seen before.

Ms Robbins had taken many photographs during the morning's excitement, and the headmaster demanded not only the film, but the camera itself be handed over to him. According to Graham Simmonds, she reluctantly did so.

Earlier on the day of the sighting, Paul Smith, a former Westall High student, was working in a market garden situated between the High School and The Grange. He, along with his boss, were pulling carrots getting them ready for market:

> I looked up and I was facing this object in the sky. My boss turned around and he saw it, too. We stood looking at it for several minutes. A few moments later, the children came over from the high school and they noticed us. It took a while [for them] to make up their minds if they would come on to our private property, and they decided they'd come in anyway. They ran straight over, across the market garden and walked down to this corner [indicating The Grange].

About twenty minutes later, trucks turned up. They were khaki-colored trucks covered with camouflage, long trucks that carry quiet a few people and about twenty guys got out, men in khaki uniforms, and a couple of jeeps. The Army guys questioned my boss. He said he never saw anything, but he did. [Paul Smith, *Westall '66* documentary]

Jacqueline Argent was a Westall student in Form 2A in 1966. A day after the sighting, she was called from her classroom to attend the Headmaster's office. Inside two well-dressed men confronted her. Here's her filmed account of what followed:

Only one man spoke, and he started off with: 'We would like you to go through what you saw happen yesterday' and began firing questions at me. Then he went into 'And I suppose you think you saw a flying saucer?' I said, 'I didn't say that. I saw an 'object' then he said 'And we suppose you saw little green men?' I felt very, very angry. [Jacqueline Argent, *Westall '66* documentary]

Part of the reason Jacqueline felt so intimidated and threatened during the interview was that her headmaster, Mr. Samblebe, was in the room and didn't intervene to protect her from this hostile grilling. Finally she was told 'We don't want you talking about this outside the school. There are no such things as flying saucers, and it is not going to be good for you if you talk about this outside the school. You are not to talk about this!' It was the theme of the school assembly being repeated.

Jacqueline recalls bursting into tears. She ran from the office and all the way home.

Another filmed witness, Kevin Hurley, an Engineering student at nearby Monash University at the time, heard about the Westall sighting around 4.00 p.m. on the day it happened. 'Guess what?' his uncle asked him on the telephone, 'The kids have seen a UFO at the school! It landed there!' Kevin arranged to meet his uncle so they could inspect the site together, and then rode his bicycle the 10kms (6 miles) to the rendezvous:

The area we walked through was knee-high grass; it wasn't scrubby like it is today. The grass was flattened down in a circular area, like something had come down, twisted a little bit, and flattened the grass in a circular fashion – in a clockwise spiral pattern – and four indentations. [Kevin Hurley, *Westall '66* documentary]

That evening Kevin saw the Westall interviews on the Channel 9 news, and told his mates about it. They all decided to visit the site together the next day:

We got to the long grass and came across a barrier marked 'Stay Away' right around the area. A man in uniform, a very aggressive chap, yelled at us 'Go away! Don't come here!' We saw a number of khaki-covered trucks, and men going around the paddock with what looked like Geiger counters or metal detectors. [Kevin Hurley, *Westall '66* documentary]

A week later – after Easter – Kevin Hurley decided to ride his bike down to the site again. Much to his surprise, all the grass had been mown 'to an inch high' and the location of the 'landing circle' had been destroyed by fire.

Kevin rode his bike home and wrote a letter of complaint to a Melbourne morning newspaper.

Les Medew was an apprentice mechanic in 1966. His account appears to over-lap part of Kevin Hurley's testimony. Les hid behind some low tree branches at the Grange with his younger sister – a Westall High student – and saw a farmer on a tractor cutting the grassed area:

> We observed two Army trucks, two men in camouflage and two men in blue uniforms. It appeared that a soldier was using a metal mine detector; he was walking around sweeping back and forth. They started kicking violently at the ground … they went back to the trucks and were gone. We had no idea what those Army men were doing, [but] to have the Army there, it was something important. [Les Medew, *Westall '66* documentary]

When Shane Ryan approached Channel 9 hoping to get access to the original 1966 news footage with the girl students, it had vanished from the network's film archives. Despite on-going searches, no trace of it has been found. It may have simply been thrown out or incorrectly shelved.

In 2011, however, Shane Ryan was fortunate [or sufficiently determined) to track down the TV newsman who conducted the interviews for Channel 9, and who provided the following recollection:

> Shane, I remember this story so very well. There were lots of Flying Saucer stories being reported at the time, but there was no story like this! This happened in broad daylight; there were so many witnesses; it happened at a school; and when we got down there the reaction of the kids – they were running around, they were very excited, they were all wanting to talk to us about what they'd seen, and they wanted us to know that it was something extraordinary – they really had seen a flying saucer! [Shane Ryan, *Podcast UFO* with Martin Willis, 26 December 2013]

Fifty of the initial witnesses commemorated the 45th anniversary of the original sighting in April 2011.

Former pupils and teachers gathered on the sporting oval at Westall with their friends, and retraced their steps from the schoolrooms, to the playing fields, and finally to the pine trees at The Grange. The media were also in attendance.

There was no longer any need for secrecy. In 2013, The Grange underwent a wonderful transformation. Today it has a UFO-themed playground and family picnic area – perhaps a 'world first'. Its main attraction is giant flying saucer that children can enter and soar off into the stratosphere in their imaginations (and exit via one of it's twisting red slides or a rope net).

More importantly, a nearby information board tells of the mass sighting of UFOs in 1966 and includes large breakout quotations by several eyewitnesses.

It is an important public acknowledgement that something significant happened at the spot ... something that involved the bullying of children and the heavy-handed subversion of the apparent truth by authorities.

On his Westall Flying Saucer Incident page on Facebook, Shane Ryan mentioned that he 'still gets new witnesses every few months coming forward to share what they recall about the Westall Incident.'

On April 2, 2017, Victorian UFO Action [VUFOA] held an all-day conference 'Westall – The Witnesses Speak.' The event was widely publicized and attracted several interested 'first-timers.' Over 200 attended to watch the Rosie Jones documentary and hear the Westall witnesses' testimony directly.

Eight student and civilian witnessed took to the stage, along with Shane Ryan and Rosie Jones. Each witness gave their account of their Westall experience from over 50 years ago. Further witnesses sitting in the audience, one from Westall Primary school, stood and identified themselves, and contributed their recollections of the encounter, adding confirmation to the accounts of others.

The audience listened quietly and appreciatively, fully involved.

One witness, Colin Kelly, invited those interested to join him on the morning of 6th of April – the 51st anniversary of the initial sighting – at Westall High for a conducted tour of the sites involved.

About twenty-five people joined Colin ... for a fascinating, articulate and informative two-and-a-half hour tour of the Westall '66 scene, starting with a tour of the High School pin-pointing the locations of the Channel Nine interview, the 'Tanya' ambulance location, the scene of the school assembly and other key locations in the story, along with recollections and comparisons of the school buildings and grounds 'then and now'...
[James Rigney, *Westall Flying Saucer Incident* website, 6 April 2017]

Colin Kelly lead the group on to the school oval where he had been playing football back in 1966 at the time of his own sighting. 'As it happened, the group was on the sports oval at the precise time and on the precise day of the 51st anniversary of the event,' James Rigney wrote, 'a fact I believe we all overlooked at the time!'

The group made it's way down to the Grange where we met up with witness Paul Smith (the market gardener) for another one hour session, this time from both Colin and Paul, including Colin's identification of the landing site ... and Paul's fascinating account as viewed from the adjacent market garden, with lots of questions from the spellbound group.
[James Rigney, *Westall Flying Saucer Incident* website, 6 April 2017]

*

Fittingly, the final word goes to Shane Ryan, who has done more than anyone in the last fifty years to keep the Westall incident alive and ripe for explanation:

When I first started I really thought I'd be able to crack the Westall mystery within about twelve months or so, and I wouldn't have been surprised if I found a very prosaic, ordinary explanation to what it was, but I haven't. It may be a life-long task. [Shane Ryan, filmed *VUFOA interview*, May 2010]

NOTES:

1. *The Clayton Calendar* was a magazine of the Brown's Road State School (later named Clayton State School, then Clayton Primary School, now closed). This article appeared in Term Two, 1966, and was written by Geoff Holland, a former student of this school but attending Westall High at the time of its publication.

2. The prefect Bill Chalker refers to here was school captain Graham Simmonds.

* *

UFOs DOWN UNDER

Postscript:

How's this for a coincidence?

Precisely one year after the Westall sighting in April 1966 another school on the other side of the world had a prolonged daylight sighting of its own!

The Crestview Elementary School in Opa-Locka, Florida, U.S.A. encounter shared several astounding similarities with that of Westall High:

* The sightings were both in broad daylight

* Both schools have aerodromes nearby

* Teachers and students saw the craft

* Local residents also witnessed the sighting

* High tension power lines passed near both schools

* The objects had no markings or portholes

* Students said the objects disappeared behind trees

* Some children were frightened by the experience

* Light aircraft showed great interest in the visitors

The following story is taken from the *Miami Times* and tells of 42-year-old John Wolf's experience three days after the initial sighting when his daughter Judy announced that the UFOs had returned:

So Wolf got his binoculars and went over to the field just past the Crestview School... there were 30 or 40 people standing around ... looking north...

It looked like three or four things were out there, Wolf said. They were hovering just behind a line of trees...on top there seemed to be a dome — like the glass dome on a coffee pot... Every time a plane approached one of them something astounding happened. There would be no motion but the thing suddenly just was not there anymore. When the plane left, the thing always reappeared — almost in the same spot. They were like pogo sticks, jumping all over the sky...

John Wolf watched them for about an hour and a half. So did a few dozen other people, mostly adults. They all saw the same things ... [Bill Barry, *The Miami News*, April 13, 1967]

*

For an example of a more enlightened approach exercised by a school authority than that demonstrated at Westall High, we look briefly at a more recent school sighting on another continent.

On September 16, 1994 at around 10.15am., at the Ariel elementary school near Harare in land-locked Zimbabwe, southern Africa, sixty-two students were playing outside during their morning break when they saw three silver balls or 'spaceships' flying over their school.

The balls disappeared in a flash of light and reappeared nearby. They repeated this on-and-off routine three times before following a line of electricity pylons and moved lower towards an uncleared bushland portion of the school-grounds, which the children were forbidden to enter.

One 'ball' either landed or hovered in this rough piece of country, about 100 meters from the edge of the playing field.

A small figure, about one meter high, appeared standing on top of the 'silver ball'. He, or a companion, then moved to the ground and walked a short distance on the rough ground before becoming aware of the watching children and promptly disappeared. The ball or 'spaceship' took off immediately and rapidly vanished from view.

The children's ages ranged from 5 to 12 years; and they came from different cultures (black, white, and Asian). The children gave similar reports of the incident, although some were more observant. Their teachers were attending a staff meeting and saw nothing of the 15-minute event.

Ariel's headmaster, Mr. Colin Mackie, does not believe in UFOs but said he believed the students had seen what they claimed.

Three days after the incident Mr. Mackie permitted a BBC television crew to interview up to a dozen of the older children. He also encouraged the children to draw what they had seen.

John Mack, Professor of Psychiatry at Harvard Medical School in Boston, U.S.A., traveled with his research assistant to Zimbabwe as quickly as possible. John had over forty years in professional psychiatric practice, and was closely involved with supporting those who had experienced the alien abduction phenomena (which was not suggested in the Ariel case).

John Mack was killed in an automobile accident in London in September 2004 but Dominique Callimanopulos, John's research associate, wrote the case report on the UFO Evidence website:

> Even in their state of fear, many of the children reported also being curious by the strange beings they saw, whose eyes in particular commanded an intense attention ... The twelve children we interviewed over the course of two days all described the same event with a steady consistency of detail. [Dominique Callimanopulos, *UFO Evidence — Scientific Study of the UFO Phenomenon* website]

The Ariel elementary school in Zimbabwe has high-tension power lines along one of its boundaries, just as both Crestview School in Florida and Westall High in Melbourne do.

Why is this significant?

John G Fuller (1913-1990), American journalist and author, who is perhaps best remembered for his ground-breaking Betty & Barney Hill book *Interrupted Journey*, researched his *Incident at Exeter* book following a series of well-publicized UFO sightings near Exeter in New Hampshire, USA.

He noticed one recurring theme in the interviews he personally conducted with people claiming to have UFO sightings. Fuller noted:

> I was pouring through the 203 pages of transcript of the tape recordings. The words 'power lines' or 'transmission lines' appeared on an alarming number of pages ... there were 73 mentions in various locations by various people. [John G Fuller, *Incident at Exeter* (Putnam, 1966) p.229]

Coincidence? Maybe ... but many people who have studied the phenomena don't think so!

22. New Zealand Teachers see Strange Object

'Something from another dimension'

First we had a mass UFO sighting at Westall school, in Melbourne on April 6, 1966, followed precisely a year later by another event at Opa-Locka, Florida, U.S.A., again witnessed by students and teachers.

Then, three years later, it was New Zealand's turn.

The *Napier Daily Telegraph* headlined it:

MYSTERY SKY OBJECT SEEN BY TEACHERS AND 400 CHILDREN

> A huge unidentified flying object which appeared as a 'hole in the sky' as it hovered near Napier was watched for up to twenty minutes by the headmaster, teachers, and more than 400 children at Richmond School, Maraenui, yesterday afternoon. [*Napier Daily Telegraph*, May 8, 1970]

A subsequent New Zealand report on the sighting was written by Norman Alford for the Aerial Phenomena Research Organization (APRO) of Tucson, Arizona and appeared in their May-June Bulletin, 1970.

Other than those two sources, little else seems to have appeared in print about the sighting.

Just after 2.00pm, Richmond school's headmaster, Mr. W Billing, was watching the children at play when he noticed something unusual in the southern sky.

At first he thought it was an aeroplane, but he soon realized it had stopped moving. He drew the attention of several teachers to it, and soon the children stopped playing and watched 'awed and fascinated by the saucer-shaped object.'

> It was like a huge wingless plane with the sun glistening on it. But what amazed us was that it was also glistening on the side away from the sun. [W.Billing, in *Napier Daily Telegraph*, May 8, 1970]

Alford's APRO report said another Richmond teacher, Mr. A Coveny, commented that the object first appeared in the south as an opaque hole in the blue sky, low on the horizon, and presented as elongated or oval in appearance.

The object moved towards the school and stopped just below the sun.

> Billing and Coveny guessed the object was hovering between Westshore and Tongoio, and they said they watched a plane landing at Napier Aerodrome while the object was in clear view. 'There was definitely no comparison between the two', Billing said. [Norman Alford, *APRO Bulletin*]

After hovering for several minutes the object began moving away.

In describing what happened next, *Napier Daily Telegraph* again quoted Mr. Billing:

> It then moved at right angles, and the next thing we knew it was like a round ball with the middle a transparent-like sheen. It then flattened out again and continued to move away in a straight line to become like a bright star.
>
> All of a sudden it seemed to light up again, like an extremely brilliant planet, and then fade again before it moved away at speed. [W.Billing, in *Napier Daily Telegraph*, May 8, 1970]

The object was last seen at 2.23pm

Norman Alford's report in the APRO Bulletin attributes the following observations to headmaster Billing:

> Billing ruled out a balloon as a possible explanation because of the object's change of shape from round to oval and vice verse, which indicated a round flat configuration. He also said the object definitely impressed him as being solid and metallic. [W Billing, in *APRO Bulletin*]

When interviewed by Norman Alford, Mr. Coveny expressed surprise that comparatively few people had witnessed the event. He felt at least half of Napier's population should have seen it.

"Here at the school everyone stood with their mouths open trying to work out a logical explanation," he said.

When one of the students asked him if it was a flying saucer, Mr. Coveny said it was — because he couldn't give any other explanation.

> When asked by Alford to compare its apparent size in the sky with an object at arm's length, he said it was huge –like a basketball at arm's length, as it changed from oval to round. Coveny's own words to Mr. Alford were that it appeared to be 'something out of this worldly concept – something from another dimension.' [A Coveny, *APRO Bulletin*]

Despite Alford's best efforts, the pilot of the National Airways plane which had landed at Napier whilst the object was in sight was never tracked down. Further, no comment about a possible radar sighting at the time has been found.

*

Move back now twenty months earlier – to September, 1968.

Relocate your thoughts from Richmond school to just ten kilometers/6 miles away – the Taradale shopping center.

Meet two lads aged 19 and 17, John Alfred Dow and Paul Franklin. They had been buddies at high school, and still hung around together. Dow was an apprentice joiner and owned a 1957 Austin A55 motor car. Franklin, despite being younger, was a smartly-dressed, well spoken, 'non-bogie'-type who was the 'initiator' of the pair.

> On Friday, September 5 [1968], John Dow and Paul Franklin were driving around the Taradale area... when they noticed lights hovering above the city dump. They described the lights as 'dozens of reds, greens and blues darting around'.
>
> While sitting in their car watching this display, they were startled by a tremendous explosion from the direction of the dump, followed by rumblings and vibrations which shook the car. The lights then appeared to group and speed off. [*Flying Saucer Review 69*, Vol. 15, No, 2,. p.3]

Thinking they had seen flying saucers, they drove immediately to the Taradale police station and reported the incident to the duty officer. He was interested, and passed no judgmental comment.

The next evening the pair returned to the same spot, hoping to witness further unusual phenomena, without success.

On Sunday, September 8, they again visited Taradale and saw an object which shot off a beacon of light, although they could not see its shape. They reported this to the Taradale police, this time finding another officer on duty who laughed at their story and who mentioned the 'salt-impregnated cable' theory causing the flashing as a result of wind. The only trouble with this theory – so the boys said – was that there was no wind! [*Flying Saucer Review 69*, Vol. 15, No, 2. p.3]

They were in the Taradale shopping area again on Monday evening. Over the Puketapu Hills to the west, they saw a light that commenced glowing and suddenly shot straight up into the sky. As they were tiring of the derision they anticipated receiving, John and Paul did not make a police report of this sighting.

The next evening, Tuesday the 10th, they were keen to get to the bottom of the 'lights and rumblings' business. Little did they realize this was to become an expensive exercise!

Firstly they drove towards Puketapu on the Puketapu Road, then turned into Omaranui Road to drive back towards Taradale.

While they were on this road, they saw a lighted object in the sky in the [southerly] direction of Hastings. In addition to frequent color changes from white to red to orange to blue, this airborne object kept sending out a beam of white light.

The young men decided to drive towards the object, but it disappeared behind a cloud, so they drove to Taradale, crossed the bridge, and entered the main street.

The area before crossing the bridge has an electricity sub-station which distributes power from the Tuai Hydro to Fernhill, Pakowhai, Napier and Taradale – in layman's terms, the area has four high-voltage overhead transmission lines crossing nearby roads – and the young men drove under each of them.

Near the Taradale camping grounds, Franklin, who was sitting at right angles [turned on the front passenger's seat], saw the object again through the car's rear window, this time across the river whence they had come.

The object appeared to pick up speed as though it had seen them, at the same time becoming brilliantly white. Franklin called out, and Dow glanced around.

> Franklin then shouted: *"Bail out, it's got us,"* and both leapt from the car on the passenger's side. As the car was then doing 30-40 m.p.h. both boys fell badly, suffering abrasions and bruises. [*Flying Saucer Review 69*, Vol. 15, No, 2. p.3]

Franklin landed on his back and immediately shielded his eyes with his hands because the 'unbelievable intense whiteness' of the object was blinding him.

His mate, driver John Dow, had landed face down on the ground. The last he saw of the object was when it was 2 or 3ft. away from the back of his car when he dived out.

The object hovered just two feet above the sprawled lads, and suddenly shot off skywards.

Their car, meanwhile, crashed into a fruit shop on the other side of the road, smashing the plate glass window. A small crowd gathered, attracted by the noise of the crash, and found two dazed young men complaining about being attacked by a UFO!

> The object, the boys claim, was a 'spheroid' about 2½ft/76cm. in diameter, and although glowing brilliantly, did not cast any light whatsoever. Instead, they have the impression of a translucent brilliance with the light pointing into the object. [*Flying Saucer Review 69*, Vol. 15, No, 2. p.3]

The time was 8.50p.m.. The police arrived on the scene within fifteen minutes and took statements from both Dow and Franklin. There was no suggestion that the boys had been drinking and no evidence of liquor. Constable Barry Martin-Bus conceded that the boys' account sounded 'sensible and logical, in spite of their excited state' — although he considered the phenomena was a fireball.

The weather had been fine and cool, the *Flying Saucer Review* report said, and inconsistent with that required for the 'fireball' phenomena.

The police booked John Alfred Dow on a charge of dangerous driving.

The case was dismissed. The Magistrate concluded that 'it was evident the accused had got himself into such a state of mind that he acted involuntarily when something distracted him.'

23. The Melton Police — UFO Fiasco

'The acute sensitivities of a security 'breach'

This bizarre encounter with two unknown aerial craft took place at Melton, a satellite suburb on Melbourne's north-western fringe, in 1983.

It wasn't so much the nature of the craft or even the people who witnessed their strange conduct that sent authorities into a frenzy, but the perceived threat to a nearby national security installation.

In what started as a normal night-time police patrol, Constables Raymond Ellens and Peter Ferguson were driving their divisional-van along the Keilor-Melton Road when, around 12.40am, they noticed a bright stationary light low in the sky.

As it began to move, they took up position about a kilometer behind it and followed at a safe distance.

Using their police radio, they notified Sgt. Barry Harman on watch-house duty at Melton police station of their activities. At around 1.00am, he in turn contacted Air Traffic Control at Melbourne's Tullamarine airport who told him 'No known aircraft in the area.'

They had another message for him as well:

> They had observed something on radar in the vicinity of Melton, only momentary, and they were attempting to set their radar equipment in an endeavor to locate it.

The Police Air Wing then contacted Sgt. Harman by telephone stating that they had received information from Air Traffic Control tower concerning the craft, but they were unable to assist with an aircraft of the Police Air Wing for a search. ['The Melton Police Encounter' by John Auchettl, *Australian UFO Bulletin*, December, 1983]

But the escapades of the unidentified airborne visitors were far from over.

> The object slowly turned around and headed west to the Regional Shopping Center [Melton], where it descended to about 500m [550yds] and hovered. It had two bright lights in front and a red flashing light at the rear. It made a whirring sound and the two constables thought it was a gyrocopter. [*The Mail-Express* (Bacchus Marsh- Melton), 27 July 1983. p.1]

Constables Ellens and Ferguson parked their vehicle at the shopping center and stepped out. Using the police van spotlight, they took a closer look at the object.

Constable Ellens reported:

> The light from the spotlight shone on its tail section that was of tubular framework construction with a fin at the rear. The object had two bright white lights at the front and a single red light at the rear. It was hovering over the shopping center. The object made a low-pitched humming sound quite different to a helicopter or aero engine.

The UFO moved away to the south-east, towards Leakes Road, Rockbank. The officers jumped into their car and pursued it. Next, it returned back over Melton continuing on to the area of Fogarty's Airfield some 8km/5miles away, with the police divisional van not far behind. Then it swung right towards Toolern Vale.

The two officers saw the object 'land' near a paddock at the rear of the Toolern Vale Stud Farm, but although they inspected several paddocks in the area, they could find nothing.

> 'It would land with its lights off, we get to within 100m/110yds of it and we thought we've got it this time. But the next thing we knew, it was in the air and behind us again,' Constable Peter Ferguson said. [*Daily Telegraph* (Sydney), July 22, 1983]

[The police] chased it until about 2.40am when it disappeared. It was picked up twice on air traffic control radar at Tullamarine, but most of the time the radar could not detect it ... the constables said the object was playing games with them and appeared to land several times: 'at one stage it slid behind a hill.'

'When we turned around to go back, it did a U-turn and came up in front of us, with two lights beaming straight at us,' Constable Ellens said. 'The whole night we were thinking we were going to grab this thing,' said Constable Ferguson, 'It got a bit frustrating.' [*The Mail-Express* (Bacchus Marsh- Melton), 27 July 1983. p.3]

After they lost sight of the object again, the constables returned to their station and busied themselves doing paperwork.

Then they went out again on a further patrol, this time intending to go westwards from Melton.

In the words of Constable Ray Ellens, 'We went out on patrol towards Bacchus Marsh and we saw it again hovering over the regional shopping center. This time it was low, about 60m/200ft. We got out and shone the spotlight on it to get a good look, and it looked the same as it had before. Then it took off and we continued this cat-and-mouse game of chasing it for several hours.' [Bill Chalker, *The OZ Files – the Australian UFO story*, (Duffy & Snellgrove, 1996) p.179]

At about 4.40am, the game changed.

The UFO returned, disappeared briefly, and made a sudden reappearance on the other side of the horizon. The lights were much brighter and it was only when the police van got closer that the two constables realized they were following a second, much larger object. [*The Mail-Express* (Bacchus Marsh- Melton), July 27, 1983. p.3]

At 5.00am Chief Inspector Paul Hickman started duty at Melton. He and Sergeant Barry Harman, the watch-house duty officer, heard a radio call that the object was flying low in the direction of the police station. Sgt. Harman reported:

Both Inspector Hickman and myself ran onto the roadway in front of the Melton Police Station, and immediately I looked into the direction of the Regional shopping center and observed the object. My immediate observation was that of two large round lights, very similar to the lights of a motor car, approaching the police station at a very low altitude.

It appeared to be maintaining an even altitude, speed and direction towards the police station … as the object passed by at close range, I reckoned its shape to be similar to an inflatable life raft approximately 12m/40ft long. A red flashing light, not rotating, was situated in about the center of the undercarriage. There were no visible wings or tail similar to an aircraft, nor did it make any sound similar to an aircraft or helicopter. The only sound audible was that of a very quiet wind noise. [Bill Chalker, *The OZ Files – the Australian UFO story*, (Duffy & Snellgrove, 1996) p.180]

Melton Police

Constable Peter Ferguson corroborated this assessment:

> The object came closer and eventually passed directly overhead; we shone the spotlight onto its underside and observed it to be a gunmetal gray in color and to have the appearance of a very large rubber raft with two lights inset in the front, and two white lights on the rear and a red flashing light in the center. [The Melton Police Encounter (John Auchettl), *Australian UFO Bulletin*, December, 1983]

He added: 'It made a low pitched humming sound and appeared to be traveling at about 70 — 80kph (46mph). The object was approximately 200 ft [61m] above us and was illuminated by the spotlight.'

In his official report Constable Ray Ellens said that while he and Constable Ferguson were traveling in the police van, they saw the object traveling towards them:

> Between the object and our position was the Australian Army Rockbank Receiving Station. The object appeared to be traveling towards the [installation's] antenna array. The object appeared to be below the height of the antenna and if it continued on its path a collision would have occurred. However, it turned about, and started to arc again to the north. After a few minutes we lost sight of the object over the far horizon. [Bill Chalker, *The OZ Files – the Australian UFO story*, p. 179]

Bill Chalker later explained the vital significance of the Rockbank facility to Australia's military intelligence efforts. It is where Defense Signals monitoring occurs as Australia's part in its signals alliance with the U.K. and the U.S.A. – the site is linked with a nearby facility that has direct satellite communications with the NSA and CIA.

> In this light, one can understand the acute sensitivities with the security 'breach' that occurred that night. In intelligence parlance, one could suggest that the Melton UFO showed 'clear intent' in its intrusion at the Defense Signals Directorate Rockbank aerial array. We probably don't know the full story of that night's events. [Bill Chalker in *UFOs Sub Rosa Down Under: the Australian Military & Government Role in the UFO Controversy*]

Friday 22 July was, as the local Melton paper suggested, a 'bad day' to report minor offences to the Melton police station.

News of that day's early-hour escapades had reached the media and a frantic scramble had begun to 'catch the police who had seen the airborne visitors before they [the police] went off night shift.'

UFOs DOWN UNDER

The media rush started at 7am with newspapermen and breakfast television crews jostling for answers. According to the local *Mail-Express*: 'The [police] station's routine activities had to soldier on through a deluge of phone calls and TV cameras.'

Sergeant Barry Harman, who had been in constant contact with those in the chasing police-van, and had himself witnessed the UFO fly overhead at close quarters, personally took over the media inquiries after the others went home, their shift finished.

> There were calls from Canberra, Sydney, France, England: "BBC calling ...beep, beep, beep," mimicked [a constable] as the fifth English radio station rang for an interview. [*The Mail-Express* (Bacchus Marsh- Melton), 27 July 1983. p.1]

Sergeant Harman went off home around midday and was woken after an hour's sleep by television helicopters overhead. His mind was too busy for further sleep so he returned to the police station to see if things had settled down, and "was instantly connected" to a live Melbourne talk-back radio show!

Bill Chalker, keen seeker of physical UFO evidence, said it was a "complex, multiple-witnessed" encounter. He spoke with some of the officers soon after the incident and was impressed with "the seemingly bizarre nature of the affair," but there was no physical evidence offering.

Sydney's *Daily Telegraph* afternoon newspaper carried of the Melton encounter the same day, 22 July 1983:

PLAYFUL UFO HAS EXPERTS BAFFLED

> Melbourne police and aviation officials are baffled over a mystery object that led police vans on a six-hour chase through Melbourne's western suburbs today. Police said the object was "obviously playing fun and games" with them as it continually appeared and disappeared over the Melton area.

Next morning, 23 July, the Melbourne's *Sun News-Pictorial* newspaper carried a page-5 story:

ET LEADS POLICE A MERRY DANCE

> Has Melton suddenly become a popular extraterrestrial tourist attraction? Or were a group of policemen on night patrol the victims of an elaborate prank which resulted in a number of UFO sightings early yesterday? The police, the RAAF and the Aviation Department are quite frankly baffled... Police said the object stayed in the Melton, Sydenham and Rockbank areas before flying to Deer Park.

UFO investigator John Auchettl of VUFORS (Victorian UFO Research Society), Melbourne was present that first day, too – and the next.

His thorough report, which included flight maps, drawings and reports by witnesses, and subsequent interviews with Inspector Paul Hickman, Department of Transport, Bureau of Air Safety and RAAF spokespeople, plus an exploratory visit to Air Traffic control, took four months to complete.

In his 'Conclusion', John Auchettl wrote:

To date [December, 1983] no-one has found the craft, found a hoax, or seen the craft come back.

The Dept. of Transport has not been able to locate any information of the UFO to close their investigation. This also applies to the police investigation.

I have met and talked to now over 34 people involved in this encounter. We have looked in every area that an aircraft or airship may land or hide. This work has accumulated over 200 miles of travel.

Every avenue of investigation has been looked at over the past 4 months, yet I can only conclude that the object seen that night was a genuine UFO.

Something of great importance happened that night and in my opinion, this encounter should be regarded as one of the greatest Australian encounters ever, and held up to the level of importance as the Frederick Valentich encounter is now held.

Until this UFO is found, or Valentich is found, both will remain a great mystery.

24. Spooks: "You Saw Nothing! Got it?"

'You entered a no-fly zone!'

An urgent medical evacuation from Australia's most isolated Antarctic outpost in 1985 made American intelligence operators jittery. The rescuers — an American crew flying a Lockheed C-130 with ski-equipped landing gear — made a 5,000-mile (8050kms) round-trip over the South Pole with a critically injured Australian worker.

The following day, Wednesday, October 30, *The Canberra Times* reported:

> The first phase of a three-nation Antarctic rescue of a badly burned Australian was completed successfully last night.
>
> A US Air Force Hercules [incorrect identification] was able to land on a hastily prepared sea-ice strip at Davis Station, where a building foreman, Mr. Stephen Bunning, lay with burns to 70 per cent of his body.
>
> ... the sea-ice landing was only just possible, because at one point the ice thickness was just inside the tolerance level for the military transport.
> [*The Canberra Times,* October 30, 1985, p.3]

So why were the American intelligence officers jittery? What had the rescue team done to upset them? Surely, the aircrew and medical team deserved to be commended, not condemned?

However, a US Navy Flight Engineer who participated in this event reported that their aircraft entered a 'no-fly' zone and saw things they weren't supposed to see. On their return from their rescue mission, 'the entire crew was told to report to the skipper's office':

> We all had to sit in this room and this guy came in that nobody had seen before. The only way I can describe him is a kind of intelligence-gathering type of individual. We were sitting down and he said, 'Okay, you guys saw this thing. But you did not see it.' ['Brian', *Nexus New Times Magazine*, Volume 22 No. 3, April-May, 2015 p.66]

This witness, who retired in 1997 after 20 year's service, had spent time with a US Navy squadron called the Antarctic Development Squadron based in California, with forward operating bases at Christchurch, New Zealand and McMurdo Station, Antarctica.

In January 2015 he wrote to Linda Moulton Howe. She is widely known in UFO circles as an award-winning investigative reporter, producer, documentary film-maker, editor and author — her earthfiles.com site is packed with high-strangenesses. Linda Moulton Howe conducted a speaking tour of Australia in 1997 and again in 2011.

In order to protect his identity, this witness chose the name Brian:

> I have been wanting to write to you for a long time about my experience on the Antarctic continent with flying vehicles that I was told not to talk about. ['Brian', *Nexus*, April/May 2015, p.64]

Brian then went on to report several interesting experiences involving flying silver discs, missing scientists, and a large hole in the ice surface close to the South Pole.

Further, he told of a designated 'no-fly' zone, which he alleged, kept unwanted eyes away from a joint human and extraterrestrial scientific research base built under the ice surface near the South Pole. This latter claim appears to rely on aircrew scuttlebutt over a few beers in leisure hours.

Needless to say, as an award-winning journalist, Linda Moulton Howe contacted 'Brian' soon after receiving his letter and interviewed him to seek clarification of his claims.

Before the month was over, Linda had posted her full interview with 'Brian' on her earthfiles.com website (tinyurl.com/nsv7pjh), and written a précis which appeared in the April-May, 2015 issue of *Nexus* magazine, from which some material in this chapter is drawn.

A mountain range known as the Transantarctic Mountains divides East Antarctica from West Antarctica — Australia's Davis Station is on the east, America's McMurdo Station on the west.

The Transantarctics are one of the world's longest mountain chains, running about 2,200 miles (3,500kms), and mostly buried beneath the ice with their peaks showing through.

Lockheed C-130s usually fly across these mountains at an altitude of 25 to 35,000ft/9kms to reach the South Pole, where the U.S. maintains a supply base including aviation fuel.

'Brian' said:

On several flights to and from the South Pole, our crew viewed air vehicles darting around the tops of the Transantarctics in almost exactly the same spot every time we would fly by aircraft. ['Brian', *Nexus*, April/May 2015, p.64]

During his interview with Linda Moulton Howe, 'Brian' went further:

...all we could see on the initial sighting was the shiny reflection in the silvery things darting around down there.

I remember turning to my aircraft commander and pilot and saying, 'What are those things down there?' He got on the intercom and said, 'Well they are not ours: that's all I can tell you.' ['Brian', Nexus, April — May 2015, p.65]

'Did any one of them ever approach your plane?' Linda asked.

No, they were always below us, always stayed below us. ['Brian', *Nexus*, April/May, 2015, p.65]

The 'no-fly' zone applied to a designated area around 5miles/8kms from the Geographic South Pole. 'Brian' recalled being told it was because the area was an 'air-sampling' station and jet exhaust would contaminate the samples. He found this amusing because 'you're air-sampling on the ground' and 'we fly kind of high!'

Brian's first incursion into this 'no-fly' area happened during the medical evacuation of badly burned Stephen Bunning from Australia's Davis Station in October 1985. As Davis is on the opposite side of the continent to Brian's base at McMurdo, this operation required their Lockheed C-130 to refuel at the South Pole on both the forward and return legs.

The direct course to Davis from the refueling camp was right over the 'no-fly' air-sampling station. Because it was an emergency, the LC-130 flew the most direct route.

Here are Brian's recollections of those few minutes:

> The only thing we saw while going over this camp was a very large hole going into the ice. You could fly one of our LC-130s into this thing. It was after this medivac mission that we were briefed by some spooks from Washington, DC, and told not to speak of the area we overflew. ['Brian', *Nexus*, April/May 2015, p.65]

The public face of the medical evacuation from Davis Station in October 1985 presents only a positive reflection on the parties involved:

> A squadron LC-130 carried out a dramatic medical evacuation mission to the sea ice off Davis Station, an Australian base where no aircraft had ever landed before. [extract from 'United States Navy Antarctic Development 6: USAP air logistic support for the 1985-1986 austral season']

The heading of a brief news announcement on page 3 of *The Canberra Times* on October 31, 1985 read:

BURNS VICTIM DIES

> Mr. Stephen Bunning, 34, building foreman, of Avoca Beach, NSW, died on Tuesday night while being transported from Davis in the Antarctic in a U.S. Air Force Hercules [incorrect identification] to the McMurdo base. He had suffered burns to 70% of his body.

The other instance when 'Brian' went close to the 'air sampling' station was due to their aircraft having a navigation and electrical failure. They were told to leave the area immediately and report to their squadron's commanding officer on return to McMurdo.

'Our pilot got his butt chewed,' Brian wrote.

'There were many other times when we saw things that were out of the ordinary,' 'Brian' said, adding that on one occasion scientists and equipment were dropped at a distant camp and were not heard from for two weeks.

When an LC-130 flew back to the camp to find out why there had not been any communications, they found it deserted.

The camp radio was in full working order, so the crew contacted McMurdo, reported their findings, and were ordered back to their base.

Seven days later, McMurdo received a call from the scientists saying they were ready to be picked up from their camp. 'Brian' was among the crew sent to retrieve them:

> None of the scientists would talk to any of the crew on the plane, and to me they looked scared. As soon as we landed back at McMurdo, the scientists were put on another of our squadron aircraft and flown to Christchurch, New Zealand.
>
> We never heard about them again. Their equipment that we brought back from the camp was put into quarantine and shipped back to the United States, escorted by the same spooks that debriefed us about our fly-over of the air-sampling camp/large hole in the ice. ['Brian', *Nexus*, April/May 2015, p.65]

From these incidents, 'Brian' and some his fellow flight crew-members drew some remarkable conclusions ... but conjecture isn't evidence.

Here's how 'Brian' expressed those ideas to Linda Moulton Howe:

> Talk among the flight crews was that there is a UFO base at the South Pole, and some of the crew heard talk from some of the scientists working at the pole of EBEs (extraterrestrial biological entities) working with and interacting with the scientists at that air-sampling camp/large ice hole. ['Brian', *Nexus*, April/May 2015, p.65]

High strangeness, indeed. Brian's full interview with Linda Moulton Howe is posted on her earthfiles.com website (which attracts a subscription fee.

25. Maureen Puddy at the 'Meeting Place'

'I was petrified. I thought "I'm gone this time!"

'Have you ever been interested in UFOs?' the researcher asked. 'No. Not at all,' Maureen Puddy replied.

'Ever read anything about them?' he pressed.

'No.'

'Why do you think they chose you?'

Maureen paused, then offered, 'The only reason I can give is that I was alone, on a lonely road, with no one else about. I don't know, I can't explain it.'

The 37-year-old mother of two was living with her wheelchair-bound husband Jack in the beachside holiday village of Rye on the Mornington Peninsula, about 100kms south of Melbourne. Their son, aged seven, had broken his leg at school when a cupboard fell on him and he was whisked away to the Royal Children's Hospital in Melbourne by helicopter.

Maureen Puddy drove their Holden station wagon to the city three days a week (Mondays, Wednesdays, and Fridays) to visit her convalescing boy, often stopping off at her mother's for a cup of tea and a chat during the long drive home.

Driving home after her visit on July 3, 1972, she approached the Moorooduc railway crossing about 10kms/6miles south of Frankston, Victoria when a blue light from overhead lit up the roadway around her.

'My first thought was that it was a helicopter like the one that took my little boy to hospital, because it had a blue light under it,' Maureen later recalled, 'I thought at the time he was flying too low.'

'I got out of the car and looked up, and saw this enormous flying saucer. 'It was approximately four times wider than the road ...it could not have come down on the road without flattening light poles and fences on each side,' she added, 'the whole thing was glowing iridescent blue, it was illuminating the whole road.'

Maureen's immediate reaction was to get back into her car and move out of harm's way. She drove off at high speed, aware that the object was maintaining its position just above and behind her vehicle as she drove.

'It followed me for eight miles' — towards Dromana, where she intended reporting the incident to the police.

As she drew closer to the Dromana township, checking in her rear-vision mirror, Maureen saw a bright blue light streaking off behind her, going in the opposite direction. The chase was over.

'There was no policeman [on duty] at the police station at Dromana, so I left a note inside, got back in the car and went on to Rosebud' — a larger beachside town 9kms/5.6miles further around Port Phillip Bay.

'Maureen went into Rosebud police station and said 'I've been followed home.' The officer suggested they go outside, but Maureen warned 'You won't catch anything — it's a flying saucer! So I told him all about what I'd seen. I wanted to make an official report. I think he thought I'd gone off!' Assuring her that he would report it to the authorities, the policeman suggested she should go home.

'I came home and told my husband what I'd seen. He made a cup of tea.'

Next morning, Maureen contacted the Royal Australian Air Force (RAAF) at Laverton air base, Melbourne, and reported her sighting to them. 'They informed me that I had probably seen some sort of phenomenon' — a masterful understatement — 'and that they would send me a questionnaire to fill out and send back.'

Maureen Puddy

When the forms duly arrived, Maureen was struck by their complexity. 'You need to be an astronaut to fill them out,' she said. But fill them out she did, thirty-one questions in total; then she added a hand-written note and 'a drawing I did on arriving home while it was still very clear in my mind. No portholes or windows, only very bright light.'

She signed and dated the forms on 7 July 1972, and sent them back.

But destiny held more unexpected phenomena in store for Mrs. Maureen Puddy.

On Monday, July 24, a day usually scheduled for her trice-weekly drive to visit her son in hospital, circumstances kept Mrs. Puddy at home. A general petrol shortage caused Maureen to restrict her visits that week to two only, Tuesday and Thursday, so she busied herself at home that evening making clothes for her daughter's doll.

'I thought I heard someone call my name,' Maureen later recalled, 'I said to my husband "someone's calling me" and he went out the back, and there was no-one there. We live on a corner and I thought at the time it could have been anyone passing in the street. I didn't give it any more thought.'

'I went to bed normally at eleven o'clock, and the whole night long I was kept awake by this voice continually calling my name, Maureen, Maureen, over and over again.'

'Twice I got up to check on my little daughter, she is five, I went into her bedroom. She was sound asleep, wasn't at all upset.'

'There's an old lady who lives at the end of our block, and I thought she might have fallen over, she might be sick and she was out calling us. So I went out into the backyard and there was nobody there either.'

'I came inside, locked up, went back to bed again, dozed off to sleep again, but the continual voice went on calling all night long.'

Her husband, Jack Puddy, slept soundly throughout. He heard nothing.

'I rang my neighbor early in the morning to see if she was alright — I thought there may have been something wrong — but she was fine. I can't explain it, it just happened — that was on the Tuesday morning — then, on the Tuesday night, I had the second sighting.'

After visiting her son in the Melbourne hospital on Tuesday July 25, 1972, Maureen Puddy followed her usual routine of calling in on her mother to report on her son's condition and share a pot of tea, before continuing the long drive home to Rye.

At around 9.15 p.m. her route took her again to the familiar Moorooduc railway level crossing — the site of her earlier encounter — where she had to give way to 'a man with torch leading a cow on a rope' — as Maureen described them.

'I got four or five hundred yards (about half a kilometer) past the man when the road lit up again. I knew what it was straight away! I put my foot on the accelerator and off I went! I was determined this time that I wasn't going to stop for anybody.'

'I suppose I went about half a mile (almost 1km) going at high speed when the engine cut out — completely cut out. I had no control of the car at all. I couldn't steer it, I couldn't stop it, and even though I turned the ignition key off, I couldn't start it either. I was stopped on the side of the road.'

'I was petrified. I thought well, I'm gone this time!'

'This is hard to explain.' Maureen told one interviewer, 'what happened was like sitting in a vacuum ... like sitting in a cube. I had a feeling like I was closed in. No sound, not a breath of air.'

'I had a feeling that I was receiving a message from this 'thing', which was above the car, I could see it over the car. I knew I was getting some sort of message, but I didn't understand it. I felt I was receiving a message in a foreign language.'

'There were no words said, not a sound, just a deadly quiet. Then the letters were translated into English — beautifully spoken English. Very clear, without hearing a voice, no sound. I couldn't tell whether it was male or female, it was just a voice stating a message.'

These audio impressions formed in Maureen Puddy's mind, they were not words she heard in the normal sense of hearing them spoken, as she explained later.

The first part of the message was: 'All your tests will be negative' — then there was a pause — and it said 'Tell the media. Do not panic. We mean you no harm.'

> Then there was a long pause, and then it said 'You now have control.' The car started up all by itself, I still had both hands on the steering wheel. The blue light went out, it [the 'thing'] was gone. I just sat on the side of the road with the car engine ticking over. No sounds, it was totally dark. I put the car in gear and off I went.

I didn't panic like I did the first time. My first thought was I must get to a house, to a telephone, and ring the police, there may be some sign of this thing still about if they can get here in time.

Maureen passed several homes set back off the road and drove, she estimated, seven miles (11kms) before she found a house close to the road. She got the occupiers out of bed and asked to use their telephone to call the police, but they didn't have a telephone connected to the premises.

Deciding to waste no further time, Maureen then drove to a place where she knew there was a telephone — the Rosebud police station where she had reported her first flying saucer encounter seen in the almost identical spot twenty-two days earlier.

She was greeted with 'Oh, no. Not you again!' She told him she had seen this object and that she'd received a message from it, and didn't know what to do with it.

"I wanted to make an official report, as I thought the people should know what it was about.'

After filing her statement, Maureen Puddy drove the remaining 8 miles/13kms to her home at Rye. She told her husband what had transpired, and telephoned the RAAF straight afterwards, knowing it would soon lead to more forms to be completed.

Next morning, Wednesday July 26, following the message received the previous evening to 'tell the media', Maureen contacted three Melbourne TV stations ('two laughed and hung up, one sent a team of reporters for an interview'). She also contacted talk-back radio station 3AW in Melbourne. This call changed that station's talk-back topic for the morning to UFOs and drew some interesting responses.

'Three or four people rang in from the [Mornington] Peninsula [where her encounters occurred] to say they had seen the light from this object,' Maureen said, 'One lady rang who said that her husband had seen the object, and he'd gone inside to get binoculars, but by the time he came out, it was gone.'

On July 28, Maureen completed the RAAF questionnaire, signed it, and mailed it back. She mentioned the man with torch leading a cow on a rope as a possible witness, and described her sighting in detail, including the message.

Eventually, according to Judith Magee of the Victorian Unidentified Flying Object Research Society (VUFORS), 'the man's wife contacted her [Maureen Puddy] 'and confirmed that he had seen the light. Mrs. Magee re-emerges shortly in this narrative.

In veteran UFO researcher Keith Basterfield's cold case investigation of the Puddy encounters, he mentions locating the official RAAF files relating to this second incident in the National Archives of Australia. It identifies six witnesses who saw an 'object' in the sky around the same time in the evening from three different local points.

Of these, one couple had been in touch with the very same Senior Constable at Rosebud who took Maureen Puddy's statement that night. The policeman described Mrs. Puddy as 'a rational woman not given to great flights of fancy.'

Three weeks after Maureen Puddy's second sighting, and after an hour-long telephone discussion with Judith Magee of VUFORS, she became guest speaker at a VUFORS meeting.

'For more than an hour she held an audience of 200 spellbound,' Judith Magee reported, 'the hall was crowded, there were even people in the lobby listening through the speaker system — thoroughly fascinated!'

Further contact lay in Mrs. Puddy's future ...and Judith Magee was one of two first-hand witnesses.

The other witness was Magee's long-term associate and VUFORS researcher, Paul Norman. He was born in the U.S.A. and migrated to Australia in 1963. His hard-nosed attitude and ceaseless energy were valuable assets for a UFO researcher.

About six months after the second sighting Maureen Puddy began hearing a series of further distinct short messages: 'Maureen, Maureen, come to the meeting place.' As before, the message came from a persistent, disembodied source. Maureen tried unsuccessfully to telephone Garry Little and Bill Stapleton whom she had met during the investigation of her previous experiences. So she rang VUFORS and spoke to Judith Magee instead.

We rely here on the published account, written by Judith Magee in the *Flying Saucer Review* — a magazine published in England for the serious study of the aerial phenomena — of November 1978, part of which is paraphrased here:

> Both Judith Magee and fellow researcher Paul Norman agreed to meet Mrs. Puddy at an arranged time and place and travel with her that evening to the 'meeting place' — just south of the Moorooduc railway crossing.

Maureen Puddy

It was already dark when Maureen drove up, stopped her car, and came running to the waiting researchers shouting that she had nearly ran off the road. Maureen said that an entity, completely clothed in a gold tinfoil suit, had appeared sitting beside her as she drove to the rendezvous. She was so startled she almost ran off the road.

Judith Magee then traveled with Maureen Puddy to the Moorooduc railway crossing area; Paul Norman followed in his own vehicle. Norman parked his car and joined the others, sitting in the rear seat as they discussed the tinfoil-clad entity.

Maureen suddenly grabbed Magee's arm and pointed across her car exclaiming, 'There he is, can't you see him? He's in the same clothes.' Judith Magee told Maureen she couldn't see anything, and Maureen responded with 'You must be able to!'

The entity was now standing by the front left headlight of the vehicle, according to Maureen, and Paul Norman agreed to get out of the car and walk around it. As he came to where the entity was standing Maureen said it moved back to allow Paul to pass between him and the car.

Maureen was asked by her companions to see if she could make the entity appear to them as well. She asked, but the entity shook his head 'No'. Next, the entity motioned to Maureen to follow him, which she adamantly refused to do. Judith Magee offered to go with her, but to no avail.

Suddenly Maureen started to describe the interior of a spacecraft, and said the entity was there too, pointing to a large 'mushroom' in the room's center. Maureen described the 'mushroom' as being fixed to the floor, taller than the average person, and like a constantly shaking jelly.

Maureen was apparently looking around the room when she became very agitated, crying out 'I can't get out! There are no doors or windows. I can't get out!' [Judith Magee in *Flying Saucer Review*, November 1978]

Judith Magee, sitting in her car, put her arm around Maureen Puddy's shoulders, trying to calm her as she was becoming increasingly upset.

Bravely Judith directed her thoughts to the entity and, thinking Maureen might have a nervous collapse, silently requested the entity to show her some pity.

Suddenly Maureen announced: 'He wants me to close my eyes.'

Judith suggested it was a good idea, and felt Maureen relax

immediately she shut her eyes. Maureen continued describing the craft's interior and again became agitated when finding no doors or windows.

After a brief period Maureen's consciousness returned to her companions in the car. They turned on the interior light and offered her a cup of tea from their vacuum flask. As Judith handed her the cup, she said 'Oh, I'm back in there again' and calmly added 'He's gone. This time he's really gone. I can tell. It feels different.'

Maureen had no recall of anything she had said, or where she had 'been' since seeing the tin-foil-clad entity first approach her vehicle.

Judith Magee and Paul Norman told her what they had witnessed, and they all agreed to accompany Maureen to her home at Rye. They arrived around 10.30-11.00pm. and discussed the evening's events with Maureen's husband, Jack, over another tea and biscuits, before Judith and Paul drove back to Melbourne.

'About a week later,' wrote Keith Basterfield in his cold-case review of the Puddy encounters forty years later, 'Maureen was out driving with her son, who by this time was out of hospital.'

'The man from the room [the tin-foil-clad entity] suddenly appeared, sitting between Maureen and her son, on the front bench seat of Maureen's car. The 'man' then simply disappeared. They were on the Moorooduc Road at the time.'

26. Kempsey man Sucked through Glass

'The man could not run from the object of his fear'

The first incidence in this sequence of unusual events happened a week before its bizarre and mind-stretching conclusion. It started at a seaside village, South West Rocks on Australia's east coast, where the Macleay River flows into the Pacific Ocean.

A local resident, Mrs. A Laws, experienced an event during the evening of Thursday, March 25, 1971, which she had been reluctant to discuss because 'people would say I was mad.'

When she read of similar happenings in her local newspaper, *The Macleay Argus*, over the next few weeks, Mrs. Laws felt sufficiently encouraged to disclose her own experience, and those of her sons, to the newspaper.

She had been in bed on the night in question and, at around 10pm., had been awakened when a brilliant burnt-orange color lit up her room:

> I got out of bed and pulled back the blinds and saw a huge, bright light eight or ten feet [3 meters] in diameter near the bowling club. I thought the club was on fire and then I saw this was a great ball of light like a beautiful sunset.
>
> I thought that it might have been a flare from a ship in distress, ... or that I was having a nightmare. Then I saw the light come down slowly to earth and disappear behind the bowling club. I didn't see it again.

I watched this beautiful light for five, maybe ten, minutes. I have never seen anything like it before. [*The Macleay Argus,* April 17, 1971]

When Mrs. Laws' youngest son, Doug, returned home from work after 10pm., he woke his brother because, like his mother, he thought it may have been a distress flare from a ship at sea. He reported the incident to the local pilot station and was reliably told that no one would use flares like he had described.

The largest town in the Macleay valley, where these incidents were reported, is Kempsey (South West Rocks is 35kms/22miles to its north). Kempsey is an historic river town, once the center of red cedar timber exports but now focused on beef and dairy cattle farming. Kempsey's local newspaper is *The Macleay Argus,* from which all the direct quotations in this chapter are drawn.

A week after the South West Rocks incident, Mrs. Ailsa Summerville, who lives in Kempsey in a house overlooking the Macleay River, had a similar experience to Mrs. Laws.

Mrs. Summerville told *The Macleay Argus* she saw a brilliant pink light, with lighter tonings on the outer parts of the sphere, as it passed outside her window. It happened around 6.00 p.m. on 2nd April, and she watched it for several seconds before it disappeared:

> The light was no more than 50 — 60ft [about 17 meters] from the house and about 40ft [12 meters] from the ground. The light was so intense that I could see the outline of a parachute. It seemed to be attached to this glowing ball by cords or some other material. These were also very distinct.
>
> The light glided smoothly past the house and seemed to go towards trees. I kept watching it until it went out of sight. I wasn't frightened, just fascinated by the brilliance of the color. [*The Macleay Argus,* April, 15, 1971]

Mrs. Summerville told her husband what she had seen, and he conducted a search in the area where she saw the light disappear. He looked along the riverbank and among nearby undergrowth without finding anything.

Other Kempsey residents appear to have witnessed the same mysterious bright light on that evening of 2nd April, as reported in *The Argus* of April 8.

One party, Mrs. Ina Murray along with her son David, daughter Rowan and nephew Ric Cooke, described seeing a light, 'reddish in color with purple overtones', traveling low in the

Sucked Through Glass

north-western sky at 6.10pm. David watched the light through binoculars, and claimed he saw a smoke trail following the light.

They had originally thought the light came from a helicopter landing, but realized it was far too bright for that. This group said the light made a controlled and deliberate descent before it disappeared from view 'somewhere near the hospital.'

The area 'near the hospital' was mentioned in other reports of the April 2 sighting.

About the same time as Mrs. Murray's sighting — 6.10pm. – Mr. Arnold Nelson was farewelling his sister-in-law, Mrs. Adamson, on the front verandah of his home, when they saw a reddish light over the Macleay River.

They watched it slowly descend into the river between West Kempsey reservoir and the local hospital. Mr. Nelson said the light was very low and appeared to be about 4ft/1.2m in diameter. He also said that he saw a smoke trail following the descent.

Other witnesses included Mr. and Mrs. Andrews, who live opposite Mr. Nelson, who saw the light while they were driving in the area.

Mrs. Andrews said it was in the south-western sky and was 'a beautiful red light like the setting sun' hanging between two black clouds. She called her husband's attention to the sunset, only to be tersely reminded that the sun sets in the west, not the south.

Mrs. Richard Blight and her children also saw the light, watching it for 15 seconds before it disappeared. They thought it was a flare dropped by an aeroplane coming in to land. Subsequent enquiries revealed there were no planes in the area, and no civil defense exercises taking place.

Four other witnesses had the light under surveillance for about five minutes. They were a taxi-driver and his three passengers, all of whom preferred not to be named, according to *The Macleay Argus*.

The taxi-driver described the event:

> It seemed to be a rusty orange color like a sunset. We thought it was an aircraft, but the light went over the aerodrome and traveled towards Greenhill. It disappeared at Greenhill — we knew it was Greenhill because we could see the [street and house] lights there. [*The Macleay Argus*, April 15, 1971]

The final witness to come forward to the *Macleay Argus* was

Mrs. Dulcie Rossiter who lived near Greenhill. Mrs. Rossiter said she had the 'huge, bright light' in view for five to ten minutes:

> When I first saw it, I thought it was an aeroplane, but the light was too big and too bright. It was deep orange in color and then turned to red as it drew nearer.

She used binoculars to watch it and says she saw a trail of smoke behind the light.

> The light appeared to go behind some trees on the river bank between the town reservoir and the hospital. As it disappeared from view, I could still see the trail of smoke. [*The Macleay Argus,* April, 15, 1971]

The similarities of descriptions, directions, timing and locations of the Kempsey incidents of April 2, 1971 seem sufficient, despite their minor variations, to substantiate the claim of a genuine, multiple-witnessed, unidentified aerial phenomenon of some description.

The most bizarre incident potentially associated with these sightings was still a few hours away — around 10pm. on that same Friday night, April 2, 1971.

A 34-year-old Aboriginal man living at Greenhill claimed he was sucked out the closed kitchen window of his home by an unknown force, landing on his back after falling over seven feet [2 meters] to the home's external rear steps.

His wife said her husband had been drinking early in the evening and, although affected by liquor, was not drunk.

He vowed never to live in the house again and moved to Sydney, while his wife and children stayed on at Greenhill.

His wife's account of the incident reveals even further surprises:

> We came home from the neighbors at about 10 o'clock after watching television. My husband went to bed and was playing with the baby. He got up and went into the kitchen to have a drink of water.
>
> He didn't turn on the light, but he said afterwards he tipped his head back [to drink from a tap?] and saw this little face pressed up against the window. It had no hair and it looked like a small saucer. It had features but he did not describe them.
>
> He doesn't remember much about going through the window. He said he was sucked out by some force. He fell out at the bottom of the [outside] steps on his back.

Sucked Through Glass

I ran outside. I thought he would be stunned, but he wasn't. He jumped up and ran like hell down to the gravel (a stockpile near the Greenhill houses). I ran after him and he was crying and shaking. I thought he had the horrors and told him so. I went to go back to the house and he asked me not to leave him there, he was so frightened. [*The Macleay Argus,* April 8, 1971, p.1]

With his wife, the man attended the local hospital and had a stitch inserted into a cut in a finger of his right hand. The wife then returned home to be with their children. Later, the police were called and took the man away and kept him in a cell overnight.

He insisted to his wife that he was not mad, and that he had really seen something. She believed him, saying: 'I know he saw something. He's not superstitious. He doesn't believe in ghosts or men from space, [but] he does now.'

The *Macleay Argus* reporter attended the scene of the incident on April 7 to clarify a few several puzzling details:

The man, about 5ft3ins/160cm tall and weighing about 8½ stones, (119lbs or 54 kilograms) was standing at a sink about 18in/46cm. wide. His wife insists that he was in a horizontal position going through the window and that he was not struggling or thrashing about at all.

The man's trajectory had cleared the dishes in the sink, passed horizontally through an 81cm x 25cms [32inx 10in] pane of glass, and landed him practically unharmed on his back at the bottom of the rear steps, below the window. The reporter concluded that the feat would be impossible for anyone standing in the kitchen by the sink to undertake.

The man repeatedly told his wife of his terror, yet could not run from the object of his fear. [Instead] he went to it. [*The Macleay Argus*, April 8, 1971]

The final press story was supported with two black and white photographs of the broken glass in the widow — one from inside the kitchen over the sink and tap, the other from outside the house by the rear steps showing the broken window pane and the depth of the fall.

Unexplained aerial phenomenon continued spasmodically in and around Kempsey over the next four and a half years (at least). Ten further sightings were reported during that period.

27. Kelly Cahill's Abduction

Australia's own Betty and Barney?

On the night of September 19-20, 1961, New Hampshire, (U.S.) couple Betty and Barney Hill experienced a close encounter with an unidentified flying object and two hours of 'lost' time while driving south on Route 3 near Lincoln. They filed an official Air Force Project Blue Book report of a brightly lit cigar-shaped craft the next day, but were not public with their story until it was leaked in the Boston Traveller in 1965. This was the first widely reported UFO abduction report in the United States.*

> *The above wording is from a highway marker on Route 3 at Indian Head Resort in North Lincoln, New Hampshire, USA, opposite a granite stone face called 'Indian Head' – which features in the Betty & Barney Hill encounter in America

Thirty-two years later, across the Pacific, an Australian couple, Kelly and Andrew Cahill were driving on a quiet country road through a mountain range outside Melbourne at night when they, too, experienced a close encounter with an unidentified flying object. Kelly's account of her encounter and alien abduction, with its several unique features, achieved worldwide notice.

The husband and wife in each couple came from different cultural backgrounds; the wives were intelligent and feisty, while the husbands appeared reluctant to discuss their experiences. There was one core variation, though. The Hills used their own given names (Betty and Barney), while the Australians protected their persona with pseudonyms (Kelly and Andrew Cahill), i.e. not their real names.

The Australian couple's account pivots on Kelly's public assertions — in her book *Encounter*, her appearances on local current affair TV shows, her participation in local and overseas TV programs and podcasts, magazine articles, and her lecture tour through parts of the United States and Canada, some of which may still be seen on-line over two decades later.

In August 1993 Kelly, a 27-year-old mother of three, was driving with her husband, Andrew, from their Gippsland home to visit a friend, Eva, who lived at Monbulk in the Dandenong Ranges, 50 kilometers east of Melbourne. The journey usually took 1½ hours.

On the way, as Kelly wrote in her book:

There was a break in the trees that lined the road, and through the break I could see a big paddock, going right back to some low hills. The paddock was cleared, there were no obstructions, and no buildings in the vicinity. We were just on the outskirts of Belgrave South, before you get into the township.

I saw a row of orange lights in the paddock: unusual lights that were produced by an object on the ground. A fluorescent mist surrounded them and they weren't natural, that was instantly obvious.

This object was like nothing I had ever seen before — it was a couple of hundred meters back from the road and low on the ground, and the lights were large.

What I saw had a distinct circular shape, and the outside was rimmed with the lights. By the time this caught my attention, I had maybe two or three seconds to look at it, then it disappeared from view behind the trees as we drove on ... Without saying anything at first, I looked at Andrew, to gauge whether or not he had seen it. He hadn't, because he was concentrating on the road. [*Encounter*, (HarperCollins, 1996) p.34]

Next, from an interview Kelly had with UFO researcher Robb Tilley and incorporated into a Bill Chalker article in *International UFO Reporter* of Sept/Oct 1994, she said:

But a couple of minutes up the road I said, 'I swear I saw a UFO.' He [Andrew] said, 'Don't be stupid! It was probably a helicopter.' I said, 'It wasn't making any noise. It was just sitting on the ground.' Anyway, after a few jibes at me, he forgot all about it, and we arrived at [my girlfriend's place]. [from *An Extraordinary Encounter in the Dandenong Foothills*, Bill Chalker article in *International UFO Reporter* of Sept/Oct 1994]

Andrew dropped Kelly off at Eva's and drove on alone into the city to spend time with his buddies, while Eva and Kelly attended a local bingo game together. He returned to Monbulk ahead of the girls; they arrived back at Eva's place around 11pm. According to Kelly, the Cahills departed Eva's around a quarter to midnight for their hour-and-a-half drive home.

Traveling back along the road they'd driven only six hours earlier, Kelly and Andrew noticed something unusual. The following extract is from a television program *'OZ Encounters — UFOs in Australia'* hosted by Martin Sachs and produced by Debbie Byrne:

> About a kilometer [around 0.6m] or so in front of us, about twice the height of the tree tops, we could see this object which I thought was a blimp — it had the shape of a blimp — but it was a light. As we got closer to it the lights seemed to separate, but it was actually a row of round orange lights.
>
> It appeared like there were silhouettes standing in those orange circles — people, but you could only see their black outlines. I said to my husband, 'There's people in there, 'and the minute I said that, it shot off to the left of us, and in one or two seconds it was gone completely.'

But that was only the first early morning surprise for Kelly and Andrew Cahill:

> When we had driven no further than a few kilometers (say 1.8miles), our eyes were greeted by a brilliant light, like a shining sun, directly in front of us. It seemed to block off the entire road, and its brightness was so intense that I found it necessary to use my hand as a shade in order to peer through the windscreen. [Kelly Cahill in *Nexus Magazine*, February/March 1995. p.61]

At that point, Kelly's recall falters ... stalls.

Next moment the couple are sitting in their station wagon, driving slowly, wondering what happened. A moment earlier Kelly's heart was racing with excitement in anticipation of seeing a spacecraft at close quarters, the next she felt unwell, dazed and exhausted.

> We were both sluggish, confused and disoriented. Yet only a second or so before he was as animated as I was, concentrating intensely on the light ahead. I looked at Andrew and he seemed somewhat dazed and distant. He was still driving slowly.
>
> 'What happened to it?' I asked. 'We must have turned a corner or something.' That was the best he could come up with. I just stared at him.

'I feel as if I've had a blackout.' This was the best I could come up with, but it didn't begin to describe how strange the feeling was.

'If we just turned a corner, how come I didn't see it? This is really weird. I feel like I've been unconscious.' 'Don't be stupid,' he said. He seemed to shake off his lethargy and docility and started driving faster. [Kelly Cahill, *Encounter*, (HarperCollins, 1996) p.53]

The couple had another dispute once they reached home. It was 2.30am. Kelly instantly recognized that their usual hour-and-a-half trip had taken over two-and-a-half hours — but Andrew emphatically denied leaving Eva's before midnight as Kelly claimed. 'I was driving, and I know we weren't driving for more than an hour-and-a-half. We must have left at 1am.'

They made coffee and, sitting in the lounge room, chatted about what they'd seen during the last eight hours. Perhaps Andrew thought Kelly was becoming fixated about their UFO sighting, or maybe he was trying to be a protective husband, as he said 'It's not good to mess around with this business ... I don't want that kind of evil stuff in this house!'

Years later, in a response to a question from Cynthia Siegel in Sacramento, Kelly explained:

You have to understand, he [Andrew] comes from a Muslim background where anything to do with UFOs or aliens were totally demonic. His idea was not to think about it, not to do anything with it. [*UFO Connection*, California]

Missing time wasn't the only thing that concerned Kelly before she went to bed:

In the toilet, the first thing I noticed was that I was bleeding, and it wasn't my time. The blood was bright red, not period blood, and it was unusually profuse. It had soaked through my jeans ... I took care of the situation ...[and] walked through the kitchen, more or less in the buff, to get a robe out of the bedroom, but when I got into the light I looked down and discovered an odd mark underneath my navel.

It was a perfect little equilateral triangle, angry red, with sharp lines. It looked like it had been burned into me, or that the first few layers of skin had been removed. It measured about a centimeter [3/8in] on each side, and was located underneath my belly button and a little bit to the right, almost touching it. [Kelly Cahill, *Encounter*, (HarperCollins, 1996) pps.58-59]

The small red triangle was only a minor curiosity to Kelly; she wondered how it got there without her knowing; and then stopped thinking about it. Her bleeding continued.

Three weeks later Kelly ended up in hospital with a womb infection. She was losing weight and, for the first time in her life, suffering severe migraine headaches. She was discharged from hospital after an overnight stay with a prescription of oral antibiotics.

Kelly was not provided with any explanation for the onset of her difficulties or even a diagnosis of her problems. She told Cynthia Siegel:

> Even on the medical records they had these little question marks beside everything ... they had no explanation for why it had actually started.
> [*UFO Connection*, California]

A few days after returning home from hospital, Kelly had an uninvited night-time visitor.

She was in bed asleep by herself when she dreamed she was in bed. She became aware in her dream of a presence in the room, a presence she couldn't see.

Next, she heard a voice telling her not to be afraid, followed by a sensation like something sucking the energy from her body ('It was as if a suction device or vacuum was attached to my chest,' are Kelly's words).

As the suction increased, Kelly awoke with a start, her eyes wide open. There, standing beside her bed, within easy reach, was a tall, black figure wearing a hooded cloak!

The figure had a very dark, long face, a pronounced slope to it cheekbones and dull red eyes. Its hooded cloak was tightly drawn covering the shoulders and down out of sight below the bed. Kelly stared at the presence; it stared directly into Kelly's eyes, not moving.

Kelly was terrified, motionless. It was as if the figure wanted Kelly to know it was real, and not a figment of her dreaming imagination. remained perfectly still, continuing to stare into Kelly's eyes.

Then it simply vanished.

Kelly tried to gather her wits and her courage. The house was quiet and she knew Andrew would be asleep on the lounge in front of the fir She raced out and shook him. 'Andrew, Andrew, wake up! I'm scared! saw something beside my bed!'

Kelly explained what had happened, and Andrew tried to pacify he 'You were probably half asleep,' he said, 'You only thought you sa something.' Eventually they retired to bed.

From then on, Kelly slept with the bedroom light switched on... every night for the next two years.

Kelly had a total of four 'visitations' by what appeared to be the same entity over the next five months.

A few weeks after her first night-time visitation, Kelly and Andrew visited some friends, Anne and George, and the subject of UFOs came up in conversation. It was suggested by their host that UFOs didn't exist.

Much to Kelly's surprise, Andrew said 'If you had seen what Kelly and I saw coming home from Eva's place, you might change your mind.'

'What on earth are you talking about?' Kelly demanded.

'Remember?' Andrew responded, 'On the way home from Eva's? Remember? It wasn't making any noise.'

'Andrew, I did *not* see anything!'

'Of course you did, Kelly. We argued about it all the way home!'

Kelly sat there speechless. She didn't know what he was talking about. If she'd seen something, surely she'd remember it — but she didn't. The whole incident had been 'totally blotted out' of her memory.

Kelly didn't press Andrew further, and the conversation moved on to another topic.

But she knew Andrew would not have said something he didn't mean. 'For the life of me,' Kelly wrote in her book, 'I couldn't remember what he claimed we had seen.' [Kelly Cahill, *Encounter*, p.101]

> A few days later, all of a sudden I remembered it! It hit me! And ... then I remembered going into the light, and then I couldn't remember anything else. A couple of weeks after that, it started to really bug me, because I remembered that light, and I remember arguing with him all the way home. But it was all I did remember. [Kelly Cahill, Robb Tilley interview, *International UFO reporter*]

Kelly's memories of what transpired back on August 8 returned to her little by little. One difficulty was Andrew's refusal to discuss his recollections with her. At least, she thought, he had agreed in front of friends that they'd both seen a UFO.

On the first of October, Kelly and Andrew again visited her friend Eva in Monbulk. This time it was in the afternoon and, naturally, they drove on the same road they had driven on the evening of their UFO sighting. Again, Andrew was to drop Kelly off and pick her up later, this time a day or two later. When they reached a particular portion of the road, Kelly had an overwhelming feeling:

> In that instant, I knew what had happened that night. With a sickening thud, the whole thing changed from abstract to concrete. How blithely ignorant I had been — I'd sat on a ticking bomb for eight weeks and had no idea at all.
>
> Dread and devastation are the only words to describe the sinking feeling I experienced then... My head began to spin, and a cold sweat broke out all over my body. I knew that something had happened to us, right here ... this spot, and I began to have my first inkling of what that something was...
>
> As we drove on to Eva's house, I continued to experience flashes of recollection — flashes of us stopping the car, flashes of us getting out, of me reaching back into the car to pick up my handbag. I had flashes of seeing those creatures, those beings with the big red eyes. And more. It was terrible, absolutely terrible. [Kelly Cahill, *Encounter*, (HarperCollins, 1996) pps.105-7]

Kelly didn't speak to Andrew about her memories as they drove — she was apprehensive of announcing her thoughts to him before she had gathered the whole picture in her mind. She maintained her silence, even to Eva after Andrew had dropped her off and left.

She declined her friend's invitation to attend bingo with her, choosing rather to sit alone and continue to reconstruct her recollections of her encounter. By 11.00 p.m., when Eva returned, Kelly had reclaimed the first fifteen minutes or so, and felt exhausted. She knew there was more — her 'missing time' — but was a little unsure whether she really wanted to know anything further.

> What we had actually done, we had driven into the light, but the road curved, and the road we thought was in front of us was actually to our right-hand side. It [the object] was in the field, and it was massive ... you could have driven for five minutes and not had it out of your sight the whole time...
>
> It was much larger than the UFO seen a few minutes earlier, and it was at ground level in the field at the bottom of a gully area. I asked Andrew to stop the car, and we both got out. I remember leaning back in [the vehicle], actually on the floor, pick up my handbag because I didn't go anywhere without my handbag — that's one of the sort of things that triggered off these memories...
>
> We crossed over the road. We jumped the gutter and we walked up [to the fence line]. I looked down the road, and there was another car pulled

up, a light blue car. Some people got out and went across the road ... They must have been at least a hundred meters/328ft down the road from us ... I was more interested in what was in front of me, so I didn't get any detail.

I'm standing there, and we are looking at this thing [the large UFO]. All of a sudden there is a black figure on the field. It was about seven feet/2m tall ... its eyes seemed to turn to a red fire. It started coming towards us ... it had great round red eyes, like a huge fly's eyes and they were red like ... fluorescent stop lights, a sort of real burning red.

All of a sudden I started screaming to my husband ... 'They've got no souls! They've got no souls!'

Suddenly there was a whole heap of them, and they started coming towards us, faster than a man could run, they were gliding off the ground. They got half-way across the field and split up. Some of them went towards the other people and the rest came towards us.

The next thing I know. I felt this oomph in my stomach, like I was winded. I was thrown right back — I was on my back on the ground — I sat up, with my head between my knees. I'm trying to stay conscious. I couldn't see; everything was black.

The next thing I heard was Andrew saying 'Let go of me'. His voice was all sort of cracked up with fear. I've never heard anything like that from my husband, he's not afraid of anything.

Then a male voice said 'We don't mean you any harm.' Andrew said 'Why did you hit Kelly then?' — That's the last I heard of my husband. No one else spoke except me. I heard myself saying, 'Oh, God, I'm going to be sick.' Then I must have blacked out for a little while. [Kelly Cahill, Robb Tilley interview, *International UFO reporter*]

The voice Kelly heard pronouncing 'We don't mean you any harm' wasn't telepathic, it was audible. It was the voice of the first tall figure with the burning red eyes. When Kelly regained consciousness, his was the first voice she heard. 'I was still sitting on my backside and hadn't moved,' Kelly wrote, 'The voice said, We're a peaceful people.'

Kelly says she screamed back 'If you're so peaceful, why are you doing this? Liar!'

Very calmly, and with total authority, he said. 'Will someone please do something about her?' It was so cutting, so condescending. [Kelly Cahill, *Encounter,* (HarperCollins, 1996) p. 132]

Seconds later, Kelly — who was still winded — sensed a presence beside her and decided to deliver a further tirade to the unwelcome visitors 'How dare you put terror into the hearts of these innocent people! Go back to where you came from!'

The next thing she knew, Kelly was back in the car, dreamily conscious.

All this, we are told, came to Kelly in the quietness of Eva's lounge room. She had linked one flash of recollection to another, then another, moving them around, and trying again, like completing a jig-saw puzzle. In the end it was all too real, it wasn't a dream, it wasn't a fantasy, it was, Kelly knew deep down, what had happened to her just eight weeks ago.

When Eva came home, Kelly kept her discoveries to herself ('How could she believe me if I could hardly believe myself?'). They had coffee, chatted, and retired for the night.

When Andrew picked Kelly up from Eva's on Sunday, Kelly broached the subject of her discoveries with him on the drive home.

He didn't want to know. 'Don't start that again, Kelly!' and 'What? You've got to be kidding! You're crazy!' These reactions simply increased Kelly's feelings of seclusion, so she determined to let someone in authority know about what she had experienced. Andrew forbade her to do this, but her mind was made up.

> I took the first steps the following day. It was Monday, and I was home by myself. I rang the universities one by one, getting their numbers from the telephone directory ... every university put me through to their psychology department ... Some were helpful, in that they listened even though they couldn't help, but others were downright rude and hung up on me.
>
> I eventually came across someone who was fairly knowledgeable and who directed me to the Civil Aviation Authority (CAA). I'd been hitting the phone like crazy, and when I called the CAA it started to pay off.
>
> The CAA put me touch with a UFO research group in Melbourne, and Bill Chalker in Sydney. I remember being quite surprised that there were such things as UFO researchers. [Kelly Cahill, *Encounter*, (HarperCollins, 1996) pps.143-146]

Kelly Cahill contacted Bill Chalker on October 4, 1993 seeking help in understanding her several unusual experiences over the previous two months.

Because Kelly lived in the State of Victoria and Chalker lives 870 kilometers (540 miles) north of her in Sydney, New South Wales, Bill Chalker passed Kelly's information on to John Auchettl of Phenomena Research Australia (PRA) in Melbourne and suggested Kelly contact him straight away.

Kelly rang John Auchettl that very day and was surprised to be told her experiences were 'not at all uncommon' — she had mistakenly felt she was probably the only one in the world this had happened to!

Kelly was blissfully unaware that Ufology was a recognized area of study, and knew nothing about the standard literature on the topic. Names like Betty & Barney Hill, John Mack, Stanton Friedman, Steven Greer, J Allen Hynek, and Whitely Strieber meant nothing to her.

She did, however, remember feeling for the Knowles family on television after their UFO experience near Mundrabilla in Western Australia over five years earlier [see Chapter 18.]

John Auchettl was, as Kelly put it, 'exactly what I had been looking for'. He agreed her case needed investigation, and that he would be in touch soon to arrange a meeting.

They met the following Sunday for a steak-house lunch in the Dandenong foothills where Kelly told him more of her recollections, and how she believed other people were present at the encounter.

Auchettl questioned Kelly closely, and gave her a questionnaire to complete at home and send to him. He also sought Kelly's co-operation by preparing drawings of the craft and of the tall being with the red eyes.

Once it was clear to him that Kelly was unfamiliar with existing UFO literature, he placed her on a 'book ban' — she was not to read any books on the topic until his investigation was completed. This ensured Kelly's recollections remained uncontaminated or influenced by anything written by others.

Later, he suggested Kelly start writing a journal of her recollections:

> It was like 'Write everything down, maybe one day it can be used as reference material.' It was a sort of therapy, too. I've gone back over my old journals and I was amazed at how much you forget over the years — it may be a little incident or a small insight. The book [*Encounter*] basically came from that [journal writing]... [Kelly Cahill, *'UFO Connection'* interview with Cynthia Siegel, circa 1996]

Kelly was, at first, impatient about the researcher's progress, but John Auchettl and his associates at PRA explained it was a long and thorough process, one not to be rushed.

First, they addressed the possibility of 'other witnesses' — the people in the stationary, light-blue car seen by Kelly — by placing advertisements in local newspapers. It asked if anyone had seen any unusual activity in the particular area between certain dates. The advertisements did not mention UFOs, spacecrafts or aliens, nor mention specific roads.

As a result, PRA received thirteen letters including one from a 'family that may be related' to Kelly's encounter. Another reader saw the advertisement and contacted her daughter, urging her to respond because of a conversation they had shared.

Most of the responses to PRA simply reported seeing lights in the sky.

John Auchettl now had three potential witnesses to interview and process but, for the moment, he kept Kelly to one side, telling her the barest minimum, while he went about his work.

These three people, all professionals in their thirties, were a man and his wife and a woman friend who were traveling together, with clear recollections of the incident Kelly had reported — stopping their car, crossing the road, observing the spacecraft and the tall, dark strangers.

They had parked their car some hundred meters/300ft behind the Cahills, before they crossed the road to see the craft.

They believe they'd seen a UFO, they believe they've seen an entity — an alien — they believe an incident did occur in the field — there's no doubt in their mind — *and they believe they were examined.*

But at one point their experience does diverge from Kelly's: there was no fear, no hysteria — just calm. And the two women believe somehow they were transported from the field.

> They described being in a craft of some sort, they were in a position where they are laying on their backs, they saw the roof and the tips of their toes, they can see a group of faces, there is no speech — they couldn't speak but they could hear things going on, and they seemed to be able to communicate with each other without actually speaking. [John Auchettl, in *'The Extraordinary'* with Warwick Moss]

None of them reported seeing Andrew and Kelly or their vehicle; but they remembered another man, driving alone, who pulled up behind them to have a look at the craft, leaving his headlights on. When Kelly glanced down the road and saw their parked car, the headlights of this third car had illuminated it from behind.

The first couple and their friend contacted PRA on November 17, 1993, but the third party, the lone male driver, didn't come forward until 1996:

> [PRA] didn't find out anything about him until three years down the track. Apparently, very early on in the piece they [the driver, encouraged by his wife] had gone to other researchers to tell the story and no-one had been interested... they got a little disillusioned with it and decided to keep it to themselves.
>
> It wasn't until they saw a story in a magazine, an article I'd done, that they thought 'Hold on a second, that sounds exactly like ...' [Kelly Cahill, *'UFO Connection'* interview with Cynthia Siegel]

The article mentioned here was most likely the one Kelly Cahill wrote for *Nexus Magazine*, and published in their issue of February/March 1995, Vol.2, No. 24. They headlined her story with 'Australia's Most Credible UFO Abduction Case.'

As he did with Kelly, John Auchettl asked those from the light-blue car to draw their impressions of the spacecraft and of the tall figures. When he saw the resulting sketches, John was pleased — their similarity to Kelly's drawings was astounding.

> The date, the time, the contact with the aliens, the drawings of the craft, everything matched ... only the three women involved, myself included, had any conscious recollection of direct alien contact during that night' [Kelly Cahill, *Encounter*, (HarperCollins, 1996) p.199]

Kelly did not associate the small, equal-sided triangle she found under her navel on the night of August 8 as anything to do with her alien encounter. She had noticed it, wondered about it, and promptly forgotten it.

But in November 1993, John Auchettl mentioned triangles to Kelly. 'Triangles?' she said, 'I don't know anything about triangles.' So, playing his cards close to his chest, John left the subject alone. It transpired that 'triangles' were indeed significant in this case.

By late December of that year, John Auchettl's so-called 'book-ban' on Kelly was over, and she threw herself into a flurry of reading as much as she could find about UFOs and aliens. Among the first she read was *'Transformation'* by Whitely Strieber.

While the author wrote of having a triangular scar on his arm, it wasn't until she read an account of a French doctor and his son who, after their encounter, had triangular marks near their navels, that the penny dropped for Kelly.

She excitedly rang John Auchettl and reported her own forgotten triangle mark. He was very interested. He asked to visit her with an ultraviolet camera and photograph it. But Kelly's husband didn't want another man photographing Kelly's body, and the idea was dropped.

It took several months — until June 1994 — before Kelly learnt from John that the two women in the second car carried similar marks in similar positions — and other marks as well.

> What we discovered was that they [the two women in the light-blue car] had markings just under the navel, marking on the side of their left thigh and, on one of the girls, a bruising to the left ankle like something [had been] cuffed around her leg. [John Auchettl, in *'The Extraordinary'* with Warwick Moss]

John Auchettl and PRA certainly took steps to preserve the integrity of their investigation. The three witnesses in the second car had not yet been made aware of Kelly and Andrew's existence, let alone that they had been present at the same sighting and encounter.

'Tell them, please,' Kelly begged John, aware of the apprehensions she had earlier felt, 'It's comforting to know someone else has shared the same experience.' But he held firm; there was more work to do before any report could be released.

It was time for PRA to turn their attention to the UFO landing site and search for any ground traces to further support the testament of the witnesses. Monash University in Melbourne became involved in the on-field data collection and analysis. This work took eighteen months of investigation.

> There were aerial surveys, infra-red photography from the air, and magnetic readings were taken by a portable magnetometer — $200,000's worth of equipment — so basically they went all the way.

> I've seen photographs of several acres of the field cordoned off into one-meter/39in blocks with pegs and ribbons, and samples were taken from every single block and sent to two separate, individual analysts. [Kelly Cahill, *'UFO Connection'* interview with Cynthia Siegel]

What did this expensive ground survey work establish? They found a crescent-shaped indentation in the earth at the precise spot indicated by all three women. Within that area there was an above-average sulphur content, and a rare carbon compound called pyrene.

> We found lots of unusual anomalies and magnetic problems, and lots of changes in the soil chemistry. There was also a triangle formation of dead grass within the circle, so it gave us a strong lead that something had been on the ground and was starting to destroy the grass in the area. [John Auchettl, in *'The Extraordinary'* with Warwick Moss]

> Another thing is that John [Auchettl] told me they found unusually high amounts of tannic acid in the semi-circle. He said it was strange because tannic acid should have dissolved over the months, due to the rain we'd had, but the acid was locked in by a coating of some sort of unidentifiable waxy substance. [Kelly Cahill, *Encounter*, p.215]

One further relevant piece of evidence was introduced when the lone male driver of the third vehicle came forward in 1966. He carried the bodily mark that the two women from the light-blue car had — a series of three dots on his inside thigh. Further, he had also sustained a bruising to the left ankle as if it had been closely shackled, just as one of the women had.

That particular woman recalls being strapped down to a table, according to Kelly; and John Auchettl has said the two women from the light-blue car believed they were physically examined during their abduction. By implication, the lone male driver may have been examined as well.

The lone male driver provided his account of his sighting and abduction to PRA on the explicit basis of anonymity. Andrew Cahill, Kelly's husband at the time of their encounter, withdrew his consent and participation in PRA's investigation. Finally, the three persons in the light-blue car did not wish their personal information to be made public and later took legal action to ensure their privacy.

> They all just decided it wasn't worth all the trouble of going public. They were going to leave it behind, and weren't going to do it anymore.

> There was actually a lot more to it. There was a big court case that went on over revealing their personal information in public and a lot of other things ... there were a lot more complications went on than meets the eye. [Kelly Cahill, *'UFO Connection'* interview with Cynthia Siegel]

Bill Chalker, the researcher responsible for putting Kelly Cahill in touch with PRA in the first instance, admitted that this decision of his was, in hindsight, a mistake.

In June, 2002, nine years after the encounter, Chalker wrote: 'While Auchettl & PRA may well have been thorough in their investigation, in reality there has been no way to absolutely verify this, because of their unwillingness to release their report and data on the case.'

One explanation for this could be a legal restriction on releasing any report at all; or a conclusion by PRA that without referring to the collaborating witnesses, very little not already disclosed in Kelly Cahill's 240-page book, remained — although this seems highly unlikely.

Which brings us back to Kelly. She no longer lives among the rolling hills of Gippsland. After her divorce from Andrew she first moved, we understand, to tropical Queensland and, more recently (2015), lives overseas, presumably under her real name, her anonymity no longer needed.

At its core, and accepting her book as accurate, Kelly Cahill's encounter has many extraordinary elements: four independent witnesses (three in the light-blue car and the lone male driver), plus the similarity of their drawings to Kelly's own; her now ex-husband's confirmed sighting; body markings on four persons; 'lost' time; and physical traces at the landing site.

**

Perhaps, like Betty and Barney Hill, Kelly Cahill might one day have her own road marker erected on a quiet country road in the Dandenong Ranges near Melbourne.

References Consulted

A.P.R.O. Bulletin, The, Vol. 26, No. 11, May, 1978

ABC Radio National, *Radio Eye* program, *'To Catch a Falling Star'*

Alien Files, The, Warwick Moss TV program

Aubeck, Chris & Shough, Martin, *Return to Magonia: Investigating UFOs in History*

Auchettl, John, Phenomena Research Australia (PRA)

Basterfield, Keith, *UFOs: A Report on Australian Encounters,* Reed Books, 1997

Basterfield, Keith, *Close Encounters of an Australian Kind,* A H & A W Reed, 1981

Basterfield, Keith *Several eyewitness accounts of the Westall UFO Incident,* ufoevidence.org

Basterfield, Keith, *A Catalogue of the More Interesting Australian UFO Reports,* 2012

Basterfield, Keith, *UFOs Scientific Research* blogspot

Billing, Di, Television One News, N.Z. journalist

Brooks, Roger, TUFOIC (Tasmania UFO Information Centre)

Byrne, Debbie, producer, *OZ Encounters—UFOs in Australia,*(TV)

Cahill, Kelly, *Encounter,* HarperCollins, 1996

Callimanopulos, Dominique, *UFO Evidence — Scientific Study of the UFO Phenomenon* website

Chalker, Bill, *The 'Sea Fury Incident,'* auforn.com

Chalker, Bill, *The Drury UFO Film Affair*

Chalker, Bill, *'The 1966 Tully Saucer Nest: a Classic UFO Physical Trace Case',* 1997

Chalker, Bill, in *UFOs and Government, A Historical Inquiry,* Anomalist Books, San Antonio, 2012

Chalker, Bill, *The OZ Files—the Australian UFO story,* Duffy & Snellgrove, 1996

Chalker, Bill, theozfiles.blogsot.com.au & *The Oz Files* website

Chalker,Bill, *An Extraordinary Encounter in the Dandenong Foothills*

Chalker. Bill, *UFOs Sub Rosa Down Under: the Australian Military & Government Role in the UFO Controversy*

Coast to Coast AM, US late-night radio show

Cruttwell, Rev. N E ('Nor') in *Flying Saucer Review*

Denton, B & Phillips, C A , *The Tully Report*, UFORQ

Dickeson, F & P, ofocusnz.org.nz

Disclosure Australia Newsletter

Flying Saucer Review, U.K. magazine

Fogarty, Quentin, *Let's Hope They're Friendly! 1982*

Fuller, John G. *Incident at Exeter* Putnam, 1966

Godic, V & P, UFO Research Australia, *UFO Research in Australia & New Zealand,* 1989

Good, Timothy, *Beyond Top Secret*, London, 1996

Hansard Parliamentary Record, Canberra

Hervey, Michael ,*UFOs Over the Southern Hemisphere,* Robert Hale, London

Holledge, James, Flying Saucers Over Australia, Horwitz, Sydney 1965

Hynek, J. Allen, *The UFO Experience: A Scientific Inquiry*, London, 1972

Jarrold, Edgar, *Australian Flying Saucer Magazine*

Jones, Rosie, *Westall '66 A Suburban Mystery* documentary

Journal of Scientific Exploration Vol.14, No.1

Llewelyn, Ken ,*Flight Into the Ages*, Sydney, 1991

Macleay Argus, The, Kempsey, NSW newspaper

Magee, Judith, Victorian Unidentified Flying Object Research Society (VUFORS]

McDonald, (Prof.) James E, paper ,'*UFOs – An International Problem*'

McGhee, Moira, *Contact Down Under,* INUFOR, 2016

Messenger, Paul, machinery4change.org/counter1.html

Michel, Aimee, *The Truth about Flying Saucers*

National Archives of Australia

Nexus Magazine

Paqui, Lee, UFORQ, *Tully Revisited 50th Anniversary Address*

Pinkney & Ryzman, *Alien Honeycomb: the First Solid Evidence of UFOs*, Sydney, 1980

Pinkney, John, *A Paranormal File*, Five Mile Press, 2000

Pooley, Jane, *Humalien: the Lighter Side of the Grey Alien and Human Breeding Program,* 2016

Roberts, Keith, compiler, *Tasmania: a UFO History*, TUFOIC, 2011

Ryan, Shane, *Westall Flying Saucer Incident* website

Seers, Stan, *UFOs: The Case for Scientific Myopia,* Vantage Press, 1983

Startup, Cpt. Bill, *The Kiakoura UFOs,* 1980

Stott, Murray, *Aliens Over Australia*, Sydney 1984

The U.F.O. Investigator, NICAP Newsletter, U.S.A.

The Unexplained Files. American cable TV Discovery Channel

UFO Connection, Cynthia Siegel presenter, California

UFOCUSNZ website, New Zealand

ufologie.patrickgross.org/ce3

Ufologist, Australian magazine

UFOs Are Here, video, Guy Baskin

Willis, Martin, *Podcast UFO* (U.S.)

"We all know UFOs are real.
All we need to ask is
where do they come from,
and what do they want?"
— Apollo 14 Astronaut Capt. Edgar Mitchell

ABOUT THE AUTHOR

Barry Watts, B.Ed., is an Australian writer living on the bayside south of Melbourne. Over a period of forty years, he has written numerous books for adults and children. Barry received an Excellence in Writing award at the Santa Barbara Writers' Conference in 1988. This is his first book about UFOs – a subject that has fascinated him for decades.

You can contact him at:

barrywatts@bookfellows.com.au

www.ingramcontent.com/pod-product-compliance
Lightning Source LLC
Chambersburg PA
CBHW070605300426
44113CB00010B/1409